Introduction
to the
SPIRITUAL LIFE

Introduction
to the
SPIRITUAL LIFE

LOUIS BOUYER

Christian Classics ✧ *Notre Dame, Indiana*

First published as *Introduction à la vie spirituelle: précis de théologie ascétique et mystique,* Desclée, Paris, 1960.

Translated into English by Mary Perkins Ryan, 1961.

Nihil Obstat
John A. Goodwine, J.C.D.
Censor Librorum
Imprimatur
✠ Francis Cardinal Spellman
Archbishop of New York
June 28, 1961

Introduction ©2013 by Michael Heintz

Foreword ©2013 by David Fagerberg

Founded in 1865, Ave Maria Press is a ministry of the United States Province of Holy Cross.

www.christian-classics.com

Cover image © Alfredo Dagli Orti / The Art Archive at Art Resource, NY

Cover and text design by John R. Carson.

Paperback: ISBN-10 0-87061-281-6, ISBN-13 978-0-87061-281-7

E-book: ISBN-10 0-87061-282-4, ISBN-13 978-0-87061-282-4

Printed and bound in the United States of America.

Library of Congress Cataloging-in-Publication Data
Bouyer, Louis, 1913-2004.
[Introduction ? la vie spirituelle. English]
Introduction to the spiritual life / Louis Bouyer ; introduction by Rev. Michael Heintz.
    pages cm
Previously published in English as: Introduction to spirituality / translated by Mary Perkins Ryan. New York : Desclee Co., 1961.
Includes bibliographical references and index.
ISBN 978-0-87061-281-7 (pbk.) -- ISBN 0-87061-281-6 (pbk.) -- ISBN 978-0-87061-282-4 (e-book) -- ISBN 0-87061-282-4 (e-book)
1. Spiritual life--Catholic Church. I. Title.

BX2350.3.B6813 2013
248.4'82--dc23

                    2013021998

CONTENTS

Foreword by David Fagerberg vii

Preface to the Original Edition ix

Introduction by Michael Heintz 1

Chapter 1: The Spiritual Life According to
Catholic Tradition 13

Chapter 2: The Spiritual Life and the Word of God 41

Chapter 3: Prayer 79

Chapter 4: The Sacramental Life 139

Chapter 5: The Principles of the Ascetic Life 163

Chapter 6: Christian Asceticism and Christian
Humanism 183

Chapter 7: The Asceticism of the Cross and the
Different Christian Vocations:
Lay Spirituality 209

Chapter 8: The Asceticism of the Cross and the
Different Christian Vocations: Monastic
Spirituality 235

Chapter 9: The Various Apostolic Vocations:
The Priestly Vocation and the "Religious"
Vocations 269

Chapter 10: The Development of the Spiritual Life:
Purification 307

Chapter 11: The Development and the Rhythms
of the Spiritual Life: Illumination
and Union 329

Chapter 12: The Mystical Life 359

Conclusion: Aids in the Spiritual Life 385

Notes 389

Index 395

FOREWORD

Monasticism is a species in the genus of asceticism: the latter concerns the laic as well as the monk. Asceticism may have been perfected in the sands of the desert, but it is born in the waters of the font and is incumbent on every Christian. With this viewpoint, Louis Bouyer is able to introduce the spiritual life in a way that concerns us all. Most spirituality is presented as possessing all the sturdiness of an octopus; what Bouyer presents here is vertebrate spirituality. He describes a spiritual life that allows us to walk upright before the face of the Lord. Bouyer is uniquely qualified to do this because he understands the interwoven connections between Scripture, prayer, apostolic vocation, and the mystical life. He can synthesize these numerous dimensions because he integrated several identities and insights in his own life: a Lutheran pastor attracted by Eastern Orthodox theology who ultimately became a Catholic Oratorian and brought the perspective of liturgical theology to everything he wrote about biblical studies, the eucharist, Latin and Greek fathers, and ecclesiology, always with a pastor's heart and from within the mind of the Church. He did not care about being progressive or conservative. He wished to be traditional, and here he presents traditional elements that go to create every Christian's spiritual life. He teaches us what the Church has taught about how to ascend to Mount Zion. We owe a debt of gratitude to Ave Maria Press and Msgr. Heintz for bringing this inspiring meditation back in print.

David Fagerberg
University of Notre Dame

Preface to the Original Edition

This book is a manual, a manual for practical use. This is why the bibliography has been limited to the mention of the great basic texts and of works of some special interest in relation to the various questions we are dealing with. The reader should refer to the latter for a more complete bibliography or for discussions which are of interest to specialists only. In the purpose of the book also is to be found the reason why I have been quite reticent about certain factitious problems—for example, the question of Quietism (Can there be a love of God involving no reference to self?) and detailed questions of interest only to historians, such as the myriad subdivisions, differing from author to author, which can be introduced into the three ways, or three ages, of the spiritual life. And, for the same reason, I have not gone into any of the minute classifications which frequently occupy considerable space in works of this nature, but which do not seem to prove very useful for practical purposes.

To seminarians, priests, novices, religious, and all the faithful who wish to deepen their spiritual life by going to the great sources of holy scripture illuminated by Catholic tradition, this "Introduction" is offered for what it is and nothing more: an initiation into the fundamental problems of every spiritual life and into the perennial principles governing the solution of these problems. I have consistently avoided making this a work of special pleading for any one side or school of thought, since I am convinced that there is only one Catholic spirituality worthy of the name: that of the Gospel as the Church proclaims it to us; that is, as it came from Christ himself through the apostles, "the same yesterday, today, and forever."

INTRODUCTION

BY MICHAEL HEINTZ
UNIVERSITY OF NOTRE DAME

A nother book on spirituality? One that was first written over fifty years ago, before Vatican II? Yes, the market is awash in books on spirituality—some on prayer, others on discernment, still others on the life of the virtues or states of life—but few, if any, offer the kind of comprehensive vision provided by the French convert and Oratorian priest, Louis Bouyer (1913–2004).

In 1950, Father Bouyer published *The Meaning of the Monastic Life*, in which he argued that the basic elements of every Christian life are found in the monastic vocation, going so far as to suggest cheekily to monks that they should not consider their vocation "special." Rather, he invited monastics to consider their vocation as simply the baptismal vocation embraced with a particular focus and intensity.[1] In 1958, he wrote *Christian Initiation*,[2] addressed to both practicing and potential Christians, calling them to the full embrace of Christian life and Christian truth, which he presented as coincident in the Church's liturgical life. Two years later, he authored *The Meaning of the Priestly Life*, in which he examined the nature and vocation of the apostolic priesthood (as distinct from those ordained to serve in monastic or cloistered communities). In his introduction to this book on the priesthood, Bouyer made clear that he understood these three works in relation to one another, forming something of a trilogy.[3] In the very same year (1960), he released his *Introduction to the Spiritual Life*.[4] One

1

might, on the basis of his earlier remarks, view this fourth book, *Introduction to the Spiritual Life*, as the fruit and practical application of the vision articulated in the trilogy. While including material relative to the particulars of the different states of life, the *Introduction to the Spiritual Life* is offered more generally to all the baptized, as a "practical" guide for those who desire, in Bouyer's words, "to deepen their spiritual life by going to the great sources of holy scripture illumined by Catholic tradition" and as "an initiation into the fundamental problems of every spiritual life and into the perennial principles governing the solution to these problems."[5] However, its "practical" nature is not what one might expect; Bouyer does not simply offer a collection of techniques, providing a "how-to" manual of the life of the Spirit. Rather, he articulates the ways in which baptism, being plunged into the death and resurrection of Jesus Christ, should shape the contours of an entire life. Put another way, he situates or contextualizes the spiritual life squarely in the sacramental-liturgical life of the Church, so that the believer's identity, life of prayer, active charity, etc., are but expressions of this primary, baptismal reality.[6] Bouyer's *Introduction to the Spiritual Life*, then, is a book that anticipates what the Second Vatican Council (1962–1965), in returning to and reflecting upon the sources of Scripture and Tradition (sometimes referred to as *ressourcement*), identified as the "universal call to holiness."[7]

Who Was Louis Bouyer?[8]

Raised in a Protestant family, Louis Bouyer entered the Lutheran ministry in 1936, but by the end of 1939 he had entered the Catholic Church, and in 1944 was ordained a priest of the Congregation of the Oratory. He taught primarily in France, but also visited and lectured widely, notably in the

United States over a number of summers at the University of Notre Dame. He wrote broadly in the areas of Scripture, liturgy, and the life of faith, and is perhaps best known for his multi-volume *History of Christian Spirituality* (1963–1969), still an authoritative source and guide. He served as a member of the preparatory commission for the Second Vatican Council, as well as serving as a consultor for its implementation. In the wake of the Council, he candidly offered his own perspective on its aims and intentions.[9] Because he feared that his critique of the implementation of the Council in his native France was deemed too harsh by many of his contemporaries, he declined an offer to become a Cardinal (an honor that then went to his fellow-countryman, the Jesuit Jean Daniélou). Pope Paul VI appointed him as one of the founding members of the International Theological Commission (a committee of theologians who serve in advisory capacity to the pope) in 1969, where he served successive terms. Along with Joseph Ratzinger (Pope Benedict XVI), Henri de Lubac, Hans Urs von Balthasar, and others, he founded the international journal *Communio*. Throughout the 1970s and 1980s, he continued to teach, lecture, and write. Declining health brought him to retirement in 1998, and he died in October, 2004.

Living the Mystery

Central to Bouyer's theology is the Pauline concept, *to mysterion*, the Mystery. Not an insoluble riddle or an enigma meant to reduce one to aporetic silence, this term for Bouyer, following St. Paul, signifies the saving plan of God, revealed and effected fully in Christ, the Eternal Son made flesh. This Mystery, hidden even from the "principalities and powers of this age" (by which St. Paul meant not political leaders but fallen cosmic rational creatures opposed to God's will), is at last made manifest in the saving work of Christ crucified.[10] To some, however, this Mystery remains mere foolishness and, to others, only a stumbling block (cf. 1 Cor 2): the manifest "weakness" of God in the face of fallen human and angelic "power" trumps and subverts those very forces which are bent on destruction, and reveals the true grandeur, beauty, and life-giving power of God's self-emptying love, *agape*. Christ's self-emptying *agape*, indistinguishable from his very person (since he *is* love), is communicated sacramentally to his Body, the Church. This is most succinctly expressed by Colossians 1:27, "the glory of this Mystery, which is Christ in you, the hope of glory," a Pauline phrase Bouyer repeats no fewer than sixteen times in his *Introduction to the Spiritual Life*, as both Colossians and Ephesians further develop the notion found in 1 Corinthians. This Mystery, not remaining a mere event of the past, is a living reality that continues to abide in Christ's Body, the Church, principally, but not exclusively, through its sacramental life. As he had written in one of his earliest books, "The Christian religion is not simply a doctrine, it is a fact, an action, and an action, not of the past, but of the present, where the past is recovered and the future draws near. Thus it embodies 'the Mystery of faith,' for it declares to us that each day makes our own the action of Another accomplished long ago, the fruits of which we shall see only later in ourselves."[11]

By their baptism, Christians embody, individually and corporately, this Mystery, participating in Christ and manifesting his dying and rising in their very bodies, as St. Paul had averred (2 Cor 4:10). Bouyer understood this in terms of sacramental configuration to Christ; by the life of prayer, sacraments and active charity, believers ever deepen their share in that very Mystery and are continually configured to Christ, their crucified and glorified Lord. For Bouyer, however, this configuration, as his contemporary, the Redemptorist F. X. Durrwell had also made clear, is precisely to Christ *crucified and glorified*.[12] As Bouyer puts it beautifully in the second chapter of this very volume, "The Mystery, then, is Christ living in us, causing us to partake of the reality of his life, of his new being, and thereby restoring in himself, "recapitulating" as says the Epistle to the Ephesians, the whole of creation, the whole history of a humanity dismembered by sin but now reconciled, renewed, in a world delivered from its slavery to the powers hostile to God, powers which the cross has overcome, so as to be free in the glory promised to the children of God."[13] This is what St. Paul meant by describing life "in Christ" and, conversely, what it means for Christ to live in the baptized: a participation in this saving Mystery of Jesus' dying and rising effected by the sacramental life. The Christian life, then, is a matter of allowing that Mystery to be embodied, instantiated in the lives of believers, as they are continually configured to Christ. It is important to make clear that this not simply a kind of moral imitation of Jesus, but something much more than that: through the sacramental and liturgical action of the Church, the Mystery of Christ's dying and rising is communicated and, to use Bouyer's word, *propagated*, individually and corporately, by, in, and through his Body, the Church.[14] In many ways, living this Mystery is the most basic and recurring theme of Bouyer's *Introduction*, and arguably one of the foundational elements of his entire theological vision.

Spirituality and "Spiritualities"

It is not uncommon today to hear a friend or relative profess "I'm spiritual, but not religious," usually indicating that they maintain something of an interior life with some form of relation to a "spiritual" reality or realities, but not within the

constraints of any organized or dogmatic religion. The sociolo-
gist of religion, Christian Smith, has aptly described one form
of this modern religious sensibility as "moralistic therapeutic
deism."[15] Bouyer, as if anticipating this phenomenon, begins his
Introduction to the Spiritual Life by addressing the relationship
among the "religious life," the "interior life," and the "spiritual
life." He notes that historically there were forms of "religious"
life which did not involve anything more than prescribed external actions and which involved no "interior" belief, desire, or
intellectual commitment. He refers here to the ancient pagan
religion of Rome, which was not creedal and which involved
the performance of particular rites in a prescribed manner as
expressive of religious (and social) commitment.[16] Conversely,
he mentions forms of Buddhism which are correctly described
as "spiritual," but which have no "religious" content whatsoever
(marked by a profound detachment from everything, including anything "divine"). An "interior life," one of introspective
reflectivity, may be found in any number of individuals, from
late antique Stoics like Marcus Aurelius to moderns like Wordsworth or Thoreau. But this in itself, while noble and at times
profound, cannot necessarily qualify as a "spiritual life."

What is distinctive of Christianity is that it offers and nur-
tures an interior, religious, and spiritual life, not in relation to
an impersonal "deity" but to the living God who has revealed
himself personally in Jesus Christ; as Bouyer characterizes it,
when "the 'spirit' known in the 'spiritual life' is recognized not
as 'some thing' but as 'some one,' then the 'spiritual life' will be
a 'religious life' as well. . . . From this point of view, Christianity
is seen to be a form of 'spiritual life' in which our most personal,
most interiorized relationship with God himself in his transcendent reality is fully recognized and formally cultivated."[17] For
the Christian, the spiritual life is rooted in an interior life, but
one which moves beyond the self and fully blossoms within a

relationship to God, who has revealed himself in the person of Christ, through the Holy Spirit.

Bouyer spent his scholarly life studying the history of Christian spirituality, the ways that Christians made sense of, articulated, and expressed in prayer and worship their relationship to God through Christ in the Spirit. One of his deepest and abiding convictions, from his earliest research until late in his life, was the singularity of the spirituality of the Gospel. That is, when one speaks of "spiritualities" in the plural, one does so advisedly, since in reality there exists only one spirituality of the Gospel of Christ, though this one evangelical spirituality has been expressed and concretized in different cultural situations, at distinct historical moments, and within a variety of religious temperaments. What he claimed in the Foreword to this volume, "I am convinced that there is only one Catholic spirituality worthy of the name: that of the Gospel as the Church proclaims it to us," he reiterated clearly some thirty years later, at a conference that took place in the United States.[18] In the face of the facile and all-too-neat distinctions that some historians and theologians commonly make among the various early modern "schools of spirituality," Bouyer was fond of pointing out the fact that the great Carmelite, St. Teresa of Avila (1515–1582), made use of any number of confessors: Sometimes a Jesuit, sometimes a Dominican, sometimes a Franciscan. In short, what mattered to her was not their particular "spirituality" (again, a dubious category for Bouyer, and one that would not have occurred to Teresa), but their holiness and soundness.[19]

While Bouyer asserts that none of the great founders of the religious orders had any self-conscious intention of "constructing a spirituality" different from that of the Gospel as proclaimed by the Church, he nonetheless recognizes and celebrates the pluriform ways that Christian spirituality is instantiated in the life of Christ's Body, the Church. Chapters 7, 8, and 9 of his

Introduction, for example, articulate the ways in which the one, luminous spirituality of the Gospel is refracted in the various states of life: how the lay, vowed, and ordained members of the Church embody the one Mystery of Christ, each in particular and concrete ways. The remaining chapters then treat how the spiritual life, the one spirituality of the Gospel, is to be nurtured and developed, despite the differences among the states of life. Throughout his writings on the monastic life, the priestly life, and this present volume, Bouyer makes clear that while the particulars of the spiritual life are lived out in a variety of ways, the fundamental spirituality which is at their base is one and the same: the human response, prompted by grace, yet enacted in different times and places, to God's Word, revealed ultimately and definitively in the person of Jesus Christ.

Responding to the Word of God

The *Catechism of the Catholic Church* (at 2567) speaks of the spiritual life as a "drama." For Bouyer, this drama is enacted in the course of human history (which the Fathers of the Church would refer to as the "divine economy") in God's ongoing self-communication of his Word and the often-faltering human response. That Word is spoken not "generically" to all, but personally to each, and the response of each believer must also be deeply personal. To many contemporary ears, the phrase "Word of God" is apt to suggest the written Word, the text of the Scriptures. But for Bouyer, both drawing on the living Tradition of the Church and here again anticipating the clear teaching of the Second Vatican Council,[20] the Word of God is not in the first instance a text or collection of texts, but a Living Word, a divine Person. First revealed as the creative speech of God in Genesis, God's *Dabar* ("Word" in the Hebrew Scriptures is revealed in the new covenant as God's *Logos* ["Word" in the Greek New Testament]), his Eternal Son, through whom he has continually revealed himself, and is now definitively made known in Jesus Christ, the Eternal Word made flesh. The many words of Scripture mediate this one Word in written form, and as such are privileged, authoritative, and remain very much "the soul of theology." But for Bouyer, this Word is encountered, experienced, and engaged in and through the sacred liturgy, the Church's public worship. This liturgical context is the milieu in which the Scriptures are to be heard, prayed, and meditated upon; in a sense, even someone praying "privately" the Scriptures can grasp and understand their meaning only in and through the liturgical matrix in which they were, so to speak, generated and in which their fullest meaning is made real, present, and tangible in sacrament. In fact, Bouyer cites the sentiment of Pope Pius XI (1922–1939) that the "principal instrument of the ordinary magisterium is the liturgy"[21]; that is, it is the liturgy which communicates most basically and efficaciously "the Mystery of Faith." For after all, the worship of the Church antedated (and arguably shaped) the composition of the texts known today collectively as the New Testament. It is only natural then, that having spoken of the privileged place of the Scriptures in the life of prayer (chapters 2 and 3), Bouyer then turns immediately to the sacramental life (chapter 4) which continues in human history the saving work of Christ recorded in the sacred text. The Scriptures are at the heart of the life of faith, but as Bouyer puts it in chapter 2, the "spiritual life must and can nourish itself from the Word of God *through the liturgy*."[22]

An "Eschatological Humanism"

In recent decades, there have been some popular approaches to spirituality which presuppose or even seek to exploit a perceived tension in the Christian theological tradition between creation and redemption.[23] Without perhaps realizing it, such approaches only ape the early Gnostics, who saw the two orders in opposition to one another. Bouyer recognizes the tension that seems inherent between a humanistic enthusiasm about the prospects for human flourishing and the Cross of Christ, which stands at the center of the Christian faith as an indictment of unredeemed human aspirations toward autonomy. He seeks to navigate this by a delicate balancing of what he calls a "metaphysical optimism" and a "historical pessimism."[24] Optimism in regard to the fundamental goodness of the created order, but realistic pessimism about the obvious fact of human sinfulness and the prospects of unaided human efforts to overcome this; as he puts it concisely, "it is by losing love that we were lost"— by closing in on oneself, one shuts out the possibility of being genuinely loved by another.[25] Bouyer unmasks the false opposition, however, between asceticism and humanism, between the way of the Cross and human fulfillment. For it is precisely the created order, fashioned through the agency of God's *Logos*, which is the object of God's redemptive love revealed in the *Logos*-made-flesh, Jesus Christ. In a properly Christian vision, it is creation itself which is healed, elevated, and restored by the redeeming work of Christ Crucified; creation is not overcome or undone by the grace communicated through Christ's self-denying *agape*, but rather restored and glorified by its full participation in its Glorified Lord's self-giving (and thus life-giving) love. This *agape* is experienced, indeed even tasted, within the sacred liturgy, which offers to participants even here and now a share in the *eschaton* to come. The *telos* or purposeful end of redeemed humanity is precisely *in Christ*, who reveals himself in the breaking of bread, and through the unceasing liturgical action of the Church offers a genuine participation in his own divine life, experienced in this age only enigmatically, but fully in the age to come.

Thus the Cross is not an obstacle to human fulfillment; it is rather the principal means of its fulfillment. This is why Bouyer describes a properly Christian humanistic vision as eschatological.[26] It is only in light of the *eschaton* of human history in Christ that the deepest human aspirations will be achieved; closed in on itself and apart from an in-breaking of Divine Love, a fallen creation can only endlessly recapitulate its own errors. For Bouyer (and he would no doubt argue, for the entire Christian tradition), the spiritual life is a continual movement, under the promptings of grace, toward that *telos* both revealed and made possible by Jesus Christ: a restored and glorified humanity, re-created by its sharing in the very life of God, a life understood inseparably from his death.

Chapter 1

THE SPIRITUAL LIFE ACCORDING TO CATHOLIC TRADITION

Religious Life, Spiritual Life, Interior Life

An introduction to the "spiritual life" must begin by making quite clear the sense in which this expression is to be used. We must start, therefore, by defining the spiritual life. But such a definition will inevitably prove either too vague or too abstract unless at the outset the spiritual life is correlated with two other more or less synonymous terms or expressions: "the religious life" and "the interior life."

We should note, first of all, that these three expressions are currently used in a loose way which tends to confuse them. Yet, even though the three more or less overlap, they do not exactly coincide. An effort to ascertain, as far as possible, what distinguishes them from one another and what they have in common will, therefore, prove enlightening.

We need to realize that there have existed, and still do exist, some forms of the "religious life" which imply neither any "spiritual life" nor any "interior life" properly so called. The old

13

Latin religion, that of the pagan peasants of Latium, involved nothing more than the correct carrying out of certain rites, with the exact repetition of certain formulae. Later on, as we learn from Cicero, a pontiff like Cotta could be considered beyond reproach even though he openly cast doubt on the very existence of the gods. Whether he himself was a believer or not was his own personal affair. All that was required of him was that he carry out the rites properly and properly pronounce the formulae.

Obviously, these are extreme examples. But in Christianity itself, among Catholics and among Protestants as well—even though the latter tend to minimize the essential value of external religion—men can be found whose religion, in actual fact, consists mostly, if not exclusively, of "practices" or "good works," diligence in fulfilling ritual obligations (receiving the sacraments or reading the Bible). Is not this the essence if not the whole of the piety of many Christians, who may be very sincere and even devout after their fashion? For others, religion consists chiefly in a charitable activism in which they spend themselves, without stint, on all kinds of good works and social services. Doubtless, neither the one case nor the other (and they are often found in combination) could be considered by anyone who reflects on it a little to represent an ideal form of Christianity. But this is the sum or at least the principal part of Christianity for many people, who are often excellent persons filled with good will, and by no means "hypocritical Pharisees."

Again, in that form of Buddhism which seems to be especially pure and primitive, called Hinayana (that is, "the little conveyance"), we find what might be called a "religion without God." Actually, this last term seems ill-chosen; it is meaningless: there can be no religion unless it has some sort of God as its object, even if, as with the Romans of the decadence, the real existence of that object can be questioned. Let us say instead that the form of Buddhism we are speaking of is a form of spirituality, a "spiritual life," detached from all religion. Buddha does not deny the gods: he simply detaches himself from them as he does from all distinct existence. In principle, the "spiritual life" which he preached consisted entirely in this detachment, this absolute disinterestedness in regard to all being—cosmic, human, or divine. Such a "spiritual life" may well seem paradoxical. But it does in fact exist, and it has been and remains, at least for a certain number of persons, an experience the final meaninglessness of which we must deplore without denying either its psychological reality or its grandeur.

It is no less strange, perhaps, to have to recognize that there are many people who have an "interior life" which, though very rich, has nothing religious about it and could not be considered a "spiritual life" however widely that notion were extended. Poets and artists may be complete unbelievers and even avowed materialists and, nevertheless, experience and communicate a richness of imagination, of thought, of emotion, which is all their own. They may know nothing of the "religious life" and even have no "spiritual life"—if by this we understand at least some access to a reality other than that of the sensible world and one which transcends the individual. But it cannot be denied that such people have an "interior life," nor, often, that this life is of an exceptional richness.

Think, for example, of Proust's world of a past relived, that extraordinary reconstruction of the memory in an over-sensitized consciousness. Or consider the literally fabulous development of consciousness in a novel like Joyce's *Ulysses*, a real interior epic. One of these authors felt nothing but complete indifference to religion, and the other had become passionately hostile to it; nor can it seriously be questioned that each of them deliberately shut himself up in an absolute denial of anything beyond the sensible world. The strange, even monstrous "interior life" transmitted to us in their work possesses nonetheless a reality which is not only indubitable but even stupefying. Still more strange, certainly, is the case of certain poets. The experiences which Wordsworth not only describes but evokes in the strongest sense of the term, in his verses on Tintern Abbey and in many passages of his autobiographical poems, recall—occasionally to the point of positively misleading the reader—the very forms of mystical experience. Yet, in spite of the religious considerations with which the poet often accompanies the expression of these experiences, it is very doubtful whether this poetic experience reaches out to any reality other than that of the depths of the soul that feels it.

But it is not necessary, perhaps, to bring in artists and poets in order, as it were, to put one's finger on the experience of an "interior life" which is certainly not essentially religious and which cannot strictly be called a "spiritual life." Do not many persons—all men and women, it may be—especially in certain periods of childhood or early youth, create for themselves a dream life wholly and exclusively their own?

And in this waking dream, which they people with beings and things in conformity with their most intimate desires, unrealizable or as yet unrealized in ordinary life, do they not live an "interior life," which can take over to such a degree as to discolor or even to inhibit all their exterior life?

When we consider all these facts, to which many more could easily be added, our previously fluid notions now appear to have crystallized without any forcing, of their own accord.

The "religious life," in the widest sense of the term, appears, or is maintained, whenever there is experienced, in any way, a relationship of any kind with a transcendent deity, real or supposed—a relationship which can even, in certain extreme cases, be nothing more than a survival in our behavior of something that our intelligence finds doubtful.

Conversely, there is an "interior life" when the life of a human being takes on a conscious, more or less autonomous, development.

But the "spiritual life" is not attained until this "interior life" develops, not in isolation but in the awareness of a spiritual reality, however this be understood, a reality that goes beyond the consciousness of the individual. Yet this "spiritual reality" is not necessarily apprehended as divine; this character may even be expressly denied it.

If, however, the "spirit" known in the "spiritual life" is recognized not only as "something," but as "someone," then the "spiritual life" will be a "religious life" as well. If it is not so recognized, then however lofty (or deep) its reach, the "spiritual life" will not in any way coincide with the "religious life" as such.

The Spiritual Life in Christianity

If we keep the distinctions we have thus arrived at consciously in our minds, whatever their further import may be, we cannot but be struck by one constant fact. In studying the whole of human history or trying to fathom the psychology of a particular individual, the same conclusion is evident: of its own accord, the interior life tends to develop into the spiritual life, which, in turn, orients itself no less spontaneously toward some form of religious life.

Artists and poets may be militant materialists. But their very passion to "make" a work of art a "poetic work" expresses the inherent need of every intense interior life to go beyond the enclosed cell of the individual, to become communication, communion. And nothing is more striking in the interior dream cherished by so many people than the impassioned tendency to turn toward a world possessing a reality that surpasses us, that subsists and exists independently of us.

Buddhism, on the other hand, which we pointed to as the most amazing effort humans have ever made to provide themselves with a spiritual life while dispensing with the religious life, betrays, as if by surprise, to what a degree such an effort is unnatural. Conceived precisely as a way of satisfying the human need for a spiritual life outside all religion, it has been unable to hold to its primitive "atheism." From the original Hinayana, deliberately areligious, Buddhism has developed toward the Mahayana ("the great conveyance"), that is, toward a new form of popular religion and one still capable—as in Amidism for instance—of the highest refinements. Here, the Buddha himself becomes a god: the perfect savior-god who takes the place of all the gods whom he has caused to fade from the concern of his disciples.

From this point of view, Christianity is seen to be a form of "spiritual life" in which our most personal, most interiorized relationship with God himself in his transcendent reality is fully recognized and formally cultivated.

In this respect, nothing could be more contrary to the tendency which seems inherent in all the ways of Indian spirituality, even in those which, having been dominated for sometime by Buddhism, have rejected it under one or another of its forms. In Hinduism, as in many other Far-Eastern spiritualities more or less closely related to it, like Chinese Taoism, the spiritual person tends toward an absorption of his or her proper personality in a deity which is itself impersonal. The Christian, on the contrary, tends to the full development of a life which is wholly human and at the same time wholly personal, in the discovery of a God who is not only himself a person, but the personal being *par excellence*.

Nobody, it would seem, has set out this difference, this radical opposition, in a clearer light than has the historian and psychologist of religions, Rudolf Otto. His study is all the more revealing in that all the tendencies of the liberal Protestantism with which he is imbued would tend rather to minimize as far as possible the importance of dogmatic conceptions in religion in general and in Christianity in particular. It is all the more remarkable, then, to see how in one of his most important works, he brings out this characteristic which is uniquely proper to the Christian spiritual life.

Furthermore, he intentionally took, as examples for comparison, two great spiritual thinkers the specific differences between whom, one would have thought a priori, he would find reduced to nothing or almost nothing. In Christianity, he chose Meister Eckhart, whose writings contain a profusion of expressions which seem to avow a desire for fusion, for identification, and even for the blessed losing of one's distinct personality in God. And from Hinduism, he selected the figure of Sankara, who retains as perhaps no other Oriental at the very heart of what might be called his "mysticism," the use of personal formulae to speak of the union of God and the soul.

In spite of all these conditions, then, which would seemingly combine to blur as much as possible the differences between the two spiritualities, the purely scientific and phenomenological comparison to which Otto devoted himself led to the most decisive as well as the most unexpected results. While Sankara seemed to approach most closely to the Christian experience of a personal encounter with a God who is himself personal, a fairly close analysis of his formulae show that such is not in the least the import of his statements. As he uses expressions of this kind in relation to the experience he wishes to characterize, they have none of the implications which we should be inclined to give them. In the end, there can be no doubt about the final lack of distinction in his thought between God and man, who, furthermore, have never been recognized as two beings but only as two forms of being, and of the same being. In contrast, the appearances of Pantheism to be found in Eckhart are only appearances which do not bear up under an attentive analysis. Studied objectively, Eckhart, even when he seems on the verge of a total immersion of his own personality in the abyss of a formless deity, lets it clearly be seen that, for him, however united God and the soul may become, they remain—without the possibility of confusion—two beings who are radically distinct in their very union. . . .

Yet this is still not to say enough. A Christian spiritual life is not one dominated simply by the ineradicable, indestructible *idea* on the part of the Christian that God is a person. This life flows from the *fact* that God has revealed himself to us as a person. No Christian spirituality worthy of the name can exist where the conviction has been weakened that God, in Christ, has made himself known to us by his own words, his own acts as Someone. The whole spiritual life of Christians is aroused and formed by the fact that, as they believe, God has spoken to us and that his living Word has been made flesh amongst us. In other words, in Christianity, the spiritual life does not start from a certain conception of God, not even from the idea that he is a personal God, but from *faith*, the faith which is proper to Christianity; that is, the assent we give to the Word of God, to that Word which is made known to us, which is given to us in Christ Jesus.

A very simple comparison will serve to clarify this absolutely fundamental point. We all know the story of Robinson Crusoe. In an early period of his apparently solitary existence on that island on which the storm had cast him, he believed himself to be entirely alone. Soon, however, there came the moment when he observed the traces of someone other than himself. He came upon some branches broken in such a way that it did not seem as if the act could have been performed by any being other than a man, and he was sure that he had not done it himself. He found the remains of a fire that he had not kindled. And, finally, he saw in the sand the print of a foot that was not his own.

At this stage of his story, is not Crusoe, as it were, the image of the man who, in reflecting on the world in which he finds himself immersed (or, for that matter, in reflecting on himself), has discovered that God exists and that, like himself, he is not only something but someone? At this moment, man is at the highest point to which merely natural religion can lead him: the impassioned conviction that God exists and that he exists as a reality which is not only spiritual but also personal.

But everything is changed on the day when Crusoe sees Friday coming to meet him on the beach and when he speaks with him, even though at first he does not understand his language. Now he has something quite different from the mere conviction, however firmly this had been established, that the other existed and that he was also someone. Or, rather, this conviction is no longer the logical conclusion of a chain of abstract reasoning. It has become a fact, a fact to which his own most vital experience itself commits him.

The same is true of Christianity, or of Judaism before it, as compared with the highest forms of natural religion. God, his personality, is no longer simply the object of rational conviction. He is known in the supremely personal, the interpersonal, fact of his revelation. He is known, more precisely, in the personal relationship which his own initiative in coming to meet us, and this alone, is in the process of establishing. . . .

This does not, it should be noted, suppress or lessen the value of any of the religious certitudes at which man, without the aid of the Judeo-Christian revelation, has occasionally been able to arrive. It should rather be said that these certitudes simply find themselves confirmed and also transfigured. But it must be said once and for all that Christianity and Judaism cannot, in spite of these common certitudes, be put on the same level as any other religion, even of some ideal form in which would be concentrated the best elements of all religions. The revealed religion of the Old and the New Testaments is something entirely different. It is a fact and no longer an idea—however immense may be the effects that a mere idea can have on the life of man. It is the fact of the entrance of God, no longer as an idea but as a living person, into the life of man. And it is to this fact that Christian faith adheres, just as, were this one fact eliminated, Christian faith would simply and surely dissolve.

We should realize clearly that this primordial fact is preeminently the fact that God has spoken to us. In understanding the significance of the fact, we can be aided particularly by a contemporary Jewish philosopher, Martin Buber, whose thought is nourished by the spiritual tradition of the Hassidim in which Judaism might be said to be still vibrating with an echo of the great experience of the prophets.

Buber has cogently shown that no one really becomes a person to us except in speaking, in a dialogue. Someone to whom you have never spoken and, above all, someone who has never spoken to you is not a person to you in full reality. A "he" whom you speak about but who does not speak to you or you to him is not actually someone to you but only something—even though you force yourself to think otherwise, even though you know abstractly that "he" exists, personally, as you do. It is only the "you" to whom I speak who is someone to me, and, shall we say, it is above all the "you" who has spoken to me who becomes someone to me effectively.

God, the God of Israel, the God of the Bible, the God of Jesus Christ is precisely this God and the only God who can become to us not only a "he" remaining essentially impersonal but also a "you" in full reality. And he is this "you" above all because he has manifested himself to us as supremely the "I," the one who has not waited to meet us until we should take the first step, but who has himself taken the initiative in a dialogue between him and ourselves. Thus, at one and the same time, he asserts himself as *the personality* among all others, and he creates our own selves, not merely as embryonic but as truly conscious personalities endowed with self-mastery. We are not such, indeed we cannot be such, by jealously shutting ourselves up in ourselves. Quite the contrary, we can only be our true selves in this dialogue in which the divine "I" creates us as its interlocutors, as those "you's" which can only become "I's" in their turn by taking heed of his call and responding to it.

We can see already, therefore, that it is in no way an accidental circumstance that the eminently personal, interpersonal character of the Christian spiritual life is connected with a revelation, and still more precisely, with a divine Word. In the very nature of things, these two facts are connected by a most intimate bond. They are, indeed, only two correlative aspects of that great fact which Christianity is and which constitutes the very object of our faith. God has spoken to us. He has given himself to us in his Word: this is what we believe, and this belief not only dominates our Christian spiritual life but is its very source, its unique source.

We must emphasize again, as certain contemporary Protestant theologians, beginning with Karl Barth, have done with good reason, that according to this view, it is not enough to say that God, the God who speaks, is the object of the Christian faith. We must go still further and say that this faith recognizes him from the first, in the relationship, in the dialogue between humanity and God (or, much better, between him and humanity), as the subject. For, to the Jew and to the Christian, the reality of the divine Word is not simply that of some response that God has given to the cry of the person who seeks him, but rather the gratuitous, free, sovereign initiative of God seeking even the person who has not sought him, the one who has not concerned himself or herself with God at all. As the Gospel says, "It is not you who have first loved me, it is I who have loved you." It was not Israel who chose God; it was God who chose Israel, who elected it, who created it simply by his call. In this dialogue, God is the primary interlocutor, who not only himself comes to meet the other speaker but who also creates the other and who does not cease to recreate him or her by calling to him or her in the void.

Indeed, this theme of the Word which not only saves but also creates by its own power, which saves only by recreating, is above all, to use the phrase of the prophet, "what has never arisen in the heart of man, but what God has revealed to us. . . ."

The Spiritual Life in the Catholic Church

All this could be said of any form of spiritual life, whether Catholic or Protestant, in which there remains anything authentically Christian. All this was already true of the spiritual life of Judaism: for this life too depends not only on faith in the God who speaks but also on that faith as already centered on the supreme gift of God given in his Messiah, his Anointed, his Christ—even though Christ is believed in at this stage only in hope. But the specific characteristic of a Catholic spiritual life is the additional and basic distinction that God not only actually does speak to us (as the Jews have believed since the Old Covenant), that he not only has already spoken to us in a definitive way in his Christ (as the Protestants believe together with us) but also that he continues to speak to us and to speak to us in his Christ, by and in the Church.

Here it becomes evident that Catholicism is not only one form of Christianity among others, but that it is the only form which continues to be what ancient Judaism already was, yet imperfectly: the religion not only of a Word once spoken, preserved in its meaning but no longer in its living actuality, but, on the contrary, the religion of the Word and of the definitive and total Word, which is still always living, always present, always spoken here and now.

Doubtless, the best of Protestant spirituality itself also affirms in a certain way that the divine Word, proclaimed in Christ to this world perfectly and therefore definitively two thousand years ago, is capable of remaining for us (or more exactly, of again being) always present, always intact. But Protestantism, insofar as it is opposed to Catholicism, only admits this present actuality as being wholly interiorized, and to that extent individualized. The Protestant who reads the divine Word once inspired by the Holy Spirit can find it illuminated for him or her here and now by what he or she calls the "interior witness" of that same Spirit. Thus Protestantism tends to produce a spirituality which springs entirely from the co-presence and mutual relationship between the person of God revealed in the Christ of the Gospels and the individual person of the believer.

But, for Catholicism, there is no fully authentic Christian spirituality without the realization of an equal co-presence of our fellow believers with Christ and ourselves, in the Church. And we should strongly emphasize the fact that this, in the Catholic view, is not only necessary with a necessity of means but is essential to the very goal of the spiritual life.

It might be said that, in Protestantism, everything goes on, or seems to go on, as if the Incarnation had ended with the Ascension of the Savior. The memory of that past Incarnation preserved in the Gospels seems to furnish simply an occasion for the direct contact of each individual soul with the Word that has once for all set down its human expression in these books alone.

In the Catholic vision (which, according to the opinion of a growing number of Protestant exegetes, is simply the continuation of the vision of the apostolic Church), things are entirely different. Before being set down in a written text for its definitive expression, the Word of Christ, which is one with himself, with his living presence, remains always present in the Church inasmuch as the Church is founded on the apostles. What distinguishes the apostles in their mission is, in fact, that as their name indicates, they are those "sent," in whom he who sends them remains mysteriously present. He "who hears you, hears me. . . . He who receives you, receives me. . . . Go, baptize all nations, teaching them to observe all things I have commanded you. I am with you all days, even to the end of the world. . . . "

In other words, it is not only the content of the divine Word which, in the inspired texts of which the Church is the guardian, remains in the Church. It is that Word itself, as living act, as presence. In Christ, indeed, it is evident that less than ever can the one exist without the other. For the content of the definitive Word of the Gospel is Christ himself. But Christ is the mystery of a living person who, even though he expresses himself always in the same words, can only be truly communicated in his personal presence dwelling beneath these words. This is precisely what is meant by the apostolate as we have just defined it.

Undoubtedly, a most important aspect of that unique ministry of the apostles was that, inspired by the very Spirit of Christ, they should set themselves to gathering, fixing, and illuminating the letter of what Christ had said and done, in their Epistles as well as in the written Gospels. And this does not need to be done again.

But it was an equally important aspect of their ministry, to say the least, to cause the Church which they formed to enter into a real community of life with Christ—a community of life so real, once again, that she would possess not only the memory of what he had said and done but his perpetual presence, and all this now living in her and for her.

So far as the text of the New Testament was concerned, the bishops, successors of the apostles in their apostolate, did not have to add anything but only to keep it as it was. And yet, not only in order to preserve its authentic interpretation, but still more and above all to preserve that perpetual and living reality which is so essential to the Gospel in the Church, the bishops are always assured, like the apostles and as being their successors, of this presence of Christ with them—the presence which, once again, he promised, "even to the end of the world." The fidelity of the interpretation given by the Church, according to the Spirit of Christ, to the letter of what he said and of what the apostles said by his power is itself guaranteed only by the certitude of his living presence, of his being with the bishops as with the apostles, for the whole Body of the Church even to the end of time.

Thus, it is always in the assembly of his own, which remains the same assembly as the apostolic Church because those who assemble it are the successors of the apostles themselves, those who continue their apostolate—it is always in this same definitive People of God that Christ, always with the same actuality, the same personal reality, creative of life, proclaims the Gospel: the supreme Word of God which is himself.

It is, therefore, into the Church, the true Body of Christ, that we must be incorporated in order to participate in the Spirit of Christ, and, as a consequence, to receive his words, not as a mere dead letter, but as words which remain always life-giving because here they remain always living, always uttered by the very Word of God.

That this divine Word, fully revealed, given to humanity in Christ, should wish to reach us and does reach us in this way becomes quite comprehensible when we consider the purpose it has in view. This purpose, as St. Paul tells us in the Epistle to the Colossians, is to reconcile all men and women with one another and with the heavenly Father in the very Body of his Son. Or better still, as the Epistle to the Ephesians says, it is to recapitulate all things in Christ. The Incarnation is far from being a passing phase, as it were, in the historic proclamation of the unique Word of God in the world. It must not only endure forever but also continue to be incorporated in all humanity, so to speak, beginning with the humanity of Christ. This is what St. Paul presents as the growth of Christ in us, which must continue, he tells us, "until we all meet in the fullness of the stature of Christ, in such a way as to form in him one perfect man" (Eph 4:13). And this is why in this context he defines the Church as "the fullness [of Christ], of him who wholly fulfills himself in all" (Eph 1:23).

In the perspective of all these facts it becomes clear, as we said above, that to hear the Word of God which is Christ in the Church is imposed on us today with a necessity not only of means but of end. That, by the express will of Christ, this Word always animated by his Spirit should be found only in his Body which is the Church is clearly explained when we consider that what this Word proclaims is precisely our being gathered all together in this same Body of Christ "fulfilling himself wholly in all." Here, we might say, the means and the end are not two things really distinct: the means is only the seed of the end; the end only the flowering of the means. This Body of Christ which is the Church, founded on the apostolate, takes on, by means of the apostolate, all its reality in "recapitulating all things in Christ."

To say the same thing in a different way, we could say again that the Word of God in Christ is addressed to the Church, produces the Church. It is natural, therefore, that we must be incorporated into the Church in process of being made, in order there to receive, in all its living actuality, the divine Word which is Christ.

What does this Word actually speak to us about? The love of God that urges us and desires to gather us all together as one in him. It is, therefore, in the very unity that the Word is creating that it must be heard, and we hear it effectively only in achieving, so far as we ourselves are concerned, that unity which is in the process of being brought about.

God calls us together to love him. But we cannot love him as he loves us, with the love with which he loves us, without loving inseparably from him all those whom he loves inseparably from us. We are not only to love our neighbor *after* having loved God. We are to love God *in loving* our neighbor. The experience of life in the Church is, finally, the experience of the inseparability of these two loves.

Catholic Christianity, then, is simply integral Christianity. Catholic spirituality is simply Christian spirituality in its fullness: a spiritual life in which our own most interior, most personal life opens out and develops, only in the development of that personal relationship which God wishes to establish with us in speaking to us in Christ. But this Word of Christ, this Word which is Christ, which reveals to us the love of God in revealing to us the Trinitarian life of the divine persons, reveals this to us only as it extends this love to all men and women, as, in the Church, it opens out, so to say, the holy society of the Trinity to all humanity.

It is impossible clearly to define even in the most limited way what this Word of God is, the Word addressed to men in Christ and in the Church which must dominate all authentic

Christian spirituality, without coming at once, as we have done, to define it as a word of love. This is one of the chief objects of the present book—to define clearly what the love of God is that is announced by this Word, the love which St. Paul tells us has been "poured out in our hearts by the Holy Spirit" (Rom 5:5). But here at our starting point, we should at least bring out certain essential characteristics of the love of God revealed by the Word of God, this Word which ultimately is Christ himself.

It may be said, in fact, that the faith which is at the basis of all Christian spirituality in virtue of the welcome it gives to the divine Word is essentially faith in the love of God revealed and manifested by this Word. On the side of the God who speaks, the personal relationship that he wishes to establish with us is born of his love. On our side, it is born of the faith which we give to the revelation of that love.

But Christian faith is not faith in any kind of love of God we might conceive of. It is faith precisely in that unique love which the Word reveals to us, which it alone can reveal to us, and which, in fact, it alone has revealed to us.

It is most important to emphasize this point at the very outset. The notion of "love of God" is, in fact, essentially polymorphic. More particularly, our Western world—before Christianity and outside the Judeo-Christian revelation—had arrived at a certain idea, often very lofty, of the "love of God." We are continually in danger of confusing this idea with the idea, or rather the reality, that the divine Word reveals to us. The risk is that we then unconsciously adulterate this Word and that, even in repeating the phrase "the love of God," we lose sight of the essence of what the Word wishes to say to us and of what it alone, again, can say to us.

The first point, which distinguishes this "love of God" made known to us only by his Word, is the fact that it is the love of which God is himself the subject before there can be any question of his becoming its object. Or, if you prefer, it is not primarily the love with which God is loved but the love with which he loves. This is the basic characteristic of the properly Christian "love of God," always designated in the texts of the New Testament by the Greek word *agape*. In contrast, the "love of God" which the Greek spirituality, a stranger to Christianity, from Plato to Plotinus designated by the word *eros* was only a love which has God for object and which can never have him for subject: it is and can be only a love with which God can be loved.

Since the *agape* of which the New Testament speaks is the love with which God loves, the love which is proper to him, it is in no way made of desire as are our human loves. It does not betray any trace of a need to be satisfied in him; it is, on the contrary, the supreme gift, a pure creative gift. God does not love because he discovers in the beings he loves some quality which exists prior to his love and arouses it. On the contrary, God makes beings lovable in loving them: in fact, his love not only gives everything which is lovable about them—it gives them their very being!

Hence, this love of God is by no means simply a "spiritual love" as opposed to every form of "carnal love." Such was the *eros* of Plato. But this remained nonetheless made entirely of desire. It was a desire for "spiritual" goods in opposition to "sensual" or "material" goods. For this reason, in the eyes even of the most religious of the Greeks, the gods could not love. By definition, nothing was lacking to them; since they were gods, what did they have to desire? True enough, the Greeks too said that the "love of God" moves all things, yet as they understood it, this could not be anything but the love with which God is loved as the supremely desirable Good. Quite otherwise, when Dante spoke of "the Love that moves the sun and the other stars," he meant *agape*, the love with which God loves everything that is his work.

Thus only God can love with a love that transcends all desire. For only God can live in giving himself, in lavishing himself, he who is the source of all good and an infinite source. And so the Christian God does nothing but love with this love, which is his alone: he *is* love—this kind of love. Such is, as it were, the ultimate message of the divine Word: the meaning and the profound reality of the Word of God made flesh.

On the other hand, the supreme gift that God's love gives us—being the gift, not simply of life in general but also of his own life—this is also the gift of the possibility, the capacity to love as he alone loves. This is grace in its final essence—the free gift which the Word promises to us and gives to us. And this also is the requirement that it formulates for us.

Faith, consequently, in recognizing the love of God in Christ, welcomes this appeal that God makes to us: the appeal to love as we have been loved. And this is what is finally realized in the Church, the Body of Christ made up of all those in whose hearts the Spirit of Christ has poured out the love of the Father. Thus the Church, built up around Christ, is seen to be an extension, an opening out to all humankind of the society of the divine persons, the Trinity of the *agape*.

Mistaken Notions in Present-Day Spirituality

The principles that we have just laid out will be developed and clarified by what follows. But even now they allow us to distinguish and to correct certain errors of the day.

The first is what might be called "psychologism." By this term, we mean the temptation, so strongly felt in our age, to reduce the spiritual life to certain states of consciousness. (There is no question here of minimizing the considerable degree of assistance that religious psychology has already furnished and should continue to furnish, not only to a scientific study of the spiritual life but also to a practice enlightened by such a study.) Moreover, a certain reflexive consciousness has become so generally characteristic of modern society that it would be impossible not to take account of it in spirituality. Since the end of the Middle Ages, men and women have become accustomed to a certain self-consciousness, have become attentive to their own states of soul in such a way that their spiritual life—less, perhaps, than any other area of their existence—now cannot abstract from it. It is, in fact, the great merit both of the Carmelite school (St. Teresa and St. John of the Cross) and of the Jesuit school (following St. Ignatius Loyola and his *Spiritual Exercises*) to have succeeded in incorporating this new factor into Christian spirituality. These various spiritual leaders succeeded in giving to the normal evolution of states of consciousness throughout our spiritual development the attention that this evolution had come to claim in consequence of the growth of reflexive consciousness in souls at that period. Better still, St. Ignatius in particular knew how to reveal and to bring systematically into play the different resources of our conscious life to further the progress of the soul itself in its relations with God.

All this constitutes a very valuable gain and one which there can be no question of laying aside—even less question because it was required by a shift which may well be irreversible in the subjectivity of modern society. But the importance to spirituality acquired at a relatively recent date by these new factors should not in any way eliminate or minimize more primitive elements which remain fundamental. Above all, from the fact of this inevitable development we should not infer the fallacious conclusion that the spiritual life is reduced to certain states of consciousness and to the production of these states by the appropriate psychological means. To go more deeply into the question, we need say that those successive states of consciousness which mark out the course of a spiritual life, and especially the spiritual life of a Christian, cannot be understood by means of a purely immanent analysis alone. In other words, we must not presume that they contain in themselves their own full and complete explanation.

Let us recall in this connection that the tendency and the temptation of all the psychological studies made in the nineteenth century was to deal with states of consciousness as if they had nothing beyond them. The fact that these states are normally polarized by an object which is independent of them was apparently forgotten or considered as having no importance. In contrast, the phenomenological school has now clearly brought out the impossibility, the unreality, of a serious study of states of consciousness which neglects these objects—objects which transcend the consciousness but from which it is, as it were, wholly suspended. The "intentionality" of a consciousness, that is, its spontaneous reference to something transcending it, is not a secondary factor but a central one.

Obviously, we have here a truth which is especially enlightening and of particular importance with regard to religious consciousness and all its specific phenomena. It follows that no spirituality—Christian spirituality least of all, in view of what we have said concerning the importance to it of the personal relationship with God—can, therefore, be adequately studied by means of a purely psychological analysis. The study of the object toward which the psychology of the religious subject is oriented and in which it is centered is of capital importance here. To abstract from this is to abstract from what is essential in a spirituality, of whatever kind it may be. In particular, there can be no question of interpreting or even simply of describing the Christian spiritual life in abstraction from the God who dominates it: the God who speaks to us through Christ in the Church. The steps, the aspirations, even the movements of such a spirituality become incomprehensible if we neglect what is their moving force.

An inadequate appreciation of this first point has brought about a second error in modern spirituality: its tendency to syncretism. Actually, when one reduces the spiritual life to a simple matter of completely immanent psychology, one goes on inevitably to the idea that the "religious experience," as it is called, is, or might be, the same everywhere. From the moment that what gives a spirituality its very content is considered to be nonexistent or devoid of importance, there remains nothing more, obviously, than what belongs to the fundamental structure of the human soul, a structure which is practically invariable.

A historian and psychologist of religion like Rudolf Otto can, to be sure, by the very penetration of his analyses, succeed in escaping from such an illusion which rests on sophistry. But the ordinary student of these disciplines is easily tempted to believe that, once the depths of the soul are reached, in the last analysis, the religious experiences of a Protestant, of a Catholic (or even of a Buddhist!) are basically the same. The immediate conclusion is then drawn that spirituality causes us to be free of, and to go beyond, the frontiers of "churches" and "dogmas." Doubtless, the moderate-minded would tell us that nonetheless we should not do away with "churches" and "dogmas." These things, they would explain, can be useful to sustain beginners. And they would go so far as to say that these things have a permanent value even for the most advanced souls, but only by virtue of being symbols—in the sense of their symbolizing the permanent needs of the human soul. This amounts to saying that any particular "church" or "dogma" and, in one way or another, all "churches" and all "dogmas" move toward the same lofty realities which transcend them all.

Positions of this kind have been popularized by writings like the *Perennial Philosophy* of Aldous Huxley. They find, or seem to find, a justification in the "gnosis," as we might call it, which Jung tends more and more to impose on and confuse with his psychological analyses, which otherwise frequently give evidence of genius.

It is undeniable that any position such as this exercises a kind of fascination even on certain Catholics, and in particular on those whose interest in the spiritual life has been allowed to remain within the confines of a narrowly psychological approach. Let us note the fact that it is quite true that God is the master of his own gifts and that he can, in consequence, if such be his good pleasure give marvelous experiences to the spiritually minded outside the Catholic faith and even outside Christianity. This truth should cause us to look with respect even on what is most foreign to us in the spiritualities developed outside the Church. But it in no way justifies us in the tendency to minimize the importance of Catholic dogma for the normal development of a fully Christian spiritual life. Indeed, what has been said above should suffice to convince us that the acceptance of dogma, a living awareness of it in the bosom of the Church, is the condition *sine qua non* of a spirituality that is truly and fully Christian.

In seemingly direct opposition to these syncretist tendencies is another which is also very much alive amongst us: the tendency to favor, nay, even to create out of whole cloth, exaggeratedly specialized spiritualities. If the foregoing error was the product, not of modern psychology as such, but of a narrow abuse of it, the tendency we should now discuss briefly finds its starting point rather in history, but in a history that stays on the surface of things.

The reestablishment in the nineteenth century of the religious orders that had been banished by the French Revolution led to a thoroughgoing reconstruction in which there was, inevitably, a certain degree of artificiality. In accord with a vision of history which was often quite romantic, institutions were reproduced in the form they were thought to have had in an idealized period. In this re-creation, it must be admitted, no one knew quite where to draw a line between what had been merely ephemeral and transitory and what was permanent and essential. In the field of spirituality especially, not only each of the great orders but also each particular congregation, tended to rediscover itself and to give itself, in accordance with the work of one or another saintly founder, a physiognomy that would be proper to it. Thus not only were historical distinctions made between different schools of spirituality such as the Flemish or the Spanish—which would have been perfectly legitimate had the relativity of these distinctions even on the level of history been preserved. But there was further brought about the systematic cultivation, in and for the sake of their very distinctiveness, of a Benedictine spirituality, a Jesuit spirituality, a Carmelite spirituality, etc. There might well have been some justification for this proceeding if each order or congregation had limited itself to gathering together from its first Fathers and Mothers the teachings which could be applied to its specific tasks. But what can be said of these efforts to create for each religious "family" a complete vision of the spiritual world hermetically sealed off from any other vision and foreign, if not hostile, to those which were being developed at the same time? Such efforts, obviously, whether open or disguised, are insolubly self-contradictory. How can Teresian spirituality and Ignatian spirituality, for example, be set up as two separate edifices, when it is obvious that St. Teresa took as her directors Jesuits, Dominicans, Franciscans, as well as Carmelites, with the sole proviso that they be men of

God and good theologians? And St. Ignatius himself, although his spiritual work is so rigorously constructed, neglected none of the sources of Catholic tradition available to him, including monastic sources first of all, the ideal of which has often been made out to be radically opposed to his!

It must be said without mincing words: no great historical Christian spirituality lends itself to such test-tube development without, as a result, having its basic constituents adulterated by disciples who may be very well-intentioned but show themselves to be unintelligent descendants of the masters they affect to serve. Conversely, it must be said, a particular spirituality which would lend itself to such treatment immediately betrays the fact that it is not an authentically Catholic development of Christianity but merely a sectarian deformation. St. Benedict, St. Francis, St. Ignatius never wished—quite the contrary—to do anything other than propose to their contemporaries perennial Christian spirituality, Catholic spirituality, as simply adapted— in its presentation far more than in its ultimate bases—to the immediate needs of their contemporaries.

What are we to think, then, of these more recent spiritualities which aim from the outset to fit the narrowly specialized needs of certain environments or certain states of life? Often appearing in conjunction with developments of specialized Catholic action, they are the result of a general tendency, of which they are only one product among many.

There was first the desire to give the "diocesan clergy" a particular spirituality, conceived expressly so that they would not feel inferior in comparison with the different religious orders. Then there was the desire to work out a spirituality for the laity, which would be opposed, like the foregoing, to the spirituality of religious, and particularly of monks, and to priestly spirituality as well. In these efforts, we should realize, the good and the bad are all too easily intermingled. The inextricable confusions in which they necessarily become involved can be easily seen in connection with this desire to construct a lay spirituality as something quite distinct from monastic spirituality—for the primitive monks, the very creators of monastic spirituality, actually were, and never desired to be anything other than, devoted laypeople! As for the idea of a spirituality for the diocesan clergy, added on like one more little chapel alongside the spiritualities of the different religious orders, it might be remarked that this is in flagrant contradiction with the great ideal of priestly spirituality developed in France in the seventeenth century—an ideal directly inspired by the Fathers, especially St. John Chrysostom and St. Gregory the Great. For this ideal, as expressed in Bossuet's memorable formulation in his funeral oration for Fr. Bourgoing, was of men who wished "to have no other rules but the laws that [Christ] gave to his Church, and no superiors other than his bishops. . . ."

Coming finally to the various forms of spirituality for workers, farmers, students, etc., which have been proposed in certain circles of specialized Catholic action, we find that there seems to be a confusion here between the legitimate concern that the spirituality of the Gospel should permeate the solutions to problems proper to each particular environment and a vague and chimerical ideal which, if it were (or could be) defined, would come down to refashioning the Gospel to fit the mentality, the professional bent, the prejudices, or the current fads of one or another of these various environments. . . . At this rate, we should speedily arrive at the production of a Christianity, or rather of a multitude of Christianities, of classes or cliques, of the kind at which St. Paul's exclamation is directly aimed: "There is no longer either Greek or Jew, either circumcision or uncircumcision, either Barbarian or Scythian, either slave or free man, but Christ is all in all" (Col 3:2).

As the same apostle says, what defines Christian spirituality is not any distinction, natural or otherwise, of such and such a Christian or group of Christians, but "one faith, one Baptism, one Lord, one Spirit, one God and Savior of all." Undoubtedly, the same Spirit who works in all must demand of the different members that they each carry out different functions in the one Body of Christ; to this extent, the same spirituality must have different applications. Nonetheless, we cannot speak of different "Christian spiritualities" without always keeping in mind the fact that, if they really are Christian, they differ only on the relatively external and secondary plane of these applications, while the essence of truly Catholic Christian spirituality remains one and inalterable.

In the malformation of these exaggerated specializations, we find, contrary to first impressions, the same initial error as that of the syncretists: an imbalance between the religious subject and the object of his or her religion, with the result that the attention of the subject, which should be fixed on the object, is turned on himself or herself to the point of self-absorption. And, to the extent to which this point is reached, it is religion itself, spirituality itself inasmuch as it is religious (and even as it is "spiritual"), that fades away.

Chapter 2

THE SPIRITUAL LIFE AND THE WORD OF GOD

O ur spiritual life will be Christian to the degree to which we realize therein a life of personal relationship with God. This already implies that our spiritual life must be constructed on the basis of the Word of God and of faith: the Word by which God calls people to himself—the faith by which people recognize, accept this call.

To this basic principle, we have added—more as an explanation than an addition—the other principle that our spiritual life will be Catholic to the extent to which our personal relationship with God is developed in the Church. For the Word of God is spoken to us in the Church, and it is inseparable from the Church to the point that we cannot truly receive it except as it is communicated to us by the Church. If the Word of God is to be for us not a dead letter but a vivifying Spirit, it must be brought to our understanding in the living light of the magisterium of the Church. But, according to a golden phrase of Pius XI, the principal instrument of the ordinary magisterium of the Church is the liturgy. The first task we must undertake is, therefore, to

explain how our spiritual life must and can nourish itself from
the Word of God through the liturgy.

The Word of God as Source
of the Spiritual Life

What has already been said should have sufficiently brought out
how essential it is to the Christian spiritual life that it should be
nourished by Christian truth. This point is generally admitted
without any difficulty. But sufficient attention is not always
given to the importance, if that Christian truth is to nourish
the spiritual life, of receiving this truth in a form that we can
assimilate.

The assimilation of Christian truth is effected by meditation—a subject on which we need to dwell at length. For Christian truth cannot be assimilated in any kind of way. Modern
studies of spirituality, since the end of the Middle Ages, have
concentrated particularly on the subjective *methods* of meditation. But, in contrast to the more ancient tradition, they
have often attached little or no importance to the *objective* form
in which Christian truth should preferably be encountered in
meditation so as to be assimilated fruitfully. This may be the
reason why in our modern era, meditation appears constantly
to be threatened by a twofold danger seldom evidenced in earlier times: either it dries up in ratiocination, or it drowns in
sentimental musing.

When we are supposed to be meditating on a Christian
truth in order to develop our spiritual life, too often we are
actually only indulging in a rational (not to say a rationalistic)
consideration of this truth, from which we come away still more
dry or spiritually impoverished than we were when we began.
Or, when this does not happen, we lose ourselves, along with

the truth we are trying to meditate on, in a kind of waking dream of which this truth seems to be more the pretext than the source. The spiritual sterility of such a revery is in proportion to its artificiality.

We should pay attention to the fact that if so many people, after a loyal attempt and often a prolonged one, declare frankly that they cannot meditate, it is ordinarily because such rational reflection exhausts them, while fantastic musing distracts (or disgusts) them. But true meditation is neither of these things.

The only way to avoid the Scylla of the one and the Charybdis of the other is to begin by turning to Christian truth under the form in which God has given it to us, the form in which it was proclaimed by his chosen messengers. For God has given us this truth in the form in which it is immediately assimilable by the life of the soul.

In speaking to us, he wills to make us live, not to give us food for thought or pleasantly to occupy our imagination. We can therefore be quite sure that he knew how to present his revelation in such a way as to have it, of itself, suit the purpose for which he gave it to us.

In actual fact, it is only through a secondary process that this revelation became rationalized, and it is only by a quite understandable, though inadequate, reaction that later on it seems to have become sentimentalized, in some manner, through the play of the imagination. This is not to say that it is wrong or illegitimate to think about the truths God has made known to us so as to organize them for coherent reflection; it may likewise be good to have our imagination engaged so that these truths can take full hold of our sensibility. We should, certainly, investigate rationally all the implications of divine truth, if only to safeguard ourselves from adulterating it with all kinds of errors. And our imagination should certainly allow itself to be reshaped by this truth, if only to rid or purify itself of sinful imaginings.

Nonetheless, revealed truths have been given us by God primarily to make us live the life that God has destined for us, not primarily to equip us for the acquisition of speculative knowledge. And when we come more or less confusedly to feel that a habitual approach to divine truth through such a systematic apprehension of it is not the most normal nor the most efficacious way to gain a vital grasp of it, the best remedy is certainly not to fall back on an effort of the imagination nor on the artificial sentiments which this can awaken in us. We thereby risk adding a second mistake to the first, with still more discouraging results. The only serious remedy and, quite simply, the normal way of preventing our meditation from losing itself in a dead end is to begin by returning to divine truth as it has been presented to us by the Word of God itself.

For God, in his Word, gives us his truth precisely as a living truth, suited to making us live. Is it not, as we have said, the characteristic of every "word" to be a personal communication? The word, properly speaking, is the revelation of a person to a person, of an "I" to a "you." It is the first act whereby someone enters into the life of another someone. Consequently, it is the Word of God which is the revelation of God to us, his personal revelation. And it is by this same Word that God intends to enter into our life.

Word of God, Bible, and Liturgy

The Word of God, in the very expressions, the immediate expressions that God himself chose, is preserved for us in the Bible, that is to say, in the collection of all the divinely inspired words that have been given fixed form in writing.

Catholics have tended for too long to think that the Bible should be left to Protestants. This idea, or rather this prejudice, must be uprooted. The error of Protestantism lay not at all in the belief that the Bible is the Word of God and that it should be received as such. This is no error; it is pure Catholic truth, witnessed to by the whole tradition of the Church. The error was to wish to go back to the Bible while getting rid of everything that is essential to keep it living so that we would have it reduced to a dead letter no longer vivified by the Spirit.

It is in the Bible, then, that we should look for the primary nourishment of our spiritual life, as the Protestants insist. But we should not use it as they do. That is, we should not make use of it as a dead letter into which our individual interpretation is to infuse a new life. We should use it where it is still animated by the presence of the Person who spoke it, where the Spirit who inspired it is still active.

But nowhere, except in the Church which is the Body of Christ, does the living Word of God in Christ continue to be present among us and to speak to us today. Nowhere except in this same Body of Christ does the Spirit of Christ dwell on as a continually life-giving Spirit.

This is what we experience in a very particular way in the celebration of the liturgy. For the liturgical assembly of the Church is the assembly of the People of God called together by God himself, called first of all to hear his Word.

It should be noted that this convocation of the People of God to hear his Word is not something artificial, something which had to be brought into being, as it were, after the event in order to restore its youth to an ancient document. On the contrary, it is the very way in accordance with which the biblical texts were produced and then gathered together, the way in accordance with which they are always to be received, as they were given. To convince ourselves of this fact, it is enough to consider the decisive turning points in the history of the People of God, which are found at the same time to be the decisive turning points in the history of the Bible, as it presents this history to us.

It might be said that the People of God were created by the Exodus, and more particularly by the covenant which God made with his own on Mount Sinai, when he led them out of Egypt. Here the chaotic, unorganized horde of refugees were for the first time gathered together in a spiritual unity. Here it was that they became conscious of themselves as a people, the People of God.

How was this carried out? The Word of God, speaking through the intermediation of Moses, called the people together on the mountain. This was the first assembly of the people, what the Hebrew called the Qahal, a word which is found translated in the Greek version of the Septuagint as *Ekklesia*, and which is therefore at the very origin of our notion of the *Ecclesia*, the Church. But why was this Qahal, this embryonic Church, assembled? Precisely to hear the Word which convoked it and, having heard the Word, formally to accept it in faith, collectively pledging obedience to it.

On the same range of Horeb–Sinai, God had already revealed to Moses his name, that is to say, his intimate nature. And now, still through the mediation of Moses, the people came to receive the Law of God, the Ten Commandments, and to welcome this Law as the basis of their whole future relationship with God. The revelation of the Law flowed from that of the name: the Law had as its purpose not only to mark the people as belonging to the God who revealed himself to them, but to shape them in conformity to this God who had made them his adopted people, to stamp them with the imprint of his name, that is, what he himself is. Is not the leitmotif of the Mosaic Law the formula: "Be ye holy as I am holy"?

Such was the first act of the Qahal, the first assembly of the people on Sinai: to hear the Word of God, to receive it in the prayer of an adoring faith.

Yet this acceptance of the divine Word could not remain purely intellectual or simply passive. It implied a self-offering on the part of the people, to meet the requirements of the Word they had heard, on the basis of the promises included in the revelation of the divine name. Confidence in the promises, in the great promise of the divine intimacy opened out to man, and obedience to the revealed will of God were both to be expressed in the second act of the Qahal, to which the first led of its own accord. This second act was the sacrificial offering, the offering just prescribed by God through his Word; thus the "service of the Word" led, as its direct consequence, to the service of the sacrifice. In the latter, the people pledged themselves to obey the Law of God, believing in his promises—that is, that this people should be specifically his People—promises to which God at the same time put his seal by accepting their sacrifice. Thus was concluded the covenant between God and Israel. (See Ex 3, 19, 20, and 24 particularly.)

And the covenant thus concluded was later to be renewed under exactly parallel conditions. Settled in Palestine, Israel experienced both its own unfaithfulness to God's demands and the faithfulness of God to his promises. It was on the basis of that experience, and as shedding light upon it, that the teaching of the ancient prophets was given to Israel. The meaning of the primitive Law was found to be, as it were, renewed because interiorized. Then King Josiah convoked a second Qahal in which again is to be found the structure and, so to say, the dynamism of the first.

Again there was the proclamation of the divine Word—here in the form of Deuteronomy, that is, a reframing of the primitive Law made in the twofold and reciprocal light of experience and of the prophetic teaching of which this experience had been the occasion. And the people, having reaffirmed their adherence to the covenant by pledging themselves in obedient faith to the renewed Law, once more bound themselves to it by sacrifice—here, a particularly solemn celebration of the paschal sacrifice, commemorating and re-actualizing the first Pasch (2 Kgs 23).

A third time, after the supreme experience of the Old Testament—the trial of the Exile, the apparent abandonment by the God of the covenant—the Qahal was convoked, still according to the same pattern. When the scribe Ezra led back from Babylon into the ruins of the holy city the little community, the "remnant" purified in the furnace of that mysterious ordeal, what did he do? He gathered together the exiles and the dispersed for a solemn reading of practically the whole Old Testament Bible, as it has come down to us today. And, on this basis of this preparatory revelation with its accomplishment in the ordeal of the faithful "remnant"—a foreshadowing of the saving ordeal of the "Servant"—the people once again pledged themselves to the service of God.

But this time, it should be noted, while the promise was made to resume the ritual sacrifices when the holy city and the Temple had been rebuilt, while looking forward to this time, the Qahal was not concluded by such sacrifices. In their place appeared a prayer of a new kind: the prayer of blessing or thanksgiving, the *berakah*, which we translate as "eucharist." The people, gratefully acknowledging in this prayer everything that the divine Word had done for them, consecrated themselves to God as their response to his gifts, and especially to that supreme gift of the still-mysterious ordeal from which their own response had come forth. This "eucharistic" prayer first looked to the past in a memorial, an *anamnesis*, which included that past in its whole unity now finally revealed; then it turned quite naturally toward the future: let God himself renew, achieve, bring to final completion in the eschatological future—that is, in the last times—what he had prepared, foreshadowed, sketched out in the times of old, the memory of which was sustaining the present (Neh 8:10).

Clearly, we have here, as it were, the prehistory of the Christian Mass, where it is sketched out and where we discover its meaning in its providential preparations. Here we understand how the Mass achieves the creation of the definitive People of God. At the same time, we grasp the reason why the Mass is so essential to the life of the Church, as it is to that of each Christian in her: it is here that that life takes shape. But, above all, we see here how the People of God is created on the foundation of a collective and progressive hearing of the Word of God. As the Word is proclaimed little by little in the living tradition of this people, and, more particularly, of what we might call its liturgical life, we see that people, under the influence of that Word, being formed by sacrifice and perfected in the discovery of "eucharistic" sacrifice.

The deepening of the lessons of the Old Testament in the experience of the New, which they prepare for and illuminate in advance, shows us how we should welcome the Word of God in that liturgical celebration in which the People of God is made, and made perfect.

Liturgical "Reading" and the Traditional Interpretation of the Bible

Even in the Old Testament, the Qahal, the Assembly of the People where they were formed as God's People through hearing the divine Word, was perpetuated, so to say, in the religious service of the synagogue. And this service was already in some way a summary, a condensation of all the teaching and all the progressively formative power of the successive and decisive gatherings we have just recalled.

The synagogue service did not actually consist of one reading of the Bible each time, but of a series of readings completing and perfecting one another. First came the reading from the Torah, the five books of Moses, in which was to be found the first and fundamental revelation of God in his people, the primary and fundamental events of the intervention of God in the life of that people. Then came the reading of the prophets, giving not only their commentary on these basic truths, a commentary arising from experience, itself guided by the hand of God, but also a new and creative Word of God, leading from the primary experiences of the people to higher ones.

These ancient readings were continued in the New Testament. But the living teaching of the apostles, which took the place of the teaching of the rabbis and continued it, came to proclaim the new and definitive accomplishment in Christ of what the Old Testament had merely heralded and sketched out. This was the procedure which Christ had inaugurated in the synagogue at Nazareth: he read a passage from the book of Isaiah prescribed for that day by Jewish liturgical tradition, then he put down the book and said, "What you have just heard is today accomplished" (Lk 16:14–21).

Later on, the reading of the letters of the apostles took the place of their oral teaching, and this led up to the final reading of the Gospels, containing the very letter of the words of Jesus and his actions, as the apostolic catechesis had kept and interpreted them.

The more the scientific studies of our four Gospels are multiplied and deepened, the more clearly it appears that the three synoptics, and St. Matthew in particular, were conceived in a way particularly designed to show how the teaching and the life of our Lord were the accomplishment of what the Old

Testament had prepared. It even seems that the Gospel According to St. Matthew, with its constant references to the scriptures, was laid out in such a way that the presentation of the Gospel of Christ is modeled on the sequence of scriptural lessons in use at that time through the Jewish liturgical year.

All this shows us how the revelation of God to humanity in his Word is at once organic and progressive. This revelation is never a mere collection of abstract truths, which only need to be linked logically together. It is, through a succession of living experiences, the illumination given us by him who has engaged us in these experiences. As the Fathers of the Church call it, it is a divine pedagogy.

Like any wise teacher, God does not content himself with saying once for all what he has to say, nor with doing (and, above all, with having us do) everything all at once. Still less does he mechanically repeat the same things, like a record or a film. Instead, he makes use of experiences which are analogous, but always increasingly profound, increasingly engaging, not only our minds but our whole being, so as to have us penetrate little by little into the central truth which he has held in his heart from the beginning, waiting until we are capable of embracing it in its fullness and, above all, of truly making it our own.

This is why the first experiences which he caused his people to go through already enclosed, in a certain way, the definitive truths of the Gospel. In the first Pasch by which the people were delivered from Egypt, the passage of the Red Sea, the settling in the promised land, God already indicated that he willed to be the Redeemer of his own: the One who would deliver them by freeing them from slavery, who would set them free by adopting them, making them, as it were, the inheritors of his own goods.

But this truth, to be rightly understood, called for a new experience—that of a more profound ordeal, in which the people would come to understand the necessity for deliverance, not only from external enemies like the Egyptians, but also from interior enemies: their own egoism and idolatry. After the first Pasch, consequently, there had to be another Pasch prepared for by the teaching of the greatest prophets: the sorrowful trial of the Exile, the prelude to that veritable resurrection of the people which was the new deliverance. In this second experience, the people discovered that there is indeed no radical deliverance for humanity which is not the fruit of an interior struggle, in which suffering, distress accepted in faith, is the condition of a truly new life.

But the supreme value of this second experience lay in the guidelines it in turn laid down for a still more profound discovery. It opened out on the perspective of another death and another resurrection, no longer in figure but in all reality: the death and resurrection, no longer of the community passing through the furnace of trial, the "remnant" of Israel, but of the unique "Servant of the Lord." Thus the hope was sketched out of finding even the unjust justified in the death of the Just One, of rebuilding Jerusalem not merely for a handful of Jews returned from dispersion and exile, but for all the pagan nations, "the fullness of the Gentiles" (Rom 11:25).

And now, as in the Jews of the synagogue so in us of the Church, there must be carried out spiritually what is described by physiology as the law of all organic life. According to the well-known formula, ontogenesis must reproduce phylogenesis. This means that the same process which has brought a certain race to its present state of development must be reproduced, as if in an abridged and condensed form, in the life of each individual.

The way by which God has led his People to its fullness, by which he leads us all together toward what St. Paul calls the "fullness of Christ in his mature age" (Eph 4:3), is the way which we must all in some way take and traverse each on his or her own account. We must all, by the organic progressive teaching of the scriptures given us by the Church in her liturgy, relive interiorly the entire history of the People of God. The Church herself lives on by "keeping and going over all these things in her heart," as the evangelist St. Luke tells us of the Virgin Mary. In the Church, in giving ourselves over to the maternal pedagogy of her liturgy, in which she continually repeats, in order to "edify" us in the strongest sense of the word, the fatherly pedagogy that God realized once for all in the great events of sacred history, we discover in the Gospel the fullness of the meaning of the scriptures: the fullness of the message which God addresses to us from the times of the patriarchs and prophets and finally discloses in his only Son.

Meditating on the Bible and the Mystery of Jesus

The goal of the divine pedagogy in sacred history, and the goal of the pedagogy of the Church in the liturgical celebration, is to bring us to understand that the unity of revelation, the unity underlying the infinite diversity of the scriptures, is the unity of the mystery of Jesus.

It is in docilely giving ourselves over to this pedagogy that we recognize that this living unity is not to be sought in any form of rational reflection, however sublime. Still less can it be the product of an aesthetic imagination delighting in its own exercise. It is the unity of a living exchange, or more exactly of a divine action, but of one which seeks us and engages us as a whole, completely. In bringing God to us, it must bring us to him.

The liturgy, which causes us to read the whole Bible as oriented to Christ in the way in which the apostolic teaching presents it to us, thus makes it clear, then, that this unity is the unity of what St. Paul calls simply "the mystery" (cf. Col 1:26–27). To the apostle, the mystery is finally Christ himself and, in particular, his Cross. Yet it is by no means Christ and his Cross simply set up in front of us. As St. Paul says again, it is "Christ in you, the hope of glory!" (Col 1:27).

This amounts to saying, first of all, that the mystery is Christ and his Cross seen as "fulfilling the scriptures," as completing the expression, realizing the manifestation in act of that Word, complete and final, which God from the beginning wishes to say to us, throughout the manifold preparatory words of the prophets. But this equally means that the mystery is the Cross of Christ discovered as the key both to the whole of human history and to the history of each particular individual.

More deeply, the mystery is the Cross of Christ seen in all its perspectives—including the Resurrection, the outpouring of the Spirit on all flesh, our incorporation into the risen Christ and, finally, in him, "God all in all."

The mystery is, then, Christ living in us, causing us to partake in all the reality of his life, of his new being, and thereby restoring in himself, "recapitulating" as says the Epistle to the Ephesians, the whole of creation, the whole history of a humanity dismembered by sin but now reconciled, renewed, in a world delivered from its slavery to the powers hostile to God, powers which the Cross has overcome, so as to be free in the glory promised to the children of God (cf. Eph 1 and 2).

It is when we have come to this point that we discover the true meaning of the spiritual interpretation of the scriptures, so essential to all Christian tradition. Here also we are enabled to disengage this interpretation from the expressions of it which are more or less unfortunate, or from the fallacious imitations which still too frequently interfere with our understanding it.

Properly understood, the spiritual interpretation of the scriptures means simply the way in which the Church, the People of God, understands them and relives them particularly in her liturgy. And this is also the interpretation which should, as its name indicates, enable us to live by them, to live them in the very Spirit who inspired them.

Contrary to the more or less fantastic caricatures by which it may have been supplanted, this authentic spiritual interpretation of the scriptures in no way sets aside their historical interpretation. It is not even enough to say that it presupposes the latter as its indispensable basis. We have to go further and say that it is itself the only historical interpretation of the scriptures which is integrally historical. For it is, as we have said, the only interpretation which enables us to attain their full meaning: all that is included in their most completely objective interpretation when such an interpretation takes sacred history as including all its prolongations up to our times and beyond, prolongations as yet accessible only to faith, but to the faith which the scriptures themselves formally teach.

Following the movement of the inspired thought of the last prophets and thus flowing in a development interior to holy scripture itself, this spiritual interpretation has us first go forward from the original Pasch to the Exile and to the captives' return. It leads us, that is, from a collective and external "redemption" to another which is already interiorized and to that extent individualized. In fact, one of the most characteristic traits of Hosea, of Ezekiel, or of the second part of the book of Isaiah is to make use of all the expressions, the images, the ideas first connected with the Exodus in order to express and interpret what we might call the spirituality of the Exile and of the new deliverance to which it gave place.

We have here a literary method of composition that has happily been called the anthological style: one in which the innumerable citations of classic texts become the medium of the newest, the most original revelations. But this goes far beyond a mere literary method. Behind it, in the use of it, we follow the progress of a thought nourished by a history in which truths, like the providential deeds in which they are discovered by inspired reflection, beget one another in a truly vital continuity.

Yet this first development is but a sketch of the second—a new creation, but one which is at the same time always organically linked with what has preceded and prepared for it: the fact and the proclamation of the Gospel.

From the sacrifice of the "remnant," of the few Jews who remained faithful during the ordeal with which God had winnowed them, we now go forward to the sacrifice of the one "faithful Servant," obedient to death, even the death of the Cross. The evangelist St. Luke described the voluntary death of Christ as "his Exodus which was to be accomplished in Jerusalem." And there is no doubt that Christ himself had explained to his own the meaning of his death by a twofold reference: to the paschal lamb which "takes away" the sins of the world by the shedding of its blood and to the lamb (cf. Is 53) led to the slaughter which "carries" those sins in its broken body. . . .

Yet the Gospel of Christ now invites us to carry our own cross and to follow Christ. "If we suffer with him," says St. Paul, "we shall reign with him" (2 Tm 2:12). And it is in this sense that he says of himself: "I fulfill in my flesh what remains to be suffered of the sufferings of Christ, for his Body which is the Church" (Col 1:24). It is in this sense, because Christ is to live his mystery in us, that the mystery is "Christ in you . . ." and that, consequently, a new transposition needs to be made of all the truth of the scriptures—a transposition from Christ to the Church, from Christ to each of us as his members in the Church.

But here, finally, the same glorious perspectives are opened out to us that his Cross opened out to Christ—he who, according to an interpretation commonly given by the ancient commentators to a phrase of the Epistle to the Hebrews, "did not hesitate to suffer in view of the joy that was proposed to him" (Heb 12:2). The total interpretation of the scriptures, that is, should always lead us to the eschatological perspectives of the "Jerusalem from on high which is our mother," according to the phrase of St. Paul (Gal 4:26), of that "Bride of the Lamb, coming down from heaven like a wife adorned for her husband," according to the final vision of the Apocalypse (Rv 21:2). Thus it is revealed that the mystery is not only Christ and Christ in us, but "the hope of glory. . . ."

The Meaning of Scripture

The little that has just been said indicates clearly how the Jews already legitimately saw the full sense of the scriptures as developing in a moral sense interiorized for each believer and in an eschatological, apocalyptic sense in which "the figure of things to come" was discerned in the features of the events of old. And our discussion should suffice to make clear, above all, the soundness of the threefold significance which Christian tradition recognizes in scripture now that Christ has come: going from the allegorical sense properly so called (as St. Paul defines it in the Epistle to the Galatians and all the Fathers after him) to the tropological sense, and finally to the anagogical sense—one single spiritual meaning opening out all its depths in a strict continuity.

The allegorical sense of St. Paul and the Fathers means that in Christ is definitively realized everything that foreshadowed him in ascending toward him and preparing us for him. This meaning is transferred to us by the tropological sense, which is not simply any kind of moral application of scripture to each of us, but that very definite application resulting from our faith in the life of Christ in us. And, in turn, this tropological meaning, by virtue of the perspectives it opens out to our hope—of the fullness of Christ becoming our own fullness—finds its final flowering in anagogy, the anticipated attainment of the eschatological realities. As we shall see later on, this anagogical sense becomes—in the final meaning given to the term by the Fathers, the mystical sense of the scriptures—the meaning which causes us to discover to the degree which is possible here below, the experience by anticipation of everlasting life.

These two last transferences, of tropology and of anagogy, to which we shall also return later on, are, it should be noted, intimately connected with the sacramental life of the Church. This life, as we shall soon see, is where we are to find the mystery of Christ as the life of "Christ in us, the hope of glory."

This is the teaching particularly of the Fourth Gospel. Scientific exegesis has clearly brought out the fact that, for St. John, in the sacrament, Baptism or Eucharist, "what takes place on earth" (3:12) actually has as its content "what takes place in heaven": birth of water, birth of the Spirit; not only new birth but birth from on high—eucharistic bread, bread of heaven; the flesh of the Son of man, but that flesh become "Spirit and Life" by the Cross and the Resurrection. . . . It is for just this reason that the reading of this Gospel traditionally took place during Passion and Eastertide: to reveal to us how the Cross of Christ, relived by us in the sacramental liturgy, leads us like him, with him, in him, by suffering to glory, by the elevation on the Cross to the elevation of the Ascension.

The Liturgy, School of Meditation

The liturgical life of the People of God not only teaches us objectively about the mystery of Christ in which all the scriptures converge and from which their intelligibility shines forth. This life also gives us the subjective method, as it were, whereby the divine Word is to be assimilated, the only method which enables our understanding to be an assimilation, not only intellectual but truly vital.

Indeed, the manner in which the Church, in her liturgical assemblies and above all in the Mass, reads the Bible and meditates on it teaches us in action how all spiritual reading of the holy scriptures should be pursued and how an appropriate meditation should be carried out so that we assimilate the scriptures as we ought.

The tradition of the Church does not "limit itself simply to bringing together texts of the Old and of the New Testaments in such a way as to illuminate their meaning by having us go from one flowering of the divine Word in sacred history to another, from Moses to the Gospel of St. John by way of the prophets and the apostles. It surrounds each reading of a particular text with everything apt to facilitate the living assimilation required.

It is in the most ancient forms of the liturgy of the Word, those which have best preserved the primitive pattern, that what might be called the Church's classic method of meditation can most easily be grasped. The finest examples are provided by the great reading service of Good Friday and the Easter Vigil as it used to be, before the recent abridgement reduced it to a form almost as condensed as that of most of the other Masses.

In these examples, we see how all the ancient vigils of reading the divine Word were conceived. A basic element was simply repeated a greater or smaller number of times in succession, following the ascending progress of revelation, according to the rhythm we have already explained, from the Torah to the prophets, from the prophets to the teaching of the apostles, finally culminating in the Gospel. And this last was always given a timely commentary in the homily preached by one of the successors of the apostles or one of their collaborators, a priest of the second rank.

In the structure of the basic element thus repeated, a structure which is practically invariable, is contained what we have just called the Church's own method of meditation.

Each reading is accompanied by three elements, harmoniously associated with it in such a way as to ensure its full flowering in the believing soul. These elements are responsorial chant, personal silent prayer (guided if necessary by a discreet directive from the deacon), and finally the collect prayer, in which the bishop or priest presiding over the liturgical celebration gathers together, in a brief formula publicly pronounced in the name of all, what should have been the object and the fruit of the private meditation.

As we go on to examine responsorial psalmody, the first of these complementary determinants of biblical reading, it may not be irrelevant to recall the fact that, in the tradition of the synagogue, the reading of the holy Word itself was a chant, a musical recitative. We know that the Hebrew text of the Bible in the recension called the Massoretic (that is, traditional) includes, together with the vowel points indicating the correct pronunciation, a series of accents to make the public reading of the text a true liturgical chant. This method of chanting the sacred text is explained in part as a measure for making sure that everyone in a fairly sizable gathering would be able to hear the reader clearly.

But such an explanation alone is obviously inadequate. We need to add that, in the traditional conception, first Jewish and then Christian, the reading of the sacred text is never a simple "lesson" in the sense in which we understand the word today. It cannot be reduced, that is, to the merely didactic, to a form of instruction, like that given in a class or a seminar. The reading of the divine Word in the Church is necessarily a celebration: in the simple proclamation of his Word to the world, God is glorified. To re-form this Word on our lips and to repeat it in any spirit other than this would be to profane it. It is not a Word which a man or woman can repeat in order to examine and dissect it rationally, as can be done with human words. It is a Word which of itself calls for sacred song: which is not to be uttered by any but pure lips, lips which express the holy joy, the religious fear of a heart that is not only believing and submissive but adoring.

Under these conditions, it seems quite natural that the response aroused by the divine Word in the heart of the man or woman who hears it should, from the outset, take on the form of a chant, and also that this chant, no less naturally, should take its formulae from those of inspired prayer. Pascal said, "Only God is able to speak fittingly about God." We might add, "Only God is able to speak fittingly *to* God." St. Paul emphasizes the fact that, of ourselves, we do not know what we ought to ask of God. This is why, he adds, the Spirit himself comes to the aid of our weakness and intercedes in us, for us, by ineffable sighs (Rom 8:26). If these sighs are to be expressed, how ought they to be, except first of all in the words which the Spirit himself has dictated to us?

Once again, in the dialogue between ourselves and God, it is he who takes the initiative in speaking to us. It is he alone, again, who can create in our heart the response that his Word expects from us. This is precisely the reason why prayers are included in his Word, those prayers which are the models of all others, the Psalms and other biblical canticles.

It is normal, therefore, that the first response aroused by each reading of the Word should habitually be taken by the

Church from the collection of Psalms or, more generally, from among the scriptural canticles. And it is typical that these inspired prayers should in fact be songs, words in which faith does not reason, does not even describe, but sings what it believes.

For this faith which the Word wills to create in us and which should be the first and the last utterance of the prayer that responds to the Word is neither a cold judgment nor the expression of artifically elaborated sentiments. It is the exultation of our whole being, ravished in the contemplation of the mystery discovered in the Word. For this mystery is essentially the gift of God, and this is to be understood not so much in the sense of its being one or another particular gift that God has given us of what is his, but in the sense of its being the gift of himself: a gift in which it is he who gives and he who is given.

The contemplation of this gift, a contemplation which cannot remain detached from what it contemplates, a contemplation which prostrates us in grateful adoration only to lift us up at once into a pure gladness wholly open to, wholly given over to him who has given us everything—such a contemplation is at the heart of a faith that is truly living. The Word is not truly welcomed for what it is, by a true faith, except when the prayer that welcomes it, that adheres to it, takes on this character.

This is why, although as we shall see, contemplation is the term which should be used to describe the highest states of Christian prayer, nevertheless no prayer is truly Christian unless it is fundamentally contemplative from the outset. The contemplation of which we are speaking here, it must be clearly understood, is not some kind of aesthetic exercise; this would not wholly engage us in our prayer. It is that "giving of thanks" by which, recognizing in faith the gift of God, we joyfully cry out to him in gratitude with a love responding to his own, a love that is his own love poured out in our hearts by the Spirit.

He has given us the abandonment of the whole created being to the Creator who has given us everything.

Whether the responsorial chant be of the type found in Matins or the Gradual of the Mass (which is related to that of Matins), or one like the Tract (the continued chant of a whole psalm), or simply an alleluia verse (summing up in one word the joy caused by the gift of God), this chant is always one which has been selected by the Church. This means that the living consciousness of the People of God causes us to discern in this chant, more or less clearly, more or less formally, the major theme of what has just been proclaimed to us—the theme which is to be the object of our "eucharist," of our prayer which is at once grateful and obedient, in the joy of faith.

As things are at present after the many rearrangements of the Lectionary and of the *Graduate Romanum*, the continuity of theme is sometimes very loose. But if we take the series of responses at Matins still in use along with the reading of each book of the Bible, we find here the spiritual essence of each of these books, as it were, distilled. . . . And the Alleluia, into which the linked responses before the proclamation of the Gospel usually develop, is no less revealing in its own way than the most subtly interwoven series of responses. It shows us that every meditation of the divine Word, every contemplation of his mystery, finds its goal in what is beyond expression. The "jubilus"—that is, the musical vocalization of the "a" of the Alleluia—this, and this alone, can finally translate the ecstasy of the believing soul in the face of revealed truth, truth which is ultimately not an idea but a person. . . .

This is also why, just as the Word proclaimed and received tends toward the chant of praise, this chant in turn tends toward silence. After the burst of exaltation evoked by the singing from a spiritual understanding of scripture, a silent, wholly personal prayer must be completed and consummated in us, in each one of us—the recognizing of the truth, the thanksgiving which is our only fitting response to the Word addressed to us.

This silence invites us, first of all, to make fully our own the prayer in which the Church engages us. It urges us to go with our whole selves to him whom his Word has revealed to us. Until this contact has been established, there is no prayer, properly speaking. Without question, this meeting with God is to be brought about in the Church, and for that matter, properly speaking, it is always the Church who is the interlocutor with God in the dialogue of prayer. But the Church, as believing and loving, exists only in us. The Church welcomes the divine Word and gives herself to it only to the degree to which each soul in her effectively does so. Here the task of each person is irreplaceable: no one can substitute for anyone else; the community, while transcendent to the individuals composing it, lives only by the grace in each one of its members.

Our personal assimilation of the gift of God, our personal association with the prayer of all in unity, can take many forms which we shall examine at length. It may be nothing more than the simple appropriation of a word, of a phrase of the liturgical prayer; it may give free rein to an outpouring all our own, set in motion by this phrase but overflowing it; it may lose itself in the simple gaze of mystical contemplation. This matters little; what matters essentially is that not only our mind—our intellectual attentiveness—be engaged, but also our heart: that core of our whole personality, that center not only (nor primarily) of our emotions and our feelings but of our most intimate decisions, those most thoroughly involving our whole being.

While such a prayer normally needs silence for its birth or at least its development, it should normally also end in silence. As with all conversation between persons in whom mutual affection, knowledge, and comprehension have attained a certain depth, so in such an exchange there must soon come a moment when no word can suffice to express what is in our hearts, a moment in which all words are by the same token unnecessary, being both inadequate and superfluous. It is this moment in prayer which we usually call "mystical." And there is no true prayer which does not tend toward it.

Yet, so long as we are here on earth, we cannot lose ourselves completely in this silence which is one with a perfect exchange of the Word that has gone beyond the bounds of speech. If our silence is to remain charged with spiritual substance, it needs here below, sooner or later, to resume contact with distinct words. Otherwise, the peace of the soul forgetting itself in God might, perhaps, insensibly degenerate into a simple torpor, into that vague kind of dream the emptiness of which so soon becomes equivocal and which is prey to all kinds of unhealthy "quietisms."

If only for this reason, after such silent and wholly personal prayer, by means of the "collect" which she has the priest pronounce, the Church brings us back, touching earth again, as it were, to a well-defined traditional expression, however simple, of what she expects from God, and especially of what she has given to him of herself in her gratitude for his own gifts. And for souls who are not yet raised so high, whose personal prayer is only a babbling, quite as much as for those whom an ardent facility has launched into a passionate dialogue with God, this final return to a prayer which is collective, hierarchical, and formulated by the very voice of tradition is beneficial and necessary. It alone preserves prayer both from sterility and from garrulousness.

Not that the Church wishes in any way to hold down the inspiration of her children or in any way to substitute for it. But the Spirit, within her, never ceases to teach us first of all how to pray truly, in a heart-to-heart dialogue, according to the heart of God.

Unceasingly also, the witness that he gives to himself in the assembly of his own affords us a test of our own inspirations, one which we cannot do without. Christians who take without distinction, as divinely inspired, every spontaneous impression and every more or less developed interior reaction of their own spirit face to face with the divine Word are in greater danger than anyone else of stifling the Spirit by confusing him with their own unconscious caricature. Continually referring to the sense of the Church helps such people better than anything else to distinguish what is authentically "spiritual" in themselves from what is fallacious, and thus strengthens them and assures their further progress in the ways of the Spirit. Thus—by continually going back and forth between the prayer which is most personal, least reducible to any formula however excellent and one which makes use of the most sober and pure formulae of the living tradition of the People of God—is true prayer woven, the prayer of the Christian who in one movement becomes more fully the child of God in becoming always more fully the child of the Church.

Prayer and *Lectio Divina*

These last considerations lead us straight to the heart of one of our chief concerns: that of "methods of prayer," or, if you prefer, of the ways which lead to the systematic development of fully personal prayer. But these considerations also suggest that the problem preliminary to that of methods of prayer is that of spiritual reading: what the ancients called *lectio divina*.

Actually, if Christian prayer is to be nourished as it should be by the Word of God, it should always proceed from reading. This is true even when we immerse ourselves in prayer at the outset. For such prayer will be truly Christian only to the extent to which it is fed from the living store left in our memory by the divine Word, previously read or heard. And the same prayer will remain Christian only if, throughout our lives, it is constantly renewed by the persevering practice of well-made spiritual reading.

This necessity explains the misunderstanding into which people today regularly fall when they come to study the spirituality of ancient Christianity. And it indicates also why it is that so many modern efforts toward a life of prayer, however ingeniously designed from a psychological point of view, too frequently prove spiritually sterile.

In the first place, when people today read the great spiritual texts which might be called classic, such as the Rule of St. Benedict, they are surprised to find so little said in them about prayer and this little said so unsystematically.

The reason for this apparent lack is twofold. On the one hand, the Rule of St. Benedict particularly presupposes a living liturgical celebration of the type we have just described and explained: one designed to be the most practical and effective school of prayer possible. On the other hand, the Rule insists at length on the *lectio divina*, by which the Divine Office is, as it were, extended into our most personal interior life—this reading constituting the most favorable opportunity for the full assimilation in individual prayer of the riches offered to us in the liturgy.

Too frequently today, by contrast, the most carefully worked-out methods of prayer have an unhappy tendency to operate in a vacuum. Even when the Divine Office and spiritual reading go along with one of these methods, only very rarely do they form an integrated whole with it. The Office remains, as it were, on the margin of personal interior life. And "spiritual reading" serves more as a means of feeding or distracting the intellect with religious themes than as a direct nourishment of prayer. In these conditions, the best-made prayer, from the viewpoint of psychological techniques, has little to chew on. Let us repeat: these are the conditions in which prayer begins to waver between arid ratiocination and sentimental dreaming, the conditions in which it feels frustrated by both the one and the other. The sole remedy is the return to a spiritual reading which is what it should be, carried out within the framework of a liturgical life which has been rescued from a fossilizing formalism.

Methods of Spiritual Reading

As is obviously necessary, then, we shall take up the question of methods of reading the Word of God before going into that of methods of prayer. We should realize, first of all, that there are several methods of reading—three or even four—among which we are not so much to choose as to alternate. It is from the slowly accumulated and concordant effects of these various ways that a truly fruitful prayer will finally be born—or reborn.

The first method of reading the scripture is the one exemplified in the oldest liturgical tradition, that called *lectio continua*, that is, a complete reading of the whole Bible, book by book, each book being read as a whole and the whole Word of God being read each year. This way of reading might be called the foundation on which all the rest is to be built up. The Word of God, as the Bible gives it to us, is really a whole world. This world, especially for us today, unquestionably requires considerable introduction and explanation. It demands even more strictly an illumination, or orientation, the living continuation in our midst of everything that constitutes it. This is what can be provided only by the liturgical life, and this is undoubtedly far more important to the spiritual life than cultivating a type of biblical study complete with historical and philological techniques.

But this world of the Bible demands above all and beyond all that we immerse ourselves and become absorbed therein. When we have done this, and done it perseveringly, this world begins to explain itself, to a great extent at least. In any event, as a result of our having done this, many false questions, many artificial difficulties which seem embarrassing at first sight and which, frequently, are never dissipated by the most expert exegesis, simply disappear. For we must be attuned to the Bible to hear therein the Word of God as it wishes us to hear it. And this profound accord can only be the effect of long and complete familiarity.

But we need to have this familiarity become all-embracing. And we need also to make sure that the principal details, and especially the contours of each of the great masses which go to make up this vast world, do not get lost in confusion. It is good, therefore, from time to time, to substitute for or to supplement the continuous reading—which is necessarily done by fragments, if not little pieces—with the reading of one or another whole book of the Bible and, insofar as this is possible, of a whole book at a time. This will prove to be the best remedy against a deceptive sense of mechanical progress, somewhat artificial, which may be engendered by the routine of a daily reading, a little too uniform in length, of one book after another, all broken up into almost equal small sections.

This is because the Bible is not a book but a whole library, admirably harmonized and coordinated, to be sure, but with each book having its own personality, each having an irreplaceable tonality like that of each individual instrument in even the largest symphony. Our understanding of the whole is, then, in many respects, in function of the renewed perception that we gain of the life proper to each element.

From time to time, it is necessary, therefore—perhaps during a period of recollection or retreat—to take one book and read it as we would read any book: as a unit and as a living whole. It is hard to believe how greatly the habitual reading of the whole Bible, progressively carried out and untiringly repeated, will be enlivened by such occasional reading, delivering us from routine and bringing out before our eyes, so to say, the individual glory of each flower in that immense garden.

But both the first and second kind of reading should, properly, be guided by liturgical tradition, especially as to the order followed in reading, so that each book will benefit from the clarification provided by the different phases of the liturgical year.

The season of Septuagesima, preliminary to the great annual retreat of Lent in which we prepare ourselves to relive the mystery of the redemption, is appropriate for the reading of Genesis: for reading, that is, about creation, sin, the first foreshadowings of judgment and salvation in the story of Noah, ending with the appearance of the People of God in the person of Abraham and the Patriarchs, our Fathers in the faith.

The first and the greater part of Lent is then to be devoted to Exodus, to the account of the first Pasch and what followed: the wandering in the desert and the entrance into the promised land. Passiontide proper is dominated by the reading of Jeremiah and of the "Servant Songs" in the second part of Isaiah as our immediate introduction to the Gospel narratives of the Passion and the commentary on them given by the Epistle to the Hebrews.

The Paschal season is then appropriate for the reading of the Acts, the first steps of the Church in the light of the Resurrection and Pentecost, and then of the Apocalypse, in which we catch a glimpse of the heavenly glory into which the Son has preceded us. To this season also belong the Epistles of St.

Peter, the first being a paschal liturgy and homily, as well as the Epistles of St. John and St. James.

The time after Pentecost immerses us first in the historical books, then the sapiential, and, finally, the prophets. Isaiah is reserved for Advent and Christmastime. (Its second and third parts are as fitting to Christmas and Epiphany as its first is to Advent.) Lastly, St. Paul's Epistles, the classic explanation of the Christian mystery, are more than ever in place during the weeks after Epiphany.

As for the Gospels—these should be the object of constant rereading, going along with all other reading. But the first part of the Gospel of St. John, dominated as it is by echoes of Baptism and the Eucharist, is especially appropriate to the end of Lent, and its second part, concerned with the resurrection of Lazarus and the Lord's last conversations with his disciples, to Eastertime.

It is by way of embroidering on the basic pattern of these great types of reading that quite another kind should be introduced: that of studious reading. This is most important, without any question, in order to deepen the basic readings and to prepare for their assimilation in prayer through the ultimate kind of reading, not yet discussed, which leads directly to prayer or, rather, already is prayer. But studious reading will not be a preparation for prayer unless we are prepared for it by the "lectio continua" consistently carried out within the living context of the liturgy. Lacking this, a more or less scholarly study of scripture runs the risk of wandering off toward a historicist intellectualism or toward philology for its own sake, and this the more easily when such study is pursued at secondhand. A real science of exegesis, when it is fully formed and developed—as we see from the evolution of biblical exegesis in the last fifty years even outside the Catholic Church—leads to the most spiritual rediscoveries of the Word of God. But a science derived from manuals—which is, unhappily, the science of the vast majority—unless it is ruled by the simple human vision of scripture, guided by the tradition of the Church and illuminated by it, almost invariably degenerates into a pretentious pedantry which raises an insurmountable wall between us and the divine Word. Nothing is worse than to become amused with, wrapped up in, the mere process of stripping away the coverings from inspiration, coverings which thus come to obscure it for you.

On the other hand, a study that is solid and pursued as thoroughly as the general culture and intellectual powers of the individual permit, if it remains an instrument of the spiritual search and is not pursued in a proud and sterile isolation from the living tradition of the Church, can be of priceless benefit to spirituality. This benefit may not be immediately evident. But it will reveal itself little by little in a sense of the authentic, the essential, which will preserve us from reading our own fancies into the Word of God or from retaining merely some dry scrap or first impression of it.

It is in words, bound up with deeds, that God has spoken and never ceases to speak to us. Anything which sheds light on these words, anything which places these deeds in their true perspective is, therefore, of priceless benefit to the most truly spiritual understanding of his Word.

One of the most precious benefits of modern scientific exegesis is, in particular, to give us an exact understanding of the literary genres in which the Word of God expresses itself. To be able to distinguish what is expressed in poetic form from what is conveyed more literally, history from parable, or, again, the substance of history from its figurative clothing while discerning the meaning and the import of this clothing—all this "focuses" us for understanding the divine Word, for avoiding asking it any questions which it does not mean to answer, and, at the same time, for giving ourselves effectively to what it does say, to what it does mean to say to us. And not less important is the correct historical perspective which allows us to appreciate each stage of revelation in its place in the whole and in function of the whole and, equally, in the realization of the divine plan.

When we first begin to make use of the modern exegetical studies that have provided us with such resources, it may seem as though a gap were opening out between the vision of the Bible they provide and the one we have formed by means of immediate contact with the Bible in the heart of the liturgical life of the Church. But, if the study is pursued patiently and is deepened, this impression will be dissipated after a time. Or, better, it will become transformed into an impression of renewal and deepening with regard to those great central perspectives opened out to us in the Bible by the liturgy—perspectives which meditation according to the school of Catholic tradition has already allowed us to discern.

This mutual adaptation will be the more effective, the more we avoid any one-sidedness in our study—whether it be more or less scholarly—of scripture. Sometimes it will be helpful to apply ourselves, with the aid of a good commentary, to one particular book or to a group of books, such as those of St. Paul or St. John, and, at other times, with the aid of a book of "biblical theology" or a concordance, to follow one great biblical theme throughout the whole Bible.

This latter kind of study can result in something substantial only on the basis of the former. But then, as if of its own accord, we might say, it enables us to integrate the historic and philological vision of the Bible with the traditional understanding of it, often regenerating the latter in such a vital way as to transfigure our whole personal spiritual understanding of the Bible. In watching ripen under our eyes, as it were, themes such as those of the Exodus and the redemption of Israel, the wandering in the desert and the search for the promised land,

the expectation of the divine kingdom and the revelation of
the Lord's Anointed, or of the heavenly Jerusalem finally substituted for all the cities that are only of the flesh; we enter into
that spiritual understanding of the scriptures toward which
all tradition guides us. And this, not by groping blindly, or by
the more or less successful balancing off of approximations or
mistranslations, but by the ways taken by inspiration itself to
reach and touch our heart.

It is then that we are fully prepared for the final and capital
form of reading holy scripture: the true *lectio divina* which leads
forthwith to prayer, which already is prayer. For this *lectio* is
fruitful in proportion to the spiritual culture of the person who
gives himself or herself to it. And it is to this culture that all the
other methods of reading just described should contribute. It
is the fruit which can only result from the slow, patient, persevering growth of all their interwoven fibers. Or, rather, this
culture is the tree, and its fruit is the *lectio divina* in the strict
sense of the word. Without the full growth of the tree, how can
any fruit be produced which is not sick and savorless? But, by
the same token, the most luxuriant growth will be like that of
the sterile fig tree if it does not finally produce this very fruit.

Lectio Divina Properly So Called

The *lectio divina* is the prime concern of the reflections and
counsels of ancient spiritual literature, especially that of monastic origin. Here it appears as being the basic food (and we might
also say the basic element) of all spirituality.

Such reading must always have the divine Word as its object.
Yet the material does not necessarily have to be provided by the
very letter of scripture; it can equally well be a liturgical text or
any other great spiritual text of Catholic tradition. It is essential,

however, that the text proceed from scripture and lead back to it, that it resemble the faithful echo which sometimes enables us to hear a far-off voice more distinctly and which transmits only that voice, not changing it in any way with its own resonances.

This text should preferably be brief as compared with the length of time we are to devote to it. The idea is not to launch into a swift voyage of discovery but to trace and retrace our path, to explore thoroughly, to make truly our own some part of the country hitherto known but superficially and assimilated imperfectly. Normally, we would choose a text contained in the *lectio continua* for this season of the liturgical year. Or else we could take a text more or less directly connected with the season so as to have the benefit of all the atmosphere, the environment which the liturgical life provides for our meditation.

Having made our choice, we should enter upon the reading with a quiet effort to recollect ourselves, to gather ourselves together, preparing us to approach it with the attention of our whole soul. The idea here is that of reading in order to read— not what we usually do: read in order to have read. Our greatest difficulty, perhaps, in trying to appreciate and to practice *lectio divina* as the ancients did is that we are spoiled with regard to reading, any reading. For them, books were a rarity. It was a great thing to have a book at one's disposal, and one made the most of it like a miser or, better, like a gourmet who slowly savors his small portion so as not to lose the least crumb of it. Again, papyrus or parchment was expensive. Space, then, was not to be wasted. The words followed one another with no space in between; to read a text like this was a task in itself. This is why, as we see in the Acts, the eunuch from Ethiopia, reading the book of Isaiah while riding in his chariot, was overheard by the deacon Philip as he walked along the road—people always read at least *sotto voce*. The proper sense of the Latin *meditari*, from which our word *meditate* is derived, is precisely this vocal rumination—obviously much better adapted to the purpose of impregnating us with what we read than is our kind of reading, the mere rapid running of the eyes across the printed page.

But the concentration, the special quality of attentiveness, required by *lectio divina* must take on a sacred motivation. What is said to us is the Word of God: in fact, it is God who speaks to us, who never ceases to speak to us in these words. Even though they have been fixed in their phrasing for thousands of years, he who makes us hear them today already had us in mind when he inspired them of old, and he is always present to address himself to us through them, as if they were at this instant pronounced for the first time.

Our reading should, then, be engaged in, pursued, and ceaselessly renewed as an act of faith in this God who speaks to us, faith in his actual presence, faith in the present reality of what he says to us and of the way in which he says it. While reading, we should be all adherence, all abandonment, all self-donation, in this faith, to what we hear and to him whom we hear behind the words being read or reread.

But this presupposes also that we give, together with this faith in the divine presence behind the text, our own presence, the presence of our whole selves, before him who is present to us. If we believe, as we ought, that the Word is addressed to us, to each of us, in continuing reality here and now, we must also believe that it takes into account everything we are, with all our problems, our needs, our deficiencies, and our joys as well, everything that oppresses or gladdens us, everything we do or fail to do. All this, and not merely our understanding, should be present in our reading. The Word we read is not made to remain in the head but to descend into the heart—taking the word "heart," of course, in the biblical sense: not as the source of the emotions only but as the core or focus of the whole personality at its deepest, that intimate sanctuary in which our eternity is at stake because here is where our ultimate decisions are woven and taken.

It is in this spirit, then, that we must assimilate each word, each thought of the text, going over them unceasingly until they open out and the current of the Spirit who chose them flows freely into us. *Te totum applica ad textum, rem totam applica ad te*, as the exegete Bengel said: "Apply yourself wholly to the text, and apply its matter wholly to yourself."

If we hesitate about the best way of approaching a particular text with this aim in view, it might be well to ask ourselves: What does he promise, what grace does this text offer me? What prescription does it lay down for me? The two, indeed, ultimately form but one. It is the divine promises that set us in the way of carrying out God's commandments. And these commandments in turn have no meaning other than to open us out to his promises.

Yet we must go even further. What is true of liturgical reading is also true of *lectio divina*. However great the importance of the obedience God requires of us and of the faith that nourishes itself on the divine Word so as to make this obedience truly possible, every divine word summons us beyond both commandments and promises. And even in the commandments and the promises, something more than themselves draws us and moves us, something without which our faith would be vain, our obedience a formality.

This something more, the seed of which is also at the basis of everything, is what we might call the simple contemplation of the divine Word, of the revelation of himself that God is making to us herein. In every Word of God, what matters most is God's opening his own heart to us in it, and it is by this that our heart should be touched, changed from top to bottom. When we arrive at this point, we have truly attained something at least of that "knowledge of God" which is the sole purpose of the whole of revelation, of the whole Word of God. This "knowledge" is contemplation, the absorption of self in what we contemplate, conformation to him whom we contemplate, adherence, union. . . .

When our *lectio divina* is worthy of its name, contemplation does not come as a kind of superstructure, as if from without. Contemplation is, even if obscurely, the prime mover of this *lectio* with regard to our faith and its crown with regard to the love nourished by that faith.

Chapter 3

PRAYER

Most modern works on spirituality begin by more or less emphatically distinguishing vocal prayer from mental prayer and opposing the one to the other. If what has just been said has any validity, it indicates that this distinction is not so neat as it has appeared to be and that opposing the two is the result of a misunderstanding, or rather of a series of misunderstandings.

Vocal Prayer and Mental Prayer

As the ancients saw it, vocal prayer is the food or the expression of interior prayer and so we can go quite naturally from the one to the other. Cassian, who sums up the whole spiritual tradition of fourth century monasticism, speaks of the highest forms of mental prayer in connection with the recitation of the psalms and delights in showing how the latter is illumined throughout by the former. Things began to change in the Byzantine Orient when the liturgical office became complicated and overweighted. In the West, the crisis became even more acute from the moment that the liturgical language ceased to be understood by the mass of Christians, even by the religious. But it was only in a very recent era, at the end of the Middle Ages, that mental prayer and vocal prayer (and particularly liturgical prayer) came to be considered two independent and secretly opposed realities, to such an extent that the problem of their relationship has come to seem the problem of their reconciliation rather than of their fruitful interaction.

This tendency has run its full course in a certain form of piety still too common among many religious and clerics. Reciting the Office, saying other vocal prayers unrelated to it, and meditation have each come to be allotted to different parts of the day, without any concern for (nor even the least possible perception of) the influence of any one of these practices on the others. If to this schedule is added a reading from holy Scripture and other spiritual reading, to say nothing of various pious practices such as the examination of conscience and a visit to the Blessed Sacrament, equally unrelated either to one another or to these various forms of prayer, the effect is extremely disconcerting. The day of a "man of God" or of a "pious person" comes to be a mosaic of apparently completely heterogeneous practices which, far from simplifying and unifying that day in "the one thing necessary" spoken of by the Gospel, seem deliberately designed to disrupt and disorganize it.

In practice, the spontaneous instinct of the spiritual life finds effective compensations for this state of affairs and manages to pursue one single search for God, one single thought of God that is basically more continuous than it seems, under cover of these heterogeneous practices, even if not always through them. Nonetheless, it is still a source of distress for a spiritual life to have to attain unity, if not by going against the practices that nourish it, at least in spite of them.

In this state of affairs, nothing seems more urgent than to see how the various traditional forms, the different ways of prayer, should on the contrary work together toward the same end, and for that reason ought to converge from the outset.

This requires that we begin by dispelling a more or less false notion of the Divine Office. It is quite true that the Office is the prayer of the Church in a preeminent way. But we must beware of drawing or of tending to draw from this fact the strange inference that the Office would or could be a prayer that does not directly concern the spiritual life of those who have to recite it. When it is said that clerics in major Orders and men and women choir-religious are "deputed" by the Church to recite the Office, what is really meant? Could it be that they need only, by virtue of their special function in the Church, ensure a correct recitation of the Office, which would then have an *ex opere operato* effectiveness, quite independent in principle of the personal part they take (or do not take) in it? This is nonsense.

In the first place, there is not and could not be a prayer acting *ex opere operato*. *Ex opere operato* activity is exclusively the characteristic of the sacraments inasmuch as these are primarily the acts of God himself. Even so, it must be emphasized that these divine acts call for the corresponding activity of the Church in general, and, in particular, of the minister who gives them and of the faithful who benefit from them, to such an extent that to celebrate them without this corresponding activity, at least in an elementary degree, is to commit a sacrilege. But in the case of prayer, which by definition cannot be a divine act since it is, above all, the act of a person in the presence of God, there can be no question of action *ex opere operato*. The teaching of the Sermon on the Mount on this point is blindingly clear: when a person prays, either he prays with his lips only, in which case he is a hypocrite mimicking prayer, or else he prays with his heart, that is to say with the attention of his spirit, the conformation of his deepest will to what his lips are expressing, in which case alone does he truly pray in the Christian sense of the word.

In what sense, then, should we take the statement that the Divine Office is "the prayer of the Church" and that clerics and religious are especially "deputed" to carry it out? Only the history of the Office can help us to understand this.

The Divine Office, in all its first beginnings, is the prayer of the Church in the sense that it is a prayer especially conceived and carried out by the Church in order that all her members can make it their own. This was the reason why one of the primary tasks of the clergy, together with the preaching of the Gospel and the celebration of the sacraments, was considered from the outset to be that of presiding at public prayer.

Very early, all the particularly fervent Christians, the ascetics, tended to join not only occasionally but daily in this celebration of public prayer, in which the mass of the faithful doubtless participated more or less regularly.

Later on, the development of monasticism led, among Christians of exceptional fervor, to a development of community prayer. And this in return influenced the public prayer of the Church as such. And it was at this point that it quickly took on an amplitude and a richness that were characteristically monastic.

But the counter-effect of this development was that this prayer ceased to be one in which any fervent Christian might be able to join. As a consequence, the public celebration more and more became ordinarily the affair of the clergy, the religious and perhaps of a handful of the faithful. It was only on Sunday and feast-days that the majority of the faithful still joined in, or at least joined in the primitive part of the Office, the part which from the outset had been conceived for everyone and still more or less retained this character.

At this stage, however, instead of still forming one coherent and complete whole, this fundamental part of the Office had already become no more than a detached fragment of a much larger whole, outside of which, because of the homogeneous evolution of all the parts, it had lost much of its meaning. Thus Sunday Vespers in the Roman rite, always having the same five psalms as part of a *cursus* now distributing the Psalter over the Hours of one week, finally came to seem incomplete and most monotonous to those who took part in this one Office only. It was to be feared that they would grow tired of it, as has in fact happened today.

Furthermore, when a monastic type of office became the rule in many secular churches as well, it came to seem more and more burdensome to the clergy themselves. The complete public celebration thus little by little became no longer the activity of every church, but only of certain churches provided with a particularly numerous clergy. And the clergy themselves were no longer required habitually to take part in the public Office. For them as for the religious, it was enough that they should associate themselves, at least in private by the use of the breviary, with what remained the public prayer of the Church in principle but which became less and less so in practice.

Under these conditions, there is now no doubt about the sense in which the "prayer of the Church" is to be understood as designating the Office. It means that the Office is, in principle, a prayer in which the whole Church, all her members, ought to be able to join, even though a historical development, in which is manifested the truth of the maxim that the good is sometimes the enemy of the best, has come to render such participation very unlikely.

At the same time, the exact meaning becomes clear of this "deputing" of the clergy and religious to the recitation, or rather the celebration, of the Office. What the Church expected of her clerics to begin with was that they would assure a public celebration in which all the faithful really could take part. But this very celebration, so far as the clergy were concerned, presupposed that they themselves were the first to take part, not only with their lips, but with their hearts, in the prayer into which they were to draw the other members of the Church. Today, when there is no longer any hope that they actually will draw others into it except in rather exceptional cases, what the Church still does require of the clergy, as of religious, is that they at least continue to make their own this prayer, which, in actual fact, no longer is (and, as it now stands, could no longer be) the prayer of all. And, need it be said, just as the clergy and also the religious ought to strive to the greatest possible extent to make this prayer both the nourishment and the expression of their own most intimate prayer, so they should always return to it, at least for the inspiration of the prayer in which they should be forming and guiding all those entrusted to them.

That this is still possible in spite of the imperfections of the Office in its present form can be shown more clearly than in any other way by a study of the Office, enabling us to distinguish what is essential in it from what is accidental, and thus to rediscover its fundamental meaning.

The Divine Office as the Leaven of Personal Prayer

The core of the public prayer of the Church is, obviously, that development of the service of the synagogue which still makes up the first part of the Mass. We have already explained at length how Christian prayer is here born of God's Word.

The Divine Office was developed as it were around this fundamental celebration, in such a way as to extend its echo into the whole life of the faithful.

Its origin also is found in the worship of the Old Testament. In the Temple of Jerusalem, the sacrifice of incense was celebrated each morning and evening, accompanied by prayers psalmodic in their essence. One part of the synagogal service, that which was held every morning and evening, could be considered as a means of joining in this daily sacrifice of praise. In the same way in the Christian Church up to the fourth century at least, although the Eucharist was celebrated only on Sundays and the feasts of martyrs, the faithful assembled each morning and evening under the direction of the clergy for a service of praise: Matins (in the primitive sense of the word), later in the West called Lauds, at sunrise, and Vespers at sunset.

These services were so much in the unbroken line of the analogous synagogue-services that, in all the ancient Christian liturgies of East and West, we find here the very psalms which had already been designated by the synagogue for the same hours. For Lauds (which took its name from them), these were the three great *Laudate* psalms ending the psalter. And at Vespers were used those other psalms of praise which together form what is called the Hallel.

In other words, what is proper to the morning and evening prayer of the Church is that it be a prayer of praise: a prolongation, a renewal of that "thanksgiving," that "eucharist" which, as we have already explained, is the fundamental prayer awakened by the Word of God itself as its response in the heart of the person who welcomes it with faith.

Thus the prayer with which each Christian day should normally begin and be completed is a prayer that is basically theocentric: in which the contemplation of the *mirabilia Dei*, the wonderful deeds of God, should raise the soul toward him in a praise that is fundamentally disinterested. Without question, it is fitting that in the morning we should call upon God for help during the day to come—that in the evening we should confess our faults to him and place ourselves in his hands before our night's sleep. These themes have their natural place in our prayer. But, if this prayer is what it ought to be, they should neither be the whole nor even the basis of it. To see God, by faith, as He has revealed himself to us in his Word, to wonder at him, to glorify him—such should be the first movement, the first upsurge of our prayer every morning and every evening.

The themes of this praise, provided by the series of psalms already assigned to morning and evening in the synagogal tradition and followed by all the Christian traditions of the East and West, are also very revealing. They show us how prayer, if it is to fill our whole life, should be adapted to that life and how, in return, prayer should conform life to the revelation concerning its own nature which only the divine Word has the power to bring to it.

What, in fact, is the essential theme of Lauds, of those three Psalms, 148, 149, 150, which constitute its core? It is the praise of God in his creation of the universe. Equally, the theme of the Hallel psalms, reserved for the office of Vespers, is the praise of God for his redemptive intervention in the history of humanity. In the morning, that is, when a man awakes, when he takes up a new awareness of the universe that surrounds him and of the life that animates it, he should newly remake his life in the world, his knowledge of the world, into a glorification of God as source of all being and the end toward which every being should tend. More profoundly, aided by the divine Word of the holy Scriptures, when he awakes each day he should renew the sense of things that he has only too often lost, the sense of things as divine words addressed to him; so that he will recognize God through them, and use them in return above all as instruments of praise.

And, in the evening, recapitulating and gathering up the day's experience, a man should recognize in it, under the same influence of biblical inspiration, an echo of the experience of the people of God considering their own past. Thus in all the experience of his own faults and insufficiencies intermingled with that of the divine grace which nonetheless never fails him—to the point of helping him to make his very failures occasions of new progress—in all this he should recognize and glorify divine Providence: that mighty hand and outstretched arm spoken of by Moses, by which God has aided and never ceases to aid his people, to bring them to himself through all the vicissitudes of their existence. Just as he is the creator of everything from the beginning, so in the history of each man—which is made a "sacred history" by his intervention, even though too often it is nothing but the history of our sins—he reveals himself and is finally to be recognized as the Savior. . . .

It is on this fundamental pattern of each morning's and each evening's prayer that should be woven the various other prayers which intersperse our days with incessant meetings with God, and thus, little by little, cause all our activities, even the most apparently profane, to be absorbed in one divine action.

This is the purpose of the three daily prayers, already familiar to the Jews, which constitute so many decisive stages, as it were, in the unfolding of our days: the prayers of the third, the sixth and the ninth hours, or, according to our way of reckoning, nine o'clock in the morning, midday and three in the afternoon.

In the Acts of the Apostles, we see the first Christians continuing to carry out these prayers of the synagogue. And all the spiritual authors of the first three centuries insist again and again on the importance of this threefold return to God, in the midst of the morning's work, at the noon-time pause, and at the moment when the day turns toward evening. From this universal practice, which had been private as to its form, the cenobitic monasteries of the fourth century constructed an organized and collective prayer. But even in the sixth century the Rule of St. Benedict still shows clearly that this was not a public service properly speaking, but a pause in the day's occupations to bring the soul back to God. These "Little Hours," as they are called, of Terce, Sext and None, can be, the Benedictine Rule expressly says, recited not in the oratory but in the place where one is working. This also explains why their form is brief and stereotyped, easily lending itself to recitation from memory when no book is at hand.

Also characteristic are the psalms assigned by the Benedictine Rule to these Hours. During the week, these are the Gradual Psalms, their perpetual theme being that if the Lord is not present and acting through us, "those who labor, labor in vain." But on Sunday, as a day almost wholly devoted to contemplation, these Hours are taken up with the recitation of Psalm 118 (Hebrew 119), with its one great theme—unwearying meditation on the Word of God.

And finally, toward the end of the fourth century, two other monastic "Hours" which might be termed household services, giving rhythm to the life of the community as such, were added to complete the cycle of daily prayer: the Offices of Prime and Compline. The first is designed to prepare for the day's work; in practice, it is combined with the chapter meeting in which the daily tasks are distributed. The second, in the same way, is meant to end the day and prepare for the night's rest; it is the prayer which, coming immediately before everyone retires to the dormitory, should leave the soul with a final sense of trustful self-abandonment for the night in the hands of God.

In this connection, we might add that the increasingly wide-spread use in recent years of these two prayers (Compline in particular), to the neglect of Lauds and Vespers, is very characteristic of a superficial view of liturgical tradition. However beautiful they may be, these prayers of Prime and Compline, centered on ourselves, on our needs, our activity and our rest, are only appendages to the truly traditional morning and evening prayer which has us contemplate God and praise him for his work as Creator and Redeemer.

One other basic element in the development taken on by public prayer under the influence of monasticism was the practice of holding a daily vigil, taken up with the meditative reading of the Scriptures. In the ancient Church, the whole community had devoted a part of each Saturday night (and the whole night of Holy Saturday) to preparing by such a "Service of the Word" for the eucharistic celebration on Sunday. This was the immediate origin of the first part of the Mass, as we have already noted. The monks made this vigil a daily one, separate from a preparation for the Eucharist. It was here that the practice grew up, not only of a selected reading of the most important Scripture passages—as had been the case in the Offices meant for the ordinary faithful—but of a continuous and, in principle, complete reading. And again the monastic vigil, like the other monastic services, added to this reading the chant, not only of certain selected psalms, as at Lauds and Vespers, or of certain fragments of selected psalms, as in the ancient Sunday vigils, but of a whole sequence of psalms. And naturally, for this hour at which Scripture was to be read at leisure, the great historical psalms or the sapiential psalms, meditating on that history in the spirit of the Sages of Israel, were those prescribed.

Yet this typically monastic elaboration of the vigil also originated from a private devotion which the earliest of the Fathers recommended to all the faithful, even to those who were married. This devotion was closely bound up with the eschatological expectation of the early Christians, their attitude regarding the return of Christ: holding oneself always ready to welcome him when He comes, at whatever moment this may take place—a moment which we cannot foresee. To this end, they voluntarily interrupted or deliberately cut short their night's sleep by a brief period of meditation, in which teachings of Scripture were recalled in order to maintain or reawaken this expectation of meeting God. The hours of night were prescribed as the proper time for this renewal, it would seem, on the one hand because they are the most tranquil, the most propitious for uninterrupted, undisturbed meditation; and, on the other hand, no less because it is during these hours particularly that, however little we intend to do so, we are more than ever tempted to forget in sleep, in relaxation, all our searching after God.

Once we have become aware of this complex significance of the Hours of the Divine Office, we can easily see how a proper understanding of this tradition can benefit us in our efforts toward fully personal prayer.

Let us consider how this directly concerns the priests, the clerics, the religious and the faithful who have the possibility of joining, either individually or communally, in the recitation of the divine Office as it exists today, and also how it applies more generally to every fervent Christian.

The primary emphasis should be laid on the prayer of Lauds and Vespers. The faithful, not bound by canonical obligation, who, while unable to take on the whole of the Office, wish to pray at least what is of its essence, have here the primitive core, the prayer which was designed in fact originally for all Christians, to which to devote themselves. And every Christian, even if for one reason or another he does not habitually say the prayers of Lauds or Vespers as these have come down to us today, should think of his day as enclosed within a morning and an evening praise normally centered on the two great themes inspiring these prayers in all Catholic and Jewish tradition.

Equally part of every Christian's life, whether or not he uses habitually the actual text of the breviary, should be some effort at daily meditation of the Word of God, carried out during his leisure hours—which ordinarily means at night. It matters little whether this be done before the beginning of the day's activities or as encroaching on the hours of sleep after it. But all of us, more or less, must take to heart the necessity for excerpting from our daily periods of leisure, under all circumstances, the minimum time needed to make sure that all our days are, to the greatest degree possible, fed from the spring of the divine Word.

As to the choice of texts to be read throughout the liturgical year and the spirit in which to meditate on them, the order of readings and the sets of responses given in the Breviary accompanying these readings can serve as a guide for everyone, even for those who are not obliged to recite the Office, and those who cannot or do not wish to recite it habitually.

Conversely, the clergy and the religious on whom the Church imposes this obligation, if they grasp its significance, will not be able ordinarily to content themselves with the truncated biblical readings and frequently inadequate commentaries in the present breviary. According to individual circumstances, all should be concerned with the need to fill out these prescribed "lessons" by the various kinds of readings described in the previous chapter—for which, again, the canonical readings serve at least as priming. The canonical vigil will thus be extended in a personal vigil, which will itself be the starting-point for all meditative prayer.

In the same way, the "Day Hours" will be the food or will furnish the general inspiration for the effort to extend our prayer from these set times to all the moments of the day. From this point of view, we may take inspiration from the Eastern and

Western traditions which unanimously mark the celebration of the third Hour by an express remembrance of the descent of the Holy Spirit on the apostles. At the sixth Hour, in the East today as formerly in the Gallican Office, Christ's nailing to the cross is recalled, and at the ninth Hour his death. In the Roman Office, at noon the introductory hymn simply alerts us to the struggle necessary in the middle of the day against becoming absorbed in the world and our own passions, and, when the day turns toward evening, the hymn invites our faith to raise itself above the vicissitudes of creation to the eternity of its Creator.

But all these reminders have value only as they impel us to constant prayer and facilitate it. This was the reason for introducing, in the Byzantine Orient, intermediary Hours between the three more ancient canonical Little Hours. And this is the purpose behind all the various practices, of which we shall speak in detail, designed to put prayer into the whole of life and, what is no less important, to adapt prayer to the whole natural course of that life in such a way as to orient it wholly toward Christ and toward God.

In particular, whether or not we use the canonical text of the prayers of Prime and Compline, it is desirable that our beginning work and our retiring to sleep both be undertaken under the eyes of God, and that they take on a meaning which unites both our activity and our rest with the living presence of God in us through Christ.

In the light of all this, it would seem out of the question for priests and religious to dispose of the Divine Office during low-energy periods of the day—periods more or less unavailable for anything requiring much effort—so as then to devote themselves to more or less lengthy individual prayers. The place of the Hours in the day and their essential significance (which are closely related) are to be respected so that they play their natural role of inspiring the whole with prayer, of conforming (if one can put it this way) the whole reality of our daily existence to the ideal of Christian prayer.

And, for every Christian, the liturgical tradition of the Church ought to furnish at least the outline of a prayer really inserted into life and wholly penetrating it in its most diverse aspects. It is in this spirit that we shall now examine more deeply the relationship between meditation and contemplation, then go on to the relationship between the prayer carried out during the times exclusively devoted to it and the prayer of all times, and, finally, to the relationship between praise and intercession.

Meditation and Contemplation

The majority of modern spiritual writers, beginning with St. Teresa of Avila, when they come to speak about personal prayer, mental prayer, make a radical distinction between contemplation and the meditation that precedes it. Meditation, laborious by nature, is the activity of beginners in the spiritual life, or of those who have not yet progressed very far in it. But normally, one ought to attain a phase of spiritual progress in which meditation no longer adds anything, or even becomes psychologically impossible to carry out. Then, it would seem, contemplation will flower of its own accord.

More recently, among the spiritual writers whose work is mainly one of commenting on the great authorities of the sixteenth century, especially of the Carmelite school, a supplementary distinction has appeared which has aroused a violent controversy, dividing the writers into two camps. The question raised and debated in such a lively way is whether contemplation is, as they say, always "infused" or can also be "acquired." By infused contemplation is understood one which is the effect of a pure influx of grace, taking hold of the soul independently of any effort (or at least any conscious one) of the soul. Acquired contemplation, by contrast, would be obtained by the soul itself, progressively simplifying and unifying its meditation and thus entering of its own accord, by a calm effort of concentration, into a state of spiritual tranquility which is, to be sure, the fruit of grace, but of grace still making use of the normal play of our faculties. Those who believe only in a contemplation that is infused retort that "acquired contemplation" is either a contradiction in terms or a poorly-chosen term covering a confused experience. It is of the essence of Christian contemplation, they say, according to all tradition, to be the taking possession of the soul by God; thus it is opposed to all the efforts of the soul itself to lay hold of God. One cannot without gross contradiction, therefore, speak of a contemplation acquired by human effort. What in fact this term attempts to define is probably the inadequate perception of an intermediary state in which the soul is still able to meditate and still needs to meditate, but is already oriented by grace toward a simplification and an elevation of its prayer tending to cause it to go beyond all meditation and any form of prayer in which the soul itself is the principal author. . . .

Rather than enter point-blank into these controversies, it seems urgent to begin by defining with more precision than is ordinarily used the sense in which the great spiritual writers, particularly those of the sixteenth century, opposed meditation to contemplation. This presupposes that we pay strict attention, first of all, to what they included under the term "meditation."

The study of St. Teresa in particular is most enlightening. The meditation which she was acquainted with, which she pursued so long and indeed so scrupulously without ever finding in it a fruit that satisfied her, and which finally she could endure no longer, is the type to be found in exercises like those of Garcia de Cisneros. A systematic use of the deductive reason, applied in every possible way to the object of meditation, is combined with imaginative representations deliberately called up to engage the "affections" of the soul. Meditating on the cross, for example, not only includes very detailed considerations of what it cost Christ thus to suffer, of the profit that we should draw from his sufferings, that we can draw from them if we will, but also a realistic depicting of those sufferings to quicken our sensibility and move our heart (in the modern sense, above all affective, of this last word). The desired "fruit" is to set the will in motion so that it may renounce vice a little more thoroughly and give itself to virtue a little more generously, or more deeply but through all this be, as they say, more ardently "enflamed" in its love for Christ.

There could be no question of casting doubt on the very beneficial effects that can be and still are experienced from a meditation of this type. Such meditations have proved to be very fruitful for a complete assimilation of Christian truths by the intelligence, for a realistic and at the same time a positive refashioning of the sensibility, for an efficacious exercise of the will, all this being undeniably ripened through a view of faith tending to the development of charity. They have been particularly beneficial, furthermore, since their revision and emendation by St. Ignatius and through the use of his *Exercises* by experienced spiritual directors, achieving a delicate focusing of this most ingenious exploitation of the different resources of human psychology. Moreover, this kind of meditation appeared opportunely at a period in the development of human consciousness characterized by the abrupt emergence and the swift predominance of awareness of the self. It is difficult, indeed, to decide precisely to what extent this kind of meditation is a product of this mutation in the spirit of humanity as it came to take itself for the first and principal object of thought, and to what extent it actually accelerated this maturation.

When all this has been said, the fact still remains that methods of this kind, especially from the moment when they not only became predominant in spirituality but also obliterated any other possible conception of meditation, were to manifest certain limitations, certain more or less unfortunate counter-effects.

It is quite obvious, for one thing, that this type of meditation, of which the whole of Christian antiquity was practically unaware, was itself no less unaware of what the Fathers understood by meditating. It might even be permissible to ask ourselves to what extent the development of modern meditation was not due simply to the prevailing ignorance of the ancient kind, to an actual inability to return to it.

The case of St. Teresa is particularly suggestive in this regard. Throughout her work can be perceived an extraordinary hunger for the Word of God, for holy scripture. But the lack of available translations, the lack of a culture which would have enabled her, even if she had had any translations at hand, to use them as the ancients used the Latin Vulgate or the Greek Septuagint, and, together with all this, the all too evident dangers of illuminism threatening those who, in spite of these handicaps, threw themselves into the Bible, the suspicions and the interdictions of the Spanish Inquisition—because of all these various factors, St. Teresa, like many others of the same period, was barred from that quite simple recourse to *lectio divina* from which had formerly issued a meditation unquestionably the more enriching for being entirely natural. In these circumstances, it is easy to see how helpful would be a meditation at once rational and affective, in which the imagination aided the workings of the reason to make up for the lack of immediate contact, or for the tenuousness of the contact, with the Word of God. But herein also, without any doubt, lay the reason for a considerable part of the dissatisfaction admitted by St. Teresa and by so many of her contemporaries.

The grounds for this are many. The first, and one of the most profound, is connected with whatever about the methods of meditation in question is laborious, nay, even—let us say the word—artificial. In such a way of bringing to light all the hidden resources of the human soul in order to play on them deliberately, of calling up a paroxysm of sensible impressions superimposed on what seems like an aggravated ratiocination in order that the will may, finally, be galvanized thereby—in all this, it must be admitted, a soul which is sound, concerned for truthfulness, for naturalness, might find itself ill at ease.

It should be noted that we are here concerned with a cultural phenomenon which has many equivalents in the baroque period. At that time were produced a prodigious effervescence of forms, a burgeoning which was undeniably rich and even dazzling. But behind this was a tension, a frenzy not too successfully concealing a certain weakness and disquiet. This world, in which everything human took on a new lustre, was a world impassioned but also secretly anguished. It is not a very good sign when the over-development of the intelligence tends toward the purely cerebral, nor does the sensibility coming to reinforce it improve matters when it turns to aggravating the emotions.

Indeed, behind this first impression of uneasiness, we sense a basic lack which the paroxysms excited in the activity of the religious subject do not succeed in alleviating. We mean the drying up of the sources, or the tenuous contact with them, and its consequence, the gradual fading and thinning out of the religious object.

In fact, to the extent to which the apparatus of meditation was complicated and perfected in the sixteenth century, we find as it were an impoverishment of the themes of meditation. This impression, furthermore, has provoked and still provokes

many misunderstandings. Modern meditation has frequently
been accused of having, as it were, killed its object by curiously
dissecting it. In reality, it was rather the other way around. It
was the contracting of the themes of meditation, from the end
of the Middle Ages on, which in great part called for the com-
pensatory striving for a meditation with a more tangible and
immediate psychological effectiveness.

But the truth is that this more intense forcing, like any
method of intensive culture, is of its nature incompatible with
a slow and gradual impregnation. Abrupt mutations, obtained
in such a way, may in the end reveal that they have no future.
Where superficial attitudes and behavior are so vigorously taken
in hand, the profound personality runs the risk, if not of disappearing, at least of disintegrating, simply from strain due to
the violence done to it, and from the absence of the air and
light which it must drink in unhurriedly for the sake of organic
growth. . . .

Still, the major defect here remains on the side of the religious object and its radically defective presentation and apprehension. The dangers, no doubt inherent in every method in
which a curious concentration on the human subject and his
behavior becomes more and more absorbing, would not have
been as evident if they had been compensated for by recourse
to an abundant and living objectivity.

It should be pointed out, however, that the baroque period
saw pursued and even advanced, together with the developments just analyzed, the first great "return to the sources" of
the modern era. Yet, it must still be admitted, the Renaissance
return to the sources too easily degenerated into antiquarianism,
or into fallacious reconstructions which, although they were
astonishing prodigies of erudition, were no less deficient in any
sense of intimate and living communion with the buried world
from which these treasures, submerged by the centuries, were

brought up piecemeal. As a result, the enormous and delicate mechanism which the modern type of meditation so skillfully set up too frequently found only sorry material to work on. Hence these methods—already the products of a consciousness of self too lively, perhaps, for the best assimilation of the object of meditation—seemed more and more to be turning back on themselves. Thus we can understand now, in the end, that these modern spiritualities, clever as they are, have come to seem rather like a stomach so active that it might digest itself. . . .

All this explains how it is that, in the view of so many modern spiritual writers, contemplation not only follows on meditation but is also so completely opposed to it that it is no longer clear how meditation can prepare for it—although we can very easily see how it might stifle it, since such meditation, in turn, would necessarily find itself inhibited, paralyzed by the sudden appearance of authentic contemplation.

But we see also how this state of things is the effect, in great part at least, of the exclusive practice of a very special kind of meditation. It need not follow, perhaps, that every form of meditation is so radically opposed to contemplative prayer. And at the same time we can understand better, perhaps, at least the intention of those who wished to introduce the idea—surely an ambiguous One—of acquired contemplation. It is these same writers, generally speaking, who have worked out a view of meditation which may not coincide in every respect with that of Antiquity, but which, nevertheless, no longer reduces medi-tation to this conjunction of deductive reasonings and artifically evoked phantasms, for the purpose of a kind of forcing of the will. In fact, as soon as we get away from these psychological gymnastics and try to bring meditation back to a simple and organic view of the great truths of the faith—or, better still, of the mystery of Christ, neither reduced to a blue-print for the reason nor buried under a showy and, wherever possible, startling scenery—it can be said that the effort proper to all meditation, far from being opposed to the "passivity" that marks contemplation, rather leads to it of its own accord and lends it a helping hand.

The whole question, actually, is to know whether meditation is to be organized in function of essentially fragmentary views of Christian dogma and picturesque but grossly concretized imaginative representations of the Christian reality, or whether, rather, beneath all the dogmas, beneath all the realities of the Gospel, it should tend to embrace one single mystery—the unity of this mystery being neither that of an abstract concept nor of a picture highly individualized in terms of time and space, but the mysterious yet living unity of a divine incarnate Person and of the design for our salvation in which He reveals himself to us in giving himself to our faith and our love. On an even deeper level, the distinction should be made between a meditation ordered simply toward schooling the will, and one designed to create the "new man" in us, and to do so by likening us progressively to a supernatural model not to be copied from without, feature by feature, but rather to be reproduced from within by virtue of our hidden relationship, the wholly intimate consciousness of which is re-awakened in us as our vision of the model becomes less and less imperfect.

Let us note that while the development of the modern type of meditation is not at all favorable to the ascent toward contemplation by way of meditation itself when it abounds too much in its own sense, this is not true when we avoid making it an absolute, a closed system. When systematic meditation remains an instrument as responsive to the hand that uses it as it is delicately adjusted to its proper use, then everything is different. What matters then is to afford this instrument adequate material to work with—material which, above all, possesses a life of its own so vigorous that its rhythms will stand out clearly and not be artificially cut off. This is what, in fact, has been done with the Ignatian method when, properly understood and respected in its spirit as well as in its letter, it has been nourished by a wide and deep biblical and patristic culture.

In that school described by Bremond as "Berullian Jesuit" even though it was not actually influenced directly by Bérulle but simply drank at the same sources as had he, we see this spontaneous simplifying of meditation at work, in a concentration on the life of Christ in us which is of its nature oriented and disposed toward contemplation.

Do we, then, still need to bring in "acquired contemplation" as the stage between meditation and contemplation properly so called, that is, infused contemplation?

To answer this question, we must go further into the primary problem of the relationship between meditation and contemplation, and ask ourselves what is "active" and what is "passive" in Christian prayer in general.

Passivity and Activity in Prayer

What should we think, first of all, of the idea that contemplation represents a state of prayer in which the soul is "passive" under the grace of God who acts in her, while meditation is a prayer in which it is the soul, chiefly at any rate, which is "active"? If these terms are taken in their strictest sense, this idea would superimpose on an entirely Pelagian conception of the Christian life in general a completely erroneous notion of how the divine Spirit acts within us. On the one hand, the effort of humans would be exerted with something like complete autonomy, until, at its goal, grace would crown this work of human merit—precisely the error of Pelagius. And, on the other hand, the action of the Spirit revealing itself in us would thus automatically eliminate all activity on our part.

To each of these equally over-simplified ideas is opposed the exhortation of the Apostle, paradoxical in appearance only: "Work at your salvation in fear and trembling, knowing that it is God who works in you both the willing and the doing" (Phil 2:13). This means that the laboriousness of our prayer, as of our whole spiritual life, no more opposes the action of grace in us, which must be the principle of all our good works, than the divine intervention suppresses or diminishes our own proper activity. Quite the contrary, if God acts in us, it is in no way somehow to substitute for us, but rather to foster an activity which, when it manifests itself, is not less our own from having come wholly from him.

The fact is that in all discussions of this kind we deceive ourselves completely if we think of the relationship between God's activity and our own as resembling that between two activities on the same level of existence. God is our creator, and He is the creator (especially, we might say) of what is most intimate, most personal in us. The Christian spiritual life, as we have said, fully reveals this conjunction. And now we can state precisely that it is revealed in prayer above all, for it is here that our will gives itself up to the divine will, and it is here that the divine will fructifies our created will.

It follows that it is absolutely impossible to set up meditation as a type of prayer in which our activity is primary (still less in which it would be autonomous) in opposition to contemplation as another type of prayer in which it is God who acts in us, our activity ceasing thereupon. In setting up such a contrast, we are actually betrayed into the most pernicious error possible in the realm of spirituality: as if our activity and that of God worked in strict inverse proportion, the one increasing only to the extent to which the other decreases. The truth is quite the contrary: our own activity only exists and proves fruitful in prayer to the exact measure of the activity of grace in us.

This does not, however, preclude a real distinction between meditation, in whatever way one conceives of it, and contemplation, nor an undeniable relationship between this distinction and that which may be made between the "passive" and "active" aspects of the spiritual life.

The ancients themselves, who had not worked out, let us repeat, the very special idea of meditation arrived at in modern times, recognized nonetheless a very clear distinction between meditation of the type then practised and contemplation properly so called. And for them, without any doubt, contemplation was a state in which the soul somehow escaped from itself to be as it were ravished in God. But we must clearly grasp what they themselves meant by these distinctions.

We should take note of the fact that these were worked out for the first time from the fifth to the sixth century. And this was done along lines which, though more or less parallel, still are not exactly alike. We can distinguish at least three, with some supplementary nuances. The first is connected with the writings attributed to Macarius the Egyptian, at present believed rather to be the work of a monk who was probably Syrian and a fairly close disciple of St. Gregory of Nyssa. The second was opened out by Evagrius and developed by the Pseudo-Dionysius, although not without profound modifications. The third, finally, is that of St. Augustine and, with noteworthy distinctions, of St. Gregory the Great.

In the Homilies of Macarius, there are certainly two quite distinct types of prayer, one being that of beginners, the other of those more advanced in the spiritual life. The first is a laborious prayer, an ascetic effort, pursued in relative darkness. The second, the fruit of this effort, is an ardent, luminous prayer in which the soul expands in a sense of abundance created in it by the Spirit, who, in compensation for the generous sacrifice of the goods of this life, gives it here and now the blessings of eternal life. "Macarius" states precisely that at this stage the soul lives in light because it has itself become wholly light, because it allows itself to be penetrated by this light, its faith giving itself up without reserve to the divine call summoning it to contemplation.

Evagrius sees things somewhat differently. He is the first author to distinguish sharply between three stages in the normal development of every spiritual life. In the first stage, we are absorbed by the struggle against the passions. But when we have dominated them by asceticism, the contemplative life begins—a life in which we no longer see things through our natural impressions but in the view God has of them, which He has communicated to us by his Word. Yet these phases are not simply successive and opposed to one another: the struggle against the passions of itself tends toward contemplation, and it is only by means of the contemplation then emerging that the passions are finally and effectively subjugated.

However, contemplation itself is divided into two successive levels, entirely distinct from one another. The inferior kind of contemplation, which itself includes several degrees, still knows God only through distinct ideas, however lofty and simplified these may be. The superior kind of contemplation, which Evagrius calls the "gnosis of the Holy Trinity" and also "pure prayer," on the contrary rejects and goes beyond every idea as well as every imagining, including those related to the humanity of the Savior. This is the direct vision of the place spoken of by Exodus, where God abides. And, as Evagrius himself states, this vision of God is at the same time the soul's vision of itself: here it sees itself, indeed, as restored to its primary condition of image of God, presupposing in the soul the active presence, as of the sun in a mirror, of the Model who conforms it to himself.

Pseudo-Dionysius, in turn, distinguishes three stages in
the spiritual life: the first, in which we purify ourselves; the
second, in which we are illuminated by what he calls the divine
oracles (that is, meditation on the divine Word); the third, in
which we finally enter into union with God himself. From the
point of view of prayer, this stage is also that in which we no
longer understand divine things as if from without, but rather
experience them. It is the entrance into what he calls "mystical
theology." For this, we have been prepared by "apophatic theology," which makes us realize that, strictly speaking, God is
not anything that we can affirm of him in the formulae of "cataphatic theology," which applies to him images and thoughts
drawn from our natural experience. Going beyond both the
negations of the one and the affirmations of the other, "mystical
theology" causes us to enter into the luminous cloud, into the
super-essential darkness which is one with that inaccessible light
in which God dwells.

For St. Augustine, in a third line of thought (not unanalo-
gous to the preceding, borrowing extensively, as it does, from
Neo-Platonism), the soul, guided by the divine Word, goes from
material beings and their beauty to the soul which thinks about
them and to its proper beauty; and the soul is thus drawn above
and beyond itself, to the not merely incorporeal but uncreated
beauty of him who created it and all other things, whom all
things evoke but who is above them all. Contemplation, for
St. Augustine, is this ascending movement finally reaching its
goal. But this attainment, he came to believe more and more
decidedly, can only be fleeting here below. The soul is soon
taken back by the body, by the world in which it is immersed.
Yet the fleeting foretaste it was able to gain of the divine beauty,
attracting the soul at the heart of its meditation, causes it to
resume this again with renewed ardor and effectiveness.

St. Gregory the Great, in the same tradition, states precisely
for the whole Latin Middle Ages what is to be understood by
contemplation.

He begins by recalling, in strict fidelity to the thought of
Aristotle and the majority of the Greeks after him, that all dis-
cursive reasoning, that is, all use of our power of reasoning,
should tend to a unitive vision of the thing studied, that is, to
contemplation of it. In the same way, in the domain of religion,
the more our thoughts about God are enriched and deepened,
the more they tend to give us, not any unitive and comprehensive view of him, which would be impossible, but, as it were,
a glimpse of what He is, one which infinitely surpasses everything that we can say and conceive of him. In this *excessus*, as
St. Gregory calls it, which is pre-eminently the token of grace,
the soul is for a few moments as it were, ravished from itself,
from all distinct thought. It cannot remain in this state; it must
regain contact with the world. Yet it retains a nostalgia for the
vision of God in our home-country of heaven, and its efforts
to be re-united to him there are thus invigorated.

Under various expressions, Macarius, Evagrius and Diony-
sius, Augustine and Gregory, all emphasize as clearly as possible the fact that contemplation, however they understand it, is
supremely the gift of God: the especially privileged experience
that we can have of his grace, of his very presence in us taking
possession of us, and to that extent restoring us to the primal
design of our creation to his image and likeness.

It is in this sense that contemplation can be called "passive."
Not that grace is not just as active in us from the beginning of
our meditation on the Word of God by which He is revealed
to us, and not that in contemplation we become inert under
his action. Far from that, we are then acting far more truly, far
more effectively perhaps, than at any of those moments in which
we seem, at first sight, left to ourselves and our own efforts. But

now we experience to the degree that is possible here below that, as the Apostle says, it is in fact God who creates in us both the willing and the doing. More profoundly, we here attain what St. Paul again calls "the knowledge I have of the mystery," the mystery that he further defines as "Christ in us, the hope of glory." Contemplation understood in this way is, in truth, germinally present in the most elementary act of Christian faith. And we might say that this seed develops to the degree to which faith conforms us to itself by obedience. This is why progress in prayer, causing the contemplative aspect more and more to predominate, is not so much as might appear to a superficial view the product of psychological concentration and simplification. Far more is it a progress in conforming life, and the whole inner being from which it precedes, to faith. The more the objects of our faith, or rather its great central and total object, the mystery of Christ in us, incorporates itself in our existence, from which our most profound consciousness is inseparable—or even better, the more this mystery likens us to itself—the more does faith, without losing anything of its mystery, cease to be obscure for us. To the degree to which its object becomes connatural to us, its reality becomes the more luminous with a light which progressively eclipses that of the sensible or intellectual means of knowing, which had hitherto seemed the clearer the more they were the only lights we had.

According to this view, it is quite true that the knowledge of God and of the things of God developed in us by contemplation is the supreme gift of God, is wholly "supernatural," "infused," "passive." This is not in the least to say that his grace has not already set in motion everything in us, in a sense, long before we arrive at this point. And it is not to say either that at this moment we cease to act in order to give place to him alone. It is rather to say that contemplation begins from the moment when the presence of God, the action of God in us, our life in

Christ, have so rectified, done away with, everything opposing them or screening them from us, that what had hitherto been the object of a faith in some way detached from us, and to this extent obscure, becomes the object of an experience—still mysterious, certainly, and yet nonetheless real, and even already more real than the experience of our senses or of our ordinary intellectual activity.

From a meditation more and more oriented toward the mystery of Christ, more and more absorbed in him, as the whole life of him who meditates strives to conform itself to him in faith, contemplation is born, it might be said in some sense, quite naturally—without ceasing to be, for all that, a pure grace, since it is nothing other than grace making itself felt, revealing itself to us precisely as pure grace.

We can understand also how it is that so long as our conformation to God's design for us, our restoration to life according to his image, is not complete, contemplation will appear to be evanescent. So long as we are on the way to our homeland, to the kingdom, our contemplation can be neither more nor better than a presentiment, a foretaste. Yet, as St. Augustine, St. Gregory the Great and later on St. Bernard emphasize, this foretaste will then be the most efficacious stimulant for a renewed search closely bound up both with ascetic effort and with meditative effort, to assimilate more and more perfectly, through our understanding wholly penetrated by faith, the Mystery which is the object of that faith.

We shall have to resume and deepen these considerations when we come to speak of mystical experience. But enough has been said provisionally to formulate the conclusions which have become evident with regard to the problem we are now concerned with: that of the normal relationships between meditation and contemplation. And this comes back to a definition of what meditation must be in order to lead to the contemplation which is properly Christian, and not bar or obstruct the way to it.

The ideal meditation should be continuously nourished and renewed in the *lectio divina*, as we have already described it, pursued by the light of tradition and with the aid given us by all the modern resources. It can even very well, as St. Teresa herself clearly perceived, never be anything but a sufficiently profound *lectio divina*. However, on the foundation of a living memory freighted with everything with which *lectio divina* has furnished it and already vivified by this somehow spontaneous life of the divine truth in us, meditation can, and in many cases should, profit from the psychological acquisitions of modern methods of meditation. But what is important is that these methods should always remain in their proper place as docile instruments of the soul in its search for God, and never come to imprison it, as it were, in a yoke from which it could no longer escape and one which would brand it with an ineradicable mark.

Indeed, our modern minds with their unstable power of attention, corrupted as they are with querulous thinking and encumbered with a whole kaleidoscope of images, can be greatly aided by a systematic effort at rigorous reasoning, a cultivation of the imagination which will lead it perseveringly back to representations sustaining the impetus of the soul rather than distracting and weighing it down. At the beginning of the life of prayer, this is often the only way of keeping from the vagueness of a pious but unstructural revery. At the decisive moments of existence (conversion, vocation, new progress in the interior life) which the exercises of St. Ignatius particularly have in view, such assistance can be indispensable. In the daily practice of a spiritual life it unquestionably needs to be used with more freedom, more discretion. But it will be the more necessary the more the will has still much to do in the way of self-discipline—the more the attention to God still needs to become habitual.

This is also why, in a general way, those who have little time materially at their disposal for the practices of the interior life, those who are developing it in the environment of a very distracting existence, harassed by many preoccupations, doubtless find these methods more necessary as a support than do others. But, in any case, it is vital that we be on guard against attaching ourselves to the method at the expense of the matter on which it should aid us to work the more effectively. Always and above all, we must be on the alert to renew, by the continually pursued and deepened development of the spiritual culture connected, as we have seen, with a *lectio divina* rightly made, our contact with those sources without which the best method has nothing but a vacuum to work on. Moreover, always and above all, the method, far from imprisoning us in ourselves, must help us to become more and more free and at the disposal of the appeals and the inspirations of grace.

It is in this spirit, therefore, that having finished with this question, we shall now examine some of the best known of the modern methods of meditative prayer. We shall take care to indicate precisely, following the authors who have recommended these methods, the way in which their application should be adopted, their use modified, in relation to the progress being made in the ways of prayer.

The Ignatian Method

St. Ignatius Loyola never formally taught a method of meditation. But here and there in his *Exercises,* he counsels a very personally thought-out and adjusted use of the methods current in his time. It is from these texts taken together that we can draw what is called the Ignatian method. The basic text is found as the first exercise of the first week, in connection with the meditation on sin. This needs to be completed by various other texts, particularly those found in the second and the fourth weeks.

In its most elementary form, after a preliminary appeal to God himself to guide all our intentions and our actions toward his service and his praise, the Ignatian meditation begins with two preludes. The first is what is called the composition of place. The idea is to visualize imaginatively what we are meditating on, as if it were an event taking place before our eyes. When the chosen subject is an invisible one like sin, "the composition of place," St. Ignatius himself says, "is to see with the eyes of my imagination and to consider my soul as imprisoned in this mortal body, and myself, that is to say, my body and my soul in this valley of tears, exiled among animals deprived of reason." The second prelude goes on immediately to the particular fruit which we desire from the meditation we are now entering on, at once asking God to grant it to us.

Having done this, we reach the body of the meditation, which consists essentially in the successive and detailed application of the three powers of the soul, as St. Augustine laid them out: memory, understanding, will. The memory recalls the whole of what we wish to meditate so that the understanding may examine it. The commentators explain that the latter power asks itself, for example, what practical conclusions should flow for us from what we are meditating on—why—what we have done hitherto along these lines—what we should do in the future (obstacles to be removed, positive means to undertake). Already, in the course of this labor of thought, the will should be exercised by various affections. But it is at the end of the meditation that the will should concentrate its forces and, in particular, should make its commitment concrete by definite resolutions.

The first conclusion consists in what St. Ignatius calls "colloquies": here meditation becomes prayer in a conversation with

God, with Christ, or even with the Virgin or the saints whose help we may ask in order to obtain the graces we implore. And, finally, comes a critical review of the meditation we have made, to disclose its imperfections and to put us in a position to do better the next time. It is advised, finally, to retain one single thought resulting from the meditation to which we can return during the day, which is called the "spiritual bouquet."

To this basic plan must be added various counsels of St. Ignatius applicable to the prayer of those making progress. They are advised, in the first place, to devote themselves systematically to applying their five senses, one after another, to a Gospel scene, from whence to draw the appropriate sentiments: observing the infant Jesus in the straw, the poverty of his swaddling-clothes, his limbs numb with cold . . . we should reflect that He who accepts all this for us is our God, whereupon there will be an upsurge of living faith, grateful adoration. . . .

In the second place comes what has often been called Ignatian contemplation, which is a centering of the meditation on the persons taking part in the Gospel scene we are imagining— whether they be, again, God, Christ, the Virgin, the saints, or even the witnesses of the scene. We listen to them as if they were speaking in our presence or even as if they were speaking to us personally. We see what they do, attending to all the details of their acts which could arouse salutary sentiments or reflections. But, as St. Ignatius warns: "If I find in one point the sentiments I desire to arouse in myself, I will stop there and rest in them, without putting myself to the trouble of going further until my soul is fully satisfied; for it is not the abundance of knowledge that fills the soul and satisfies it, but the awareness and the interior tasting of the truths that it meditates" (*Spiritual Exercises*, 2nd note, 4th addition).

And, finally, we come to meditations on the attributes of God, arousing each time adoration, praise, love, the total abandonment of self which these demand of us. . . .

What is most remarkable about this method, when it is rightly understood, is its adaptability. . . . It can be followed by the simplest minds, the least intellectual, and it lends itself, according to the emphasis placed on one or another of its elements, to a very supple adaptation to the progress of the soul, to its deepening apprehension of spiritual realities. . . .

The Sulpician Method

Designed for clerics, the method of prayer of St. Sulpice, elaborated little by little by the teaching of Bérulle, Condren, Olier, and finally completed by Tronson, is more particularly adapted to souls already possessing a certain spiritual formation, The outline of this method is very simple and its development natural. Olier sums it up in three celebrated formulae: Jesus before my eyes, Jesus in my heart, Jesus in my hands. The whole method, in fact, is dominated by the Bérullian idea of contemplating the "states" or the "mysteries" of the Incarnate Word, in such a way as to participate in them.

After a preparation in which, having put ourselves in the presence of God, we complete an act of contrition for our sins by the invocation of the Holy Spirit, asking him to inspire our prayer, we then begin by what is called "adoration" (Jesus before my eyes). We are penetrated by the action of Christ, by his word that we desire to meditate, admiring and adoring it for everything that faith can discover in it.

Thence we go on to "communion" (Jesus drawn into my heart). That is, we await his establishment in us of what we have contemplated in him, to be brought about by his coming into us himself. It is here that Tronson tried to clarify this method in a very practical way: insisting on "considerations" to convince us of the importance of our participation in what is proposed to our faith, and on "returns to oneself" which bring us to judge, in view of what we have done or not done in the past, what we ought to do in the future, so that this will be fruitful. These "considerations" and "returns to oneself" should, however, remain subordinated to the essential, which is aspiration toward what is proposed to us in Christ.

From here we go on quite naturally to the last part, our "cooperation" (Jesus in my hands). That is, in the presence of God and relying on his grace, we make some practical resolve that will bring into our life, in full reality, what we have adored in Christ and drawn into us by the prayer of faith. Here again, we conclude with acts of humility because of the imperfections of our prayer, of gratitude for what grace has nonetheless given us and, as is recommended along with the practice of the final "spiritual bouquet," recourse to the Virgin, so that she will protect and include in her intercession the whole fruit of our prayer.

Other Methods of Prayer

It might be said that all other methods of meditative prayer conceived in modern times are related to the two just described. The first might be considered a model of concrete psychology and of adaptation to the simplest minds; the second an ideal of assimilating our most personal life to the whole substance of the Gospel. As a simplified (but not thereby impoverished) form of the Sulpician type of meditation, we should note the formula proposed by Dom Chautard in his *Soul of the Apostolate,* which remains one of the rare spiritual classics of the nineteenth century. He himself summed it up in the three Latin words: *video, sitio, volo* (I see, I thirst, I will), adding in parenthesis, *volo tecum* (I will together with You). The first point is to contemplate, in the simplest sense of the word; that is, to let ourselves be penetrated by a Christian truth, a word of the Gospel, an example of Christ, in a state of admiring adoration. The second is to awaken in ourselves the desire to participate in it, to receive from it all the graces which can flow from it to us. The last is to make up our mind actually to do everything in our power to have this come about, not without reminding ourselves unwearyingly that it is God, in whose presence we are, who "creates in us both the willing and the doing": *volo tecum.* The most remarkable aspect of Dom Chautard's formula is its tendency to make all meditation, from beginning to end, nothing but the natural development of a single dialogue with God, with Christ.

However, after every description of these detailed methods, the advice—common both to St. Ignatius and St. Teresa—should be recalled that, for many persons, even some of those most advanced in the spiritual life, the simple recitation of a prayer formula (such as a sentence from the Our Father), slowly and patiently turned over in the mind, can constitute an excellent meditation. The whole point is to take the words one by one, drawing from each all the considerations and affections which it is capable of releasing in us, and going on, in the same way, to the next word only when the first seems to have given us all that we are capable of receiving from it for the time being.

Related to this very simple procedure is the one known to Christian antiquity, to the Middle Ages and to the Christian Renaissance under somewhat different forms. This consists in copying out selected formulae from Scripture, from the liturgy, from the Fathers, and grouping them in various "chapters" by subjects for meditation, in order to impregnate oneself with them at leisure by repeating and memorizing them. The prayers of John de Fécamp, the exercises composed by Cardinal Bona, or a little later, by the English Benedictine, Dom Augustine Baker (as an appendix to his *Sancta Sophia*) are various examples of this very simple practice which can prove very fruitful.

This leads us to the more general practice of written meditation. Especially suited to intellectuals, this presents some obvious dangers: there is always the risk of allowing prayer to degenerate into literature. Yet, on the one hand, this risk is not fatal. And, on the other, such a practice has the advantage of keeping us from the waking dream in which any meditation risks being lost. The example of the *Soliloquies* of St. Augustine and that of the *Meditative Prayers* of William of St. Thierry suffice to show both the solidity and the richness which this practice can assure to meditation through forcing it to take a definite shape. One remedy, certainly, not infallible but nonetheless efficacious, against the danger of rhetorical amplification or of composing a treatise which would no longer (or hardly) be prayer, is to keep to the dialogue form, or in any case to the use of the second person, throughout the whole course of this type of prayer.

In meditation of this kind, the slow and concentrated rereading of what we have written has, certainly, no less importance than the writing, whether this means going over the text at the end of the period of meditation during which it has been composed, or returning to it a little later. Without doubt, it is here most of all that we need to avoid the danger of turning into a mere literary exercise what should remain a spiritual one. But also, it is here that what we ourselves have thought out and expressed can set up in us all its possible reverberations. . . .

The Rosary

Since it shares in the nature of the meditation that is carried out at a determined time during the Christian day and also in that of the effort to prolong throughout the day the impulse of prayer which nourishes prayerfulness, the Rosary merits special consideration. It is probably the most generally fruitful development achieved by the inventive genius of medieval piety in the West, lending itself equally well to satisfying the elementary piety of unlettered people incapable of joining in the Divine Office (it was for this purpose that it was first conceived), and to bringing the most meditative souls to the summits of the life of prayer.

Three elements need to be distinguished in it, the bringing together and happy combination of which assure this prayer a richness, a balanced fullness certainly known to no other practice of private devotion. The first of these elements consists in the three prayer formulae on which the Rosary is constructed, in which it might be said that all the aspects of Christian prayer are given their most concentrated and sober expression. The second consists in the psychological process set in motion by the continued recitation of these formulae, in particular the central Hail Mary. The third, finally, is the very simple but very effective form of meditation to which the Rosary lends itself and which, more directly it would seem than any other form of systematic meditation, is oriented toward contemplation. Let us take up these three factors one by one.

Everyone knows that the three repeated prayers making up the recitation of the Rosary are the Our Father, the Hail Mary and the Glory be to the Father. This gives occasion for us to analyze briefly each of these formulae, of incomparable importance for anyone desiring to penetrate the meaning of Christian prayer.

It goes without saying that the importance of the Our Father is completely transcendent since it is the prayer taught us by Christ himself. Understandably, every treatise on Christian prayer left to us by antiquity includes, as the heart of its exposition, a commentary on this prayer. All the objects of Christian prayer are to be found here and, what is no less important, they are found in the mutual relationship in which they should always remain.

Everything is dominated by belief in the divine Fatherhood and in the fact that this Fatherhood wills to extend itself to us, the fact which is basic to the whole message of the Gospel.

The three first requests are but one, for the central petition here in a certain way includes both the others. The coming of the divine kingdom in this world is actually the primary object of prayer, this coming forming but one reality with the effective extension to us of the divine Fatherhood, despite all the opposing forces: sin, the power of Satan, death, etc. . . . .

Yet from the time of the Old Testament, as we have said already, the coming of the kingdom of God, the realization of the divine design in us and in the world, presents a twofold aspect corresponding to the revelation of the divine Name and the revelation of the divine Law. This is why the coming of the kingdom has for its principle the sanctification of the divine Name and for its result the perfect accomplishment in us of the divine will.

We sanctify the divine Name, moreover, to the extent to which we realize a life of sonship, a life which witnesses to our belief in the divine Fatherhood in which God is revealed to us and from which we are drawing all the consequences.

It is after this first triptych of petitions, essentially concentrated on God, that we can go on to the second, centered on ourselves, but on our new nature as children of God. Whatever the difficulties raised by the word *epiousion*, sometimes translated by *quotidianum* and sometimes by *supersubstantialem*, there is no doubt that the first petition of this second series expresses the attitude of constant and total dependence on God, the attitude in which our faith should put us. This dependence includes the whole of our life, and in such a way that whether the "bread" which nourishes it be described or not, we can be quite certain that, in the thought of Christ, the "life" which is to seek its food from God is the whole and unified life of that new person who is the child of God. The life of the body, that is, is certainly included here, but this is to be seen in the perspective of that supernatural renewal of our integral humanity which is the meaning of the resurrection.

This nourishment of the new man in us, who is the perfect man according to God, has as its necessary counterpart victory over the forces of death. The weight of past sins first needs to be destroyed. This can only come about as the divine *agape* and its infinite generosity, as it was manifested on the cross, take possession of our whole being. There can therefore be no question of our sins being forgiven, as we beg, without our forgiving *ipso facto* the debts other people have contracted toward us. Only love saves us from evil, but the love of God cannot save us from evil except by enabling us to love as God loves.

After this, but always along the same lines, victory will be possible over the temptation to which the "old" man yielded and which the new man cannot avoid encountering in his turn. Certainly, "He who is in us," as St. John says, has proved on the cross that He is "stronger than he who is in the world"—and who does not cease to tempt us in the world. Hence the final prayer to be delivered not only from evil, in the abstract and in general, but very precisely from the Enemy of God and our Enemy, the Evil One, in opposition to whom the kingdom of God must be inaugurated in our own salvation.

After this prayer—which can be called perfect, since it includes everything the Christian should ask for, in the unity of the perspective of the divine design in which his faith should place him—the Hail Mary causes us to enter into this mystery of the divine paternity and of our adoption in Christ which dominates the "Our Father." It opens out to us, in fact, the interiorization of the kingdom in her whom we might call the perfect pray-er: she whose faith could make the "Our Father" her own as could the faith of no other creature, the Virgin Mary.

Indeed, it is, under such a simple form, the whole mystery of our divine adoption through our association with the life of the Trinity that the Hail Mary salutes in the Virgin.

We hail her, first, as "full of grace," or again as she to whom, above all, grace has been given. That is to say, it is she whom the Holy Spirit, the Spirit of the Father and the Son who is the Spirit of adoption, has "covered with his shadow" before all others and for the sake of all others. In this grace of graces, in this new communication of the Holy Spirit who produces in her Maternity the birth of a new humanity, are indeed rooted all the other graces that make us sons in "the Son," thus become her own Son as He is the Son of the Father.

Therefore, we then say to her: "The Lord is with you," because she is by this very fact the creature reconciled with the Father, not only free from everything that would separate her from him, but positively and really adopted by him, in that new covenant which is the eternal covenant.

But all this finds its substance only in the redemptive incarnation, since on Mary rests the blessing belonging to the pre-eminently Blessed One, He who is here made flesh of her own flesh—which is also ours: "You are blessed among women, and blessed is the fruit of your womb, Jesus."

The medieval invocation, "Holy Mary, Mother of God, pray for us (poor) sinners, now and at the hour of our death," completes in a very happy way this contemplation of the divine adoption in Mary by transferring it, so to speak, from her to ourselves. To use the terminology of Sulpician prayer, we go from "Jesus before our eyes" to "Jesus drawn into our hearts"; from "adoration" to "communion." Let us note that, in fact, the invocation of Mary is made to her as "Mother of God"; to her in whom was realized the incarnation that makes possible our adoption. What other object, then, could her intercession have than that what germinated in her should open out in us? And we implore her intercession, looking toward this realization, for "now" and for "the hour of our death": "now"—the instant in which is unceasingly required of us the decision to open ourselves out to the design of God; "the hour of our death"—the instant in which this design should, so far as each one of us is concerned, find its definitive accomplishment.

We formulate this prayer, like every prayer, as being "sinners," but obviously pardoned sinners and, in the French formula (which is very ancient) we also add the word "poor," which in biblical terminology signifies the attitude of faith wholly detached from self—the attitude demanded of us by grace, and particularly by that redemptive grace whose special characteristic it is to be directed to sinners.

If we consider the entirely natural fashion in which all this is fused together in the Hail Mary, we must acknowledge that its fullness is not unworthy of being associated as it actually is with the "Our Father" in Catholic prayer. The objective reality of the kingdom, which the Our Father causes us to contemplate and invoke in faith, the Hail Mary interiorizes: to meditation on the significance of the divine maternity, it joins meditation on the significance of our adoption in the Son by the grace of the Holy Spirit. The complex, so essentially one, of our relationships with the divine Persons is here illuminated in the contemplation of the human person who experienced them first of all, and for the sake of all.

Let us now go on to the effect produced in us by our repeating, slowly and fervently but without artificial tension, this last formula especially. It will be better to return after this to the Glory be to the Father which, in the recitation of the Rosary, concludes each decade of Hail Mary's inaugurated by the Our Father.

The procedure of repeating again and again a brief but condensed formula in praying has not always been clearly appreciated. Until quite recently, modern men, influenced by a Cartesian notion—exclusively rational, not to say rationalistic—of intelligence, tended to look upon this practice with suspicion. Among not a few Catholic theologians, unquestionably, the Protestant objection, that the Rosary is nothing but one of those "vain repetitions" which the Gospel mentions only to condemn, found some echo. It could only be justified by reducing it to no more than a prayer good for "simple people" (not to say, more bluntly, "imbeciles"), one, it was at least tacitly admitted, from which "grown-up" or "adult" Christians should by this very fact be relieved.

Recent psychological discoveries have shown how paltry and superficial is such disdain. Obviously, the recitation of the Rosary can fall, as can that of any prayer-formula, into "vain repetition" as soon as attention and living faith are not engaged. It might be added that exactly the same thing is true of the ex tempore prayers to which extreme Protestants are reduced: these also, like liturgical or other formulae, have an equal tendency to fall into verbalism, into a rehashing, over and over, of themes that are not only not fresh but not assimilated. But it is a complete mistake to think that the systematic repetition of a formula like the *Hail Mary* has any special tendency toward this result.

The exact opposite is true: such slow and regular repetition, provided that it is accompanied by attention—which it is also preferable not to strain unreasonably—of itself produces a tranquility not only psychological but also physiological, in which the concentration, the deepening of thought, takes place as if of its own accord. The verbal rhythm, in fact, along with the simplifying and unifying of thought, simultaneously begets a calming of the nerves and encourages a psychological tranquility which closely overlap each other. In these conditions, if the distractions which, especially for the nervous and sensitive person, so easily plague every effort at meditation do not disappear straightway, they will come to seem no more than marginal, and cease to be truly disturbing.

Everything is then ready for a central thought, very unified and very rich, to absorb the mind and thus to dispose it for the highest contemplation. This will come about the more easily since the rhythm of the recitation is organized naturally around certain accents. The repeated names of Mary and Jesus, finding as it were a discreet echo in the "us" of the prayer, attract these accents to themselves. After a first and as it were preliminary concentration on Mary, in whom, as we have said, the mystery of the Trinity finds its reflection in our humanity, the name of Jesus raises this mystery to its primordial realization, its archetype, as in its source. Then, in the second formula of the prayer, we come back by way of Mary, and this time to ourselves. Nothing could be more favorable to that transition we have mentioned from the mystery contemplated to the mystery participated in.

This process, however, does not open out its whole potential fruitfulness unless the names of Mary and Jesus are charged with all the resonances which they might have for our faith. This is precisely the effect of what is called the "meditation" of the Mysteries of the Rosary. Everyone knows what these "Mysteries" are: first, the series of the five "Joyful Mysteries": the Annunciation, the Visitation, the Nativity, the Presentation in the Temple, the Finding in the Temple. Then come the "Sorrowful Mysteries": the Agony, the Scourging, the Crowning with Thorns, the Carrying of the Cross, the Crucifixion. And finally, the "Glorious Mysteries": the Resurrection, the Ascension, Pentecost, the Assumption of the Virgin, her Crowning in heaven and all the glory of the saints. The simple recalling, even quite implicit, before each decade and throughout its recitation, of one or another of these "Mysteries" and of all, one after the other, continually charges and recharges the names of Mary and Jesus for us with all their meaning, with all their reality. Thus, finally, in the single name of Jesus, united by his Mother to our humanity, is concretized everything that makes him the unique but total object of our faith: the living Word of God who creates and recreates us in his image.

In certain countries, particularly in Germany, this "meditation" is aided by the addition, either to the name of Jesus or to that of Mary depending on the context, of a brief stereotyped formula expressing the reality of the "mystery" which we have in mind during each decade: for example, "Jesus *risen from the dead*," or "Mary *crowned in heaven.*" This practice can be useful particularly for those who are not yet fully familiar with the use of the meditated Rosary. But once such use has become familiar this practice might well tend to be dispensed with, the names of Jesus and Mary alone calling up very simply the whole content of the mystery present to the thought that rests in them. At the final stage, it would even seem as if these names, above all the first, should stand out from the phrase in which they are inserted to such a point that it could lose itself in them like a river in the sea. And, equally, the distinct meditation of the "Mysteries" should normally tend to lose itself in a vision, at once very simple and very unified, of the whole of *the* mystery of Christ in us, in all its fullness. When this stage has been attained, contemplation might be said to emerge as the fruit of a meditation which contains it germinally.

Finally, by means of the Rosary or otherwise, every meditation reaching its normal goal should end in the vision, as interiorized as possible, of "God all in all," according to the expression of St. Paul. This is the meaning of the Glory be to the Father recited at the end of each decade of the Rosary, as at the end of each psalm in the Latin liturgy. According to the beautiful commentary of Cardinal Mercier, the *Gloria* makes us contemplate the glory of the divine Trinity and unites us with it—as it is in itself from all eternity: *in principio;* as it radiates from Christ in the Church: *et nunc et semper;* and as it will flow out to everything in us and in the world: *et in saecula saeculorum.* This is the anticipation "in Christ" of the eschatological times in which will he finally accomplished the perfect union of the creature with God, in the full realization of the eternal divine design.

Constant Prayer

The Rosary, the recitation of which can so easily be brought in amongst the many occupations of the day and even be carried out along with those which do not demand too close attention, constitutes a quite natural transition from meditating to praying at all times.

Meditation and, more generally, the kind of prayer carried out at a fixed time in which it is pursued at leisure, should in no way limit or as it were reduce the necessity of prayer to those times alone. On the contrary, all prayer practiced at a time especially consecrated to it and, above all, the prayer which is particularly nourishing and substantial (meditative or some other type), should be thought of as a reservoir and source from whence the whole of our days is to be watered. The point of the "spiritual bouquet," which modern authors agree in recommending at the conclusion of prayer, is precisely to gather up the best of it in a form which can most easily be kept at hand throughout the following hours.

In a more general way, the most ancient monastic authors advise the use, in the midst of varied kinds of occupations, of what are called "ejaculatory prayers." These are, as their name indicates, brief formulae of prayer which aid us to raise ourselves in one act to God. Many psalm verses, memorized, lend themselves to this practice, by which our whole life can come to be interwoven with such elevations toward God. In the periods between them, without even formulating a precise prayer, without even, perhaps, having the thought of God constantly explicit, we will remain oriented toward him in all our actions and occupations.

The choice of the formulae to be used for this purpose may either be varied indefinitely or else a single one which is found to be particularly charged with meaning may be returned to by preference. Thus the ancients had a special affection for the verse: "O God, come to my assistance; O Lord, make haste to help me," and Cassian dwelt at great length on all the meaning it would take on in a life of which it became the perpetual prayer, placing afresh, unwearyingly, as it does, every thought, every feeling, every action, in the divine hands.

In this connection, it is important to repeat what we said earlier in speaking of the Hours of the Office. Praying at all times should not mean praying in precisely the same way throughout the day. It should mean, here again, a prayer which is adapted to each particular period of time and which also consecrates the particular meaning of this period of our day by orienting all things toward the mystery of Christ.

From this point of view, it would be well if Christians were to return to a practice of the devout Jews at the time of the birth of Christianity. To go with each action of life during each day, they conceived brief prayer formulae called *berakoth:* that is, "blessings" or "thanksgivings," preserved in treatises with the same title contained in the *Mishnah* and the *Tosefta.* These formulae all begin with the exclamation: "Blessed be Thou, O Lord our God, King of the ages, Thou who hast. . . ." Then follows an appropriate citation of the divine Word, leading us to recognize the wholly loving creative initiative of God behind the precise action we are about to undertake and, by this very fact, to consecrate it to him. St. Paul is evidently thinking of this practice when he says in the First Epistle to Timothy: "Every creature of God is good and none is to be rejected which is received with thanksgiving for it is sanctified by the Word of God and prayer" (1 Tim 4:4).

The rabbis developed a whole and very profound theology of these *berakoth*, which might be considered as the basis of all Christian eucharistic theology. They emphasize that, in filling their life with such acts of "thanks," devout Jews renew the work of Adam in naming all things, recognizing, that is, the divine meaning of all things, the way in which they flow from the creative Word of God and are but expressions of it. By this word of "blessing" making the Word of creation his own, humanity gives it its final meaning: to glorify God all in all. It is thus that the human race reveals itself as priest of all creation and effectively consecrates it to God—not as if it did not already belong to him in the first place, but because the devout Jew, enlightened by the divine Word and giving it the response that it expects, is the only one who, ceasing to make the world an idol, restores it to its primary purpose as an instrument of praise. The rabbis came to say that those who pronounced the appropriate *berakah* on all things were thereby making them into so many dwellings for the *Shekinah*, the mysterious divine presence that dwelt in Israel, over the Propitiatory of the Ark, between the cherubim, in the luminous cloud.

There is all the more reason that this ideal of the universal consecration of the world should become our own, in Christ, the ideal which should animate the Christian's striving for constant prayer.

The Prayer of Jesus

Along the same line, we must finally devote a special study to a traditional practice of continual prayer, the influence of which has come to seem more and more important to historians of spirituality. This is what is called the "prayer of Jesus," developed particularly in the East, first on Sinai and then on Mount Athos, but not completely unknown in the West. We should rejoice in this universality, both because nothing could be more helpful in bringing together the Christian East and West, and because of the intrinsic value of this prayer and of the whole spiritual tradition with which it is connected.

This tradition is that of "hesychasm," a spiritual movement of the East having its roots in the tradition connected with Macarius the Egyptian and in that of Evagrius, but springing up in its most vigorous growth under the influence of the great Byzantine mystic, St. Symeon the New Theologian.

The basic idea is to "have Jesus enter into one's heart." The heart, here should be understood in its biblical fullness of meaning; that is, as the source of the whole personal life, in which thought, volition, feelings merge as one.

Very important here also is the biblical idea of the Name as the expression and donation of the personality—in particular this Name of Jesus in which it is God, in his incarnation, who communicates himself to us.

Thus the slow, perpetually repeated invocation of the evangelical formula, "Lord Jesus, Son of God, have mercy on me, a sinner," or of the kindred formula: "Lord Jesus, Son of God, be kind to me, a sinner"—is considered as "drawing Jesus into one's heart." This means that its invocation is literally to become our very breathing—breathing to be understood, according to an idea also wholly biblical, as being the very breath of our life, at once of the soul and of the body. One tends in fact, to make the rhythm of breathing accord with the repetition of the formula, in such a way that this recitation becomes one with the fundamental action of our life. Each time that we breathe in new air, the heart's attention is taken up with Jesus, his Sovereignty, his divine Sonship, and our breathing out of used air coincides with prostrating our sinful selves at the feet of the Savior, in the humility, the total self-abandonment of faith.

This practice, like that of the Rosary, though perhaps still more effectively, by the simple play of elementary physiological mechanisms helps to produce a tranquility, a physical quietude, forming, as it were, the clothing and the support of a soul made peaceful in Christ. Whence the name of "hesychasts" given to those who make this practice their own (*hesychia*—quietness).

Yet this practice gains its complete meaning only at the center or, better, at the heart, of a life made peaceful by asceticism, and already wholly oriented, by liturgical experience and the meditated reading of the divine Word, toward "Christ in us, the hope of glory," according to the definition of the mystery given by St. Paul. Then the "prayer of Jesus" will condense, as it were, into the quintessence of all this, and thus Christ will become little by little the whole of our thought, of our life. To the one who has truly made it his or her own to such a degree, not only does a permanent state of prayer become possible, but also, as the hesychast tradition affirms, a life pursued in the light of Tabor: that fight of the Transfiguration in which God appeared to us in the human face of Christ. Let us note that, at these heights, the "prayer of Jesus" is ordinarily simplified into the repetition of his Name alone; then, finally, for the Name repeated by the lips is substituted the unique and silent Presence in the heart.

Praise and Petition

All the preceding considerations lead us to one last problem posed by Christian prayer: that of its content, and, more particularly, of the relationship that should exist between these two elements at first sight opposed to one another: praise, the disinterested glorification of God, and petition, the drawing of his favors down upon ourselves.

If we grant what we have concluded up to this point, in accord with the whole of Christian tradition, that prayer should tend to contemplation as to its superior and final form, it might seem as if praise should tend to exclude petition.

Certain modern authors, in fact, Protestant or those influenced by Protestantism, wishing to rehabilitate in some way the prayer of petition, have tried to oppose it to contemplative prayer, and to oppose in the same way the "active charity" of St. Paul to the mystics' flight to God. In so doing, they are only reversing an opposition found in the philosophers of the eighteenth century and Kant in particular, already sketched out by the Greek philosophers: to the effect that the only prayer which truly honors God must, on the contrary, be "pure" praise and exclude any kind of petition.

The truth is that all oppositions of this kind hold good only in the abstract. All we need do is to look at things in the concrete for such notions to fade like chimeras.

Once more, it is a return to the object of faith that clears our vision and dispels these false problems. If there incontestably exists, as both Catholic tradition and holy scripture attest, a contemplative prayer which is typically biblical and Christian, and if this contemplation constitutes not only a superior form of prayer but the leaven of all prayer, it is quite certain that this is not just any kind of contemplation, nor, further still, is it the contemplation of just anything, no matter what. It is the contemplation of that great mystery of God that St. Paul describes as "Christ in us, the hope of glory." In this contemplation, what predominates is unquestionably what St. Paul again calls "the glory of the mystery" (Col 1:27). However, the prayer of exulting praise which this glory awakens in our hearts is inseparable, on the one hand, from our grateful acceptance of this mystery inasmuch as it involves us in its accomplishment, and, on the other hand, from an ardent desire that this accomplishment be total, around us and in us. Whence arises a particularly urgent prayer of petition which, far from being in any way opposed to praise (with which, finally, it merges as of its own accord), cannot help springing from it, so long as the mystery is not yet fully accomplished.

To be still more precise even at the risk of repetition, this mystery is the Fatherhood of God opening itself out to us in Christ. It is Christ, by his death and his resurrection recapitulating us all in himself, reconciling us all, in the body of his flesh, with one another and with the Father. How, then, can we praise, can we glorify this mystery without, at the same instant, expressing the desire that it assume, in us and in all things, its full effect, its whole reality? . . . We cannot praise the revelation of the divine design without praying that it be accomplished.

This is indicated very clearly in the quite natural development found in the *berakah*, the "eucharistic" prayer of Judaism, a development which could only be continued in the Christian thanksgiving, the Eucharist. We have mentioned these brief formulae of "blessing" which in the Judaism of later eras applied to all the actions of the devout Israelite. The first orientation of these *berakoth* is the divine praise, in what St. Paul calls "the knowledge of the mystery" (Col 2:2), inasmuch as the mystery is the will of God in all things (cf. Eph 1:9). But inseparably, these blessings consecrate what we do to God, inasmuch as obedient faith thereby gives itself up to the will of God here recognized. This is what the rabbis wish to say in declaring that by the *berakah* we prepare a dwelling for the Shekinah in all things.

In the most fully-developed formulae, consequently, like the great *berakah* for the reading of the Shema: "The Lord thy God is the only Lord and you shall adore him alone . . ." or like that for the blessing of the cup at the end of a community meal, petition is formally introduced within the "thanksgiving" itself. This petition takes into account all the needs of the people of God in general, and, in particular, those of the persons praying, exactly as the Our Father includes with the petition for the coming of the kingdom the plea for our daily bread. From the moment in which we know that the will of God, the will in which is revealed the very depth of his heart, is for our good, then our praising him for his self-revelation to us includes asking him, with a childlike confidence, for those good things He himself wishes to give us. It might be said that He wills to have us ask him for them, because He wishes us to believe without hesitation in his willingness to give them to us.

To be sure, when, in eternity, we possess all this and when all men possess it together with us, then petition, with no need left to be satisfied, will be lost in praise, as the stars vanish in the brightness of full midday. But the fact remains that praise itself, in eternity as well as here on earth, cannot be radically disinterested. Unquestionably, in the recognition that God is our good is included the recognition that He is *the* good which is primary. But it would be completely unbiblical and unchristian to emphasize this so much as to obscure or relegate to a second place the fact that He is *our* good. The God whom we are to know and adore is the God of love; he is, without question, the God who *is* love, in himself, who would be love even if we did not exist. But He is also the God who loves us, and who has manifested to us, in that love by which He created and redeemed us, the love, the *same love*, that He is in himself. To refuse to make this consideration a part, and an integrant part, of our praise in both time and eternity would be to misunderstand that very divine love which calls us to praise it by responding to it. For you do not love the person who loves you in this way if you do not include in your love for him, and as its basic motive, the love he shows to you. And this is true even if this basic motive must expand into the vision of love in its infinite fullness—overflowing us, no doubt, but always containing us.

This is why praise that is properly Christian remains "thanksgiving." Certainly, this must not be understood in the narrow sense of the mere "thank you" that easily becomes niggardly, nor even of mere gratitude for benefits received. But neither should we desire to broaden the "eucharist"—Jewish or Christian—into an over-simplified confession of the *mirabilia Dei*, into a "pure" praise so disinterested that what concerns us has no longer any part in it or only a minimum part. All the *mirabilia Dei*, in fact, concern us. The love of God has wished precisely *not* to manifest itself to us as "pure" love in itself but rather as love for us. The purity of the glorification we wish to give him by abstracting from this fact would be not only an artificial but an equivocal kind of purity. Its "disinterestedness" would be no more than the drying up of our "heart" into an impersonal kind of intelligence—and this is the exact contrary of what grace wishes to create in us.

On condition that it remain always included in the perspectives of the "eucharist," of "thanksgiving" for the divine design in its totality, the prayer of petition can (and even should) be developed freely, therefore, in Christian prayer life, without any damage to the attitude of adoring praise which normally ought more and more to predominate in it. Far from the one excluding the other, it draws it along with it.

But it is certain that the form which petition should take by preference, to remain in this way within the framework of the "Eucharist," is that of intercession: the prayer in which we pray for ourselves only within a boundless supplication which makes our own all the needs of redeemed humankind, in the perspective of the divine kingdom.

It is remarkable that the oriental liturgy, although so contemplative in inspiration, so absorbed in the divine glorification, and wholly monastic as it is in its inspiration, nonetheless gives such a large and continuous part to this intercession by means of those *ectenies* of the deacon answered by the continual *Kyrie eleison* of the people. In this connection, it is undeniable that the Latin liturgy, in the form in which we know it and celebrate it today, no longer knows this happy equilibrium. It was otherwise in former times. In the Mass, at the time of the Offertory, the *orationes fidelium* (no longer said except on Good Friday) had us make our own all the needs of humankind—humankind called to be formed into the mystical Body of Christ on the Cross. And regularly in the Divine Office, the great Litany (which we now call the Litany of the Saints), after having us contemplate all the divine mysteries, had us implore deliverance from all evils and the realization of the legitimate aspirations which God himself encourages in the heart of man. But this litany is now said only on rare occasions during the year. In fact, there no longer remain any habitual prayers of intercession in the Latin liturgy except the *Mementos* in the Eucharistic Canon. And there are even some purists who complain that these *Mementos* are opposed to the primitive sweep of the eucharistic prayer, misunderstanding the fact that even the Jewish "eucharist," far from turning away from intercession or setting it aside, not only includes it but develops into it.

Whence this regression? Doubtless (for the Great Litany in any case), through a phenomenon of decadence operating according to a paradoxical process to be observed also in many other fields of liturgical evolution. The Litany began by being overweighted with a multiplicity of invocations to the saints, then with additional psalms, with responsorial prayers which only poorly duplicated the ancient intercessions, and, finally, with an endless procession of prayers that tripled it. Thus it collapsed of its own weight, and an essential part of the liturgy, in a reaction against overloading, has disappeared almost completely.

Add to this the wearisome development, of which we shall speak again, of abstract tendencies in the modern school of mysticism, and the often too limited part that intercession has reluctantly come to play in the spirituality of many modern Catholics is explained. It has not disappeared from piety, but it frequently occupies no more than a marginal place in it. The rather bizarre, and entirely recent, practice of saying any prayer "for the intention" of a theme of intercession ignored in the prayer-formula itself is very typical. When we want to pray for the conversion of a sinner or the healing of a sick person, would it not be far more natural to ask God quite simply for one or the other, rather than to say a "Hail Mary" or any other prayer "for their intention?"

Let us note that such a practice runs the risk of degrading our most traditional prayer formulae into something like magic formularies, from which an effect is expected having no connection with the meaning. The only fully effective reaction against this insidious danger is frankly to recognize and to restore express intercession to its place in our prayer.

Undoubtedly, prayer should not be broken up into an indefinite multiplicity of human ends which would absorb us in their detail and distract us from the unity of the mystery which should finally englobe everything. But the simplification of intercession should go along with that of contemplative meditation. That is to say, it should not take the form of a simple impoverishment, entirely negative, still less of a radical sterility. It should ascend little by little into the unity of a vision of the total Christ, of God all in all, the realism of a charity which knows that God must be concerned with everyone and everything that is his work because we ourselves have come to interest ourselves in them as He himself is interested. It is here that the word of St. John: "He who does not love his brother whom he can see, cannot love God whom he does not see" (1 Jn 4:30), becomes the test of Christian prayer and of its seriousness.

Guided by liturgical prayer, intercession should normally develop out of the divine praise, the glorification of the mystery. We might say that it is the form that ought to be taken by our inevitably making contact again with the world after all our ardent turning toward God. Special themes of intercession assigned to each day, on which the mind can dwell at the end of its prayer, will often be an effective aid in the effort to make prayer realistic, as well as the familiar repetition of the great liturgical prayers of Eastern and Western tradition, particularly the original core of the Great Litany.

But what is most important is that, in our striving for continuous prayer, all our personal meetings with God throughout the day should have the character at once of thanksgiving and of intercession. A contemporary commentator on the *hesychast* tradition, on the "prayer of Jesus," has formulated this necessity very clearly by saying that we should come to place the name of

Jesus on every thing and every being on which our thought rests. Is it not in this way that even the objects of the distractions to which we are exposed in prayer will be the better reabsorbed in it and come to nourish it rather than dissipating it?

In general, to make all our cares and preoccupations not only an "intention" but an actual object of our prayer is the surest way to give everything in our life over to divine grace. Thus everything will concur toward the realization of the divine design that we must contemplate unceasingly, and by this contemplation the divine countenance will in turn be disclosed little by little to our eyes, imprinting its reflection on our own.

Chapter 4

THE SACRAMENTAL LIFE

What is, as it were, the movement of Christian prayer is the transition described in the Sulpician formula, from "Jesus before our eyes" to "Jesus in the heart." According to the startlingly similar formula of the *hesychast* tradition, we are "to draw Jesus into our hearts." Christian contemplation, in other words, inasmuch as it is contemplation of the mystery, tends to the realizing, in the strongest sense of the word, of that which the mystery is according to the phrase of St. Paul: "Christ in us, hope of glory" (Col 1:27).

Word and Sacrament

But this is possible only on the basis of the sacramental life. The divine Word presents the mystery to us as the substance of our faith. But it is in the sacraments that it causes us effectively to participate in it, and that faith can make our own the mystery here proclaimed.

Faith, indeed, is only the opening of the soul, to be achieved in prayer, to the Word of God coming to us in and by the

Church. The Word of God illuminated by the tradition of the Church is concentrated in the mystery: Christ and his Cross. But, in the Church, the mystery is not merely proclaimed. Rather, with the very authority of God, it is proclaimed as present. It is then represented, rendered present for us, in us. It is for the sacraments to apply to us this permanent presence and actuality of the mystery.

This indicates what a close bond exists between the divine Word proclaimed in the Church and the sacraments which the Church celebrates and administers to us. Yet this bond must not be understood, as the Protestants have come to do, in a way that reduces the sacrament to nothing but a visible word (*visibile verbum*). Not that this expression, which goes back to St. Augustine, is not in itself full of meaning. But it loses this meaning when, as the moderns always tend to do, *verbum* is reduced to mere phrasing and the "visible word," therefore, to mere images.

This explains to us how it was that the Protestant Reformation, in reducing the sacrament to the word, at the same time deprived the Word of its content. The entirely intellectualist character of Protestant worship, in which the church is nothing more than a classroom, increasingly gives evidence of this degradation of the Word itself which goes along, in modern times, with the absorption of the sacrament in the word. Quite the contrary, we might say, the biblical Word in its primary authenticity tends, as of its own accord, toward the sacramental reality. If God speaks, indeed, it is only to act, just as his act has a meaning, is alone capable, finally, of making us know him as he wishes to be known by us.

The Word of God is not, therefore, simply verbal expressions nor even ideas: it is always an act in which Someone reveals himself in giving himself. Finally, it is this Someone himself. This Someone, Christ, the living Word of the Father, remains present in the Church to continue to speak to us here. He is present, in fact, and he speaks to us now by the ministry of the hierarchical apostolate which he instituted, the hierarchy, that is, of which the principle is given us in the words of the Gospel: "As the Father has sent me, I also send you. . . . He who hears you, hears me, and he who hears me, hears him who sent me" (Jn 20:20; Lk 10:16).

Thus in the Church established on the foundation of the apostolate understood in this way, Christ continues to speak, and his Word, which remains his own in the very act of its being spoken, retains on the lips of his ministers the creative power proper to the divine Word. This is what happens in the sacraments.

It is in them, again, that the mystery, the object of the Word, is carried out in the Church as "Christ in us, the hope of glory." Christ, who died *for us* once for all and thereafter rose, here continues to die and to rise again *in us* so that we may rise with him forever at the end of time.

To understand in this perspective the significance and the reality of the sacraments at the heart of our Christian life, we must not think of them as merely seven parallel channels of grace. We must go back to the most traditional idea according to which they all form one single organism of the life of the Spirit in the Church. St. Thomas Aquinas gives, as it were, the vital core of this conception when he explains that the Mass is the source of the whole sacramental order because it contains the Passion of the Savior.

The Mass, Focus of the Sacramental Life

In the Mass, we go quite naturally from the mystery *proclaimed* by the word of the Gospel to the mystery *made present* by the words of consecration. These two "words" are, indeed, closely related; as we have already said, the first tends to the second. The word of consecration is but the Gospel word in the fullness of its meaning and actuality: giving us, *hic et nunc,* according to its own design, what it has begun by revealing to us and revealing to us that which is to become our own.

This is also why, conversely, we perceive the whole meaning of the proclaimed Word only in the sacramental celebration. As St. Paul says, "Whenever you eat this bread and drink this cup you *proclaim* the death of the Lord, until he comes" (1 Cor 11:26).

The Word that proclaims the love of the Father became act in the death of Christ. And the Word that proclaims the death of Christ in turn becomes act in the Eucharistic consecration. This, in return, is "the proclamation" of that death, in the fullness of its meaning and its actuality, not only by us but in us.

To understand this truth, we need to go more deeply into the sense in which Christ is present at Mass. We might say that he is here present in three complementary ways which beget one another.

In the first place, there is the presence of Christ as Head of the Church throughout all ages, the presence which manifests itself in and through the ministerial hierarchy in such a way that, according to his express will, it is he who speaks and acts as Head in and through his messengers. It is in this sense that St. Augustine can say, "Whether it is Peter, Paul, or Judas who baptizes, it is always Christ who baptizes."

In the Eucharist principally, this ministerial presence tends toward the properly sacramental presence. Under its static aspect, this is the presence of Christ himself as Glorious Victim, immolated on the Cross and triumphant in heaven. Under its dynamic aspect, it is the representation of the mystery: the Cross itself made present as our Pasch, the "passage" of God amongst us which carries us with it and leads us to him by the ways which he opened out to us "so that we may walk in his footsteps," as the First Epistle of St. Peter says (2:21).

But, as appears in the Communion of the Mass, this sacramental presence in turn does not have its end in itself: it tends wholly toward the presence of Christ and his mystery *in us*, toward the realization in us all of the mystery as "Christ in us, the hope of glory." This final unity of Christ and ourselves in the Church, becoming his Mystical Body, is, according to St. Thomas, the final reality to which the Eucharist tends and which itself has nothing beyond it: its *res tantum*.

The presence which we might say that God has in view throughout the sacramental action is, then, the presence of God himself "all in all" through his Christ. It is Christ the Head living in his members, and these in turn "carrying out in their own flesh what remains to be suffered of the sufferings of Christ for his body, the Church" (Col 1:24).

In this light, we see how the Body of Christ present in the Blessed Sacrament and the Body of Christ which is the Church are not merely two different bodies. The Body of Christ which is the Church is called so because in it we are all united in one single body by the fact of being all nourished by the Body of Christ which once died on the Cross and today nourishes the life of the mystery in us.

We see at the same time what is the nature of the reality proper to the sacramental order, the reality which faith immediately has in view. The reality of the sacraments is not a reality which somehow can subsist by itself. It is the reality of signs but of signs which communicate, in the strongest sense of the word, that which they signify. They are, as it were, the meeting place of the encounter between the reality of Christ, of his saving work, and the reality of ourselves, of our individual lives, which are to be, as it were, plunged into his death and into his new life in order to be brought to the fullness of his Resurrection. By the sacramental mystery, the sacrifice of Christ is to penetrate our entire life in such a way as to make of it, according to the formula of St. Paul, "a holy and living sacrifice, acceptable to God: the offering of our own bodies, which is our reasonable worship" (Rom 12:1). In this light, our sacrifices are not to be added to the Cross of Christ as if from without, which would be nonsense: they can take their reality only from his. It is we who are to be, not added to but incorporated in Christ, in such a way that it can be said, "It is no longer we who live, but Christ who lives in us" (cf. Gal 2:20).

This will be further explained when we examine in more detail how, according to Catholic tradition, all Christians actually take part in the sacrifice of the Mass. Here the relationship between the ministerial priesthood of the hierarchy and the royal priesthood of the whole Body of Christ is clarified in the economy of the participation of all in the unique sacrifice of the Savior.

In the document in which we see the word "liturgy" (the original meaning of which is "a public service rendered by an individual to the community") first applied to Christian worship, St. Clement of Rome tells us that the celebration of the Eucharist is carried out by the cooperation of the "liturgies" proper to the different members of the Church.

The "liturgy" of "the high priest," as he says—that is, of the bishop or the priest of the second rank who takes his place—is to proclaim the divine Word with apostolic authority and then to "make the Eucharist" by pronouncing over the bread and cup the great prayer of consecration. These two functions, as we see them in Christ himself whom the "high priest" represents in the assembly of his own, are closely connected. The one calls to the other, and, we might even say, gives rise to it.

For is Christ not the Word of God made man? In other words, the divine Word addressed in all its fullness to humanity here evokes the perfect response in his own person.

In the proclamation of the Gospel which is one with his self-manifestation to men, Christ reveals to us the fatherly love of God who calls us to become his children. And, in the Eucharistic celebration of Holy Thursday, Christ himself responded to this Word with which he is one by giving himself wholly up to it, by consecrating himself to the fulfillment of the divine design in obedience even to death, and the death of the Cross. Thus he became the Head of that new humanity which, having gratefully acknowledged the design of God and confessed his name, abandoned itself to the gift of his love and died to the life of the "old self," marked by sin, to live again to the life of the new man or woman, who is not only "called" a child of God but actually is so, in the fullest, most profound reality of his or her being.

In the same way today, the "high priest," in the assembly of the faithful, having proclaimed the evangelical Word by the very power of Christ who speaks by his mouth, at his command and by his power renews the Eucharist of Christ: he gives thanks to the Father for everything that he has given us in Christ, and, by this very fact, he carries us along in that true abandonment to the Father's will of love which was the Cross of his only Son. Thus the only Son becomes "the firstborn among many brethren," and we can all dare to present ourselves with him in his Father's presence and call him *Our* Father. . . . And throughout, the same all-powerful Word, which proclaimed to us God's design for us by opening us to the knowledge of his name, welcomed by faith in our hearts, realizes this design in us by marking us with the divine name. Christ who was "sanctified" for us (cf. Jn 17:19) "sanctifies" us in turn "in the truth" of his unique sacrifice.

Participation of the Faithful
in the Eucharist

Such is the liturgy of the "high priest." It is inseparable from the liturgy unanimously carried out by that new "chosen race," that "holy nation," that "kingdom of priests" constituted by the assembly of the faithful. If the "high priest" proclaims the Word to them all and then consecrates the Eucharist which is to be the Eucharist of all, it is in order that all may be able to pray with a prayer which will be the response expected by the Word, that all may be able to offer the matter of the Eucharistic sacrifice, and that all, finally, by communion, may be consummated in the unity of "Christ in us, hope of glory."

Let us, then, take up, one by one, these three closely related elements of the priesthood of the faithful: prayer, offering, communion.

The prayer called for here, as we have already explained at length, is that prayer which, in the dialogue between God and ourselves, is the response to his Word, the believing and obedient adherence to his design, the acknowledgment of his name invoked upon us: our abandon to the love that gives us everything.

Prayer, thus understood, issues quite naturally in offering, that is to say, our self-giving in the obedience of faith to the will of God for us as revealed in the Word, the will which we have accepted in prayer. The offering of the bread and wine of the Eucharist concretizes this giving of our whole life taken at its source, in which we acknowledge that this life proceeds wholly from God and that it should wholly belong to him.

Yet this offering is real only in the Eucharist of Christ in which he includes us with himself. Without his sanctifying himself for us, we could not be sanctified, truly consecrated to God. In the Eucharist of Christ taking possession of the material of our offering—which we cannot but present to him in a pure act of faith—we recognize, then, the supreme gift of God: that effective consecration of humanity to the heavenly Father which only the Word made flesh, the Son made man, could accomplish.

Now the bread, the wine which are given back to us are no longer simply the nourishment of our natural life. To the faith which welcomes them in communion, the bread and wine thus "sanctified" in the Eucharist are the nourishment of eternal life: the Body of Christ himself who consummated his offering on the Cross and who, now, by the power of his Cross, reconciles us all in the Body of his flesh. The divine Word which is at the heart of the Eucharist of the "new self" assures us of this fact: "This is my Body . . . this is my Blood," "he who eats my flesh and drinks my blood has everlasting life and I will raise him up on the last day. . . ."

Thus communion consummates us, not only in Christ's offering to the Father, but in the very reality of his being of Son, which is nothing but filial relationship to the Father and so eternal life in the Spirit: the Spirit of the Father and the Son, the Spirit of life, the Spirit of love.

Thus it might be said that the consecrating word, which is, as it were, the soul of the Eucharistic Prayer of the Word made flesh, re-creates us in the new self, just as the original word of creation drew us out of nothingness.

The result is that we are made all together one single Body of which Christ is the Head. As the First Epistle to the Corinthians says, "The cup of blessing that we bless, is it not communion in the blood of Christ? The bread that we break, is it not communion in the body of Christ? Since there is but one bread, we all are only one body, since we all partake of the one bread" (10:16–17).

As we have already emphasized, in this text in particular it is impossible to take the "Body" of Christ in two senses rigorously distinct from one line to the other: this "Body" of Christ which is the Church and which we all form together exists only in and by the effective participation of all in the one "Body" of Christ dead on the Cross and risen to divine life.

Thus it is also, to use the image of St. John, that Christ is revealed as the vine of which we are the branches. Thereby we become, as St. John also says, the "children" of God in his "only Son"; or, according to the different expression of St. Paul, he becomes the firstborn whose many brothers and sisters we are. But, as St. Paul himself never ceases to repeat, we are only "sons" and "daughters" by living "in the Son," "in Christ Jesus," "in Christ."

This union, however close, however intimate it may be, is nevertheless not a fusion. To the image of the Body of Christ made up of us all, St. Paul adds that of the Bride of Christ. Certainly Bridegroom and Bride are no longer more than one flesh. Yet the Bride, far from being annihilated in the Bridegroom, can find, can realize her full personality as Bride only in her union with the Bridegroom (cf. Eph 5:22–23 and 2 Cor 11:2). In other words, we become fully ourselves only in "knowing" Christ, with all that this term, as used by the prophets, connotes, not only as to intimacy, but as to conformation of one to the other and, finally, union.

It is in these perspectives that we are, in the Church, the "fullness" of Christ; that is, he completes himself in us. As the Epistle to the Ephesians, once more, says, the Church is "the fullness of him who wholly completes himself in all" (1:23). Conversely, it is only in him that we achieve ourselves: he himself is our fullness (cf. Col 1:19). And hereby, in the "fullness of times" (Gal 4:4), "the fullness of God coming to dwell corporally in Christ" (Col 2:9), God will become "all in all" (1 Cor 15:28).

The mystery of this union with Christ, and in Christ with God, is the great mystery of Christianity. As the encyclical *Mystici Corporis* has emphasized, this is a truth absolutely *sui generis*, which we must not try to fit into ready-made categories. It is something quite other than a mere moral union, consisting in the union of wills. Still less is it a physical union in the current sense of the term, supposing either the absorption pure and simple; the disappearance of one being in another; or the fusion of the two in a third, which is no longer either the one or the other. This is the mystery that Jesus expressed at the Last Supper when he said to the Father: "That they may be one, as Thou and I are one. I in them and Thou in me, that they may be consummated in unity" (Jn 17:22–23).

To this mystery, which is properly that of the Eucharist, the other sacraments introduce us and adapt us, or else they extend it to our whole existence.

Baptism

Baptism, together with Confirmation, which is, as it were, its completion or seal, conforms us to Christ dead and risen again. And so it introduces us into that "chosen race," that "holy nation," that "royal priesthood" which constitutes the People of God. Thus Baptism allows us to take part in the Eucharistic celebration by prayer, offering, and communion as has just been explained.

In other words, initiation into Christianity is one and the same reality as our engrafting into Christ himself, while our entering into the Church becomes concrete in our introduction into the eucharistic assembly. This is why, normally, Baptism is

integrated with the celebration of the Paschal Mass. During the
night of the Resurrection, in which we celebrate that mystery
of Easter which is the Christian mystery itself in its heart and
unity, the great vigil in which is summed up all the preparatory
teaching of the Old Covenant leads to the baptismal initiation.
Those who receive this initiation are thus at once ready to hear
the Gospel proclamation of the Resurrection and to take part in
the celebration of the paschal sacrifice, as the sacrifice of Christ
who died and rose again to bring us to the Father.

The essence of Baptism, as St. Paul explains it in the sixth
chapter of the Epistle to the Romans, consists in the immersion
which buries us with Christ in such a way that we die to the life
of the "old self" pledged to death by sin, to emerge from the
baptismal water risen to the life of the "new self" who is also
the heavenly person. The baptismal water is thus a symbol of
death and resurrection. It first calls up the theme of the Flood,
in which the primitive waters of chaos reappear to destroy creation radically corrupted by the Fall. But then comes the theme
of the springs of living water: the maternal water over which the
Holy Spirit spread his shadow so that new life would be born
(cf. Gn 1, 2, and 20).

Baptism, then, is a new birth, which St. John describes also
as being birth from on high: birth from water and the Spirit
(Jn 3:3–5). We might say that it is the birth of Christ in us,
or rather our rebirth in Christ. It is in this sense that St. Paul
applies to it the image of grafting (cf. Rom 2:17 ff.) and says
that we here become *symphytoi*, that is literally, "one single
plant with Christ" (Rom 6:5). Using another image, he also
says "You all who have been baptized in Christ, have put on
Christ" (Gal 3:27).

With this effect of Baptism, we should connect St. Paul's
use of Greek verbs with *syn* in order to describe everything we
now do in relation to Christ and his activity. "Conformed to

the image of the Son" (Rom 8:29), "conformed to his death" (Phil 3:10), we have been "convivified with him" (Col 2:13; Eph 2:5). "Co-risen with Christ" (Col 2:12, 3:1), we are "seated with him and in him in heaven" (Eph 2:6). In a word, in the measure to which "we suffer with him," we are also "glorified with him" (Rom 8:17), and we "reign with him" (cf. 1 Cor 4:8; 2 Tm 2:12).

More profoundly, according to one of the most typical formulae of the apostle, the whole life of the baptized person is henceforth life "in Christ Jesus." This illuminates the meaning of that other formula of St. Paul's describing Christ as the second Adam. More precisely, according to St. Paul, Christ is "the ultimate man"—not an Adam from which other men must be born by being separated from himself, but him in whom all are to find themselves again, to make henceforth only one with him and in him (cf. Rom 6; 1 Cor 15). This is what the Epistle to the Galatians expresses by saying, "All you who have been baptized in Christ, have put on Christ. There is, then, no longer either Greek or Jew, either slave or free, either man or woman, but you are all one [literally, one single person] in Christ Jesus" (3:27–28). The Epistle to the Ephesians, in turn, explains to us that the divine plan is to "recapitulate all things in Christ" (1:10), the one who is our peace, in whom we are all recreated by his death in such a way as to constitute "one single new man" (2:15), so that the building up of the Body of Christ which is the Church tends to form "one single perfect man: Christ come to the fullness of his adult age" (4:13).

Confirmation

All this is what the sacrament of the Chrism, which we in the West call Confirmation, comes to seal and complete. Indeed, to this new being, dead to the life of Adam and reborn to that of Christ, the anointing that makes him "Christ" belongs by right. By it the baptized become, in the full force of the term, "coheirs with Christ" (Rom 8:17); that is, everything that is his belongs to them but, above all, the Spirit, the very breath of the divine life. As the Epistle to the Romans says, "All those who are moved by the Spirit of God are the sons of God. For you have not received a spirit of slavery so as still to be in fear, but you have received the spirit of sonship, in which we cry: Abba! that is: Father! The Spirit himself witnesses to our spirit that we are children of God. And if we are children, we are heirs: heirs of God, coheirs with Christ, provided always that we suffer with him so as also to be glorified with him" (8:14–17).

The Epistle to the Galatians uses very similar terms, except that instead of showing how the gift of the Spirit effectively makes us sons and daughters in Christ, it explains how this adoption won for us by the Cross of Christ demands our participation in the Spirit: "Because you are sons, God has sent the Spirit of his Son into our hearts, crying: Abba! that is: Father! so that you are no longer a slave but a son, and, if a son, an heir also through God" (4:6–7).

This gift of the Spirit assures to us, in fact, the *parrhesia*, the freedom proper to children of the house, who feel themselves at home there (cf. Eph 3:12; 6:19). It teaches us from within to pray as we should (Rom 8:26), that is, as those who have entered into the ineffable mystery and can call upon God, in Christ, as their Father.

This gift of the Spirit, which is the final goal of Christian initiation, is thus finally seen to be the priestly anointing of the People of God. It is this gift that allows us, in the Son, with the Son, to be "recapitulated" in the Father himself, by the Eucharistic sacrifice become the principle of the offering of our whole life "in Christ Jesus." It is under this aspect that we understand most profoundly how the Spirit pours out the love, the *agape* of the Father himself in our own hearts (Rom 5:5).

Reconciliation

It is in relation to this sacramental whole which is Christian initiation that Reconciliation is to be understood. It is simply the sacrament which reestablishes us in the powers and privileges conferred by our baptismal and chrismal initiation when we have cut ourselves off from them by serious sin—that is, by sin which implies a practical renouncement of our baptismal faith. This is the significance of the ritual of public penance and of the reconciliation of penitents.

During Lent (while the catechumens were prepared to receive Baptism), the penitents, excluded from the Eucharistic assembly by their sin, were grounded anew, together with the catechumens, in the catechesis which they had, as it were, misprized. Then, on Holy Thursday, before celebrating the Mass in memory of the Last Supper, the banquet of reconciliation in the death of Christ, the bishop went to the porch of the Church to seek out the penitents and restore them to the assembly of worship so that they could again take part in the whole Eucharistic celebration.

Again, Reconciliation brings out the full meaning of the rites preparatory to Baptism itself: the exorcisms and the anointing with oil. These signify that belonging to Christ, entering into his mystery, is not simply a consecration but, inevitably, also a struggle, indeed a deadly struggle. In the present economy of sin repaired by the Cross, the Spirit of God takes possession of our spirit only through a victorious struggle with the spirit of evil. This struggle was first carried out *for us* on the Cross. By the exorcisms, the Church begins protecting us with the effect of the Cross. But the Cross does not enter into us, does not take possession of us through the Spirit, until Baptism. Then it is for us, now united with Christ and filled with his Spirit, to continue the struggle. This is the meaning of the anointing preparatory to Baptism with the oil called the oil of catechumens.

And this anointing is particularly associated with the confession of faith immediately preceding Baptism, in close connection with the renunciation of Satan and adherence to Christ.

All this amounts to saying that faith implies a choice and, more precisely, a breaking with a previous commitment, an evil one, as the inseparable counterpart of this adherence to Christ.

The meaning of these different rites will be explored when we come to speak of Christian asceticism, under its negative aspect of disengaging oneself from the world of sin and the Fall, so as to belong wholly to the new world of resurrection in Christ. The practice of asceticism, in other words, is above all the penitential life that must be led after Baptism by every Christian more or less, in one way or another, in order to free himself or herself ever anew and afresh from the forces of Satan. Their empire in the self, as to what St. Paul calls "the interior person," has, doubtless, been abolished. But, after Baptism, they do not cease to attack him again, by means of the world of which his own "flesh"—that is, his human nature inasmuch as it remains allied to that world—remains the accomplice. Whence the necessity for perpetual struggle and penance to mitigate the effects of the momentary defeats that still remain possible.

Holy Orders

Baptism and the anointing with chrism consecrate us for that "life in Christ" which is life in the Church, for effective participation in the Eucharistic assembly. Penance restores us to

it when we have excluded ourselves from it. The sacrament of
Holy Orders fits certain members of the Body for a ministerial
function in it, for the good of the whole.

The fullness of the sacrament of Holy Orders is realized
in the transmission of the apostolic *charisma*, by means of the
consecration of a bishop, along with the ordination of priests of
the second rank to be the bishop's coworkers. Here the imposition of hands (a gesture signifying both taking possession by
and transmitting a grace) is accompanied by words signifying
Christ's will to be represented as Head of his Body in the assembly of his own, in order to proclaim the Gospel of salvation and
dispense its sacramental mystery.

In this way are the successors of the apostles set up to feed
the flock of God. They do not take the place of the apostles in
the sense that they could build on any foundation other than
that laid down by the apostles or build something else. They
simply succeed the apostles to preserve the deposit of faith, not
as a dead letter but in the Spirit who unceasingly renews its
life. Their essential function is to preside over the Eucharistic
assembly, the gathering of the Church convoked to hear the
divine Word and to give itself to the Word in the Eucharist.
They are able to do this by virtue of the fact that the priestly
character—the character, that is, of ministers of that priestly
work of Christ which is inseparable from Christ's personal presence—enables them to speak in his name and sacramentally to
renew his holy acts. They proclaim no word other than his: it is
simply he who speaks it in them, always the same and likewise
always present and effective. They do nothing other than what
he did: it is he who makes present under their hands, by their
words thus become his own, his work accomplished once for
all so that we may be brought into it.

In the same way, like Christ himself and as continuing his
work, they engage all the People of God in prayer and offering

and gather them all in communion with one single Spirit in one single Body, that of Christ.

Ordered toward the work of this apostolic ministry, on which rests the whole life of the Church, are other ministries, the first being that of deacons. These are assistants to the bishop or the priest, and their function is essentially that of making the link between the liturgy of the "high priest" and that of the whole gathering of the priestly people. Associated with the ministerial priesthood even in the preaching of the Gospel, the administration of Baptism, and the distribution of Communion, the deacons hand on to the bishop or the priest the offerings of the faithful, whom they are to lead in the uniting of their personal prayer with that of the priest. Similarly, the deacons, under the leadership of the pastors, are to be the administrators of the charity of the faithful. Then come the subdeacons, to whom is given both a role in preparing for the Eucharistic assembly (symbolized by the care of the sacred linens and vessels, the preparation of the chalice and the paten) and, in that assembly, the role of chanters.

The lesser ministers (porters, lectors, acolytes, exorcists) ensure the right order of the assembly by caring for its natural setting, the consecrated building; by playing a secondary role in the first and second parts of the Eucharistic assembly; and by aiding in the accessory rites of Christian initiation.

It might be said that the major orders, those which are properly sacramental (including the diaconate), are the exercise of powers proper to the Head which he delegates for the good of the Body. The minor orders, on the contrary, mean the habitual exercise, by chosen individuals, of functions which any layperson, any member of the People of God, can exercise in and for the assembly of that people.

However, we must not too greatly oppose these two aspects. There is no ministerial priesthood except in and for the priestly assembly of the People of God. The bishops themselves, in consequence, exercise their sacred functions only for and in the People of God, with the accord and the cooperation of that people (as was indicated originally by the episcopal election and the ratification of the choice of the other ministers by the whole people). What is more, the priestly character of the ministers of Christ presupposes the baptismal character and is simply a development of it for the good of the whole Christian people. Actually there is no priesthood in the Church other than that of Christ. All the baptized participate in it by the very fact of their Baptism. The apostolic ministry exists only to actualize this participation unceasingly in the Catholic unity of the whole Body in its Head.

Conversely, there is no sacred action carried out by a lesser minister or by one of the simple faithful, which can be sacred except by virtue of an actual blessing of Christ, of which the sacred ministers are normally the agents. Thus it is that all the various "liturgies" of the members of Christ not only complete one another, but cooperate to such an extent that they mutually require one another and cannot exist without one another. It goes without saying that the faithful could not exist as faithful without the ministers of Christ to baptize them, teach them, unite them with his sacrifice. But the task of initiating, of proclaiming the Gospel, of carrying out the sacred mysteries on the part of the apostles themselves and their successors would have no meaning outside of the Body for which and in which this task is entrusted to them.

We need to keep all this in mind when we wish to define the spirituality of clergy or laypeople, and particularly when we wish to establish the exact relationship between "priestly" spirituality and the spirituality of all the "faithful."

Marriage and the Sacrament of the Sick

After the sacraments which make us ready for the Eucharistic celebration, come those which are, as it were, a flowering of this celebration. For the consecration of humanity and of all things to God, in Christ, through the Eucharist has as its corollary the blessing of all things. This is what the apostle means by the words already quoted: "Every creature of God is good, and nothing is to be rejected that is received with thanksgiving. For it is sanctified by the word of God and prayer" (1 Tm 4:4–5).

This, indeed, is why we find various prayers of blessing inserted in the Eucharistic Canon. Among these are two which have been made sacramental, in the most exact sense of the term, by express words of Christ: the nuptial blessing and the blessing of the oil of the sick. More precisely, marriage and the anointing of the sick are sacraments consecrated formally as being in the closest relationship with the Eucharistic celebration by these blessings given in connection with it.

To compare two sacraments so different at first sight as are marriage and extreme unction is extremely enlightening. It makes us contemplate the complementary aspects of this mystery of the Cross which is the whole of the Eucharist and which the whole sacramental life should extend to the whole of our lives.

The sacrament of marriage testifies that creation, with its positive fecundity, is found restored, consecrated, illuminated from on high in the mystery. But it testifies no less that this is done in Christ only by the laying of his Cross on all things. The teaching of St. Paul about Christian marriage and its meaning is, in fact, synthesized in that phrase: "Husbands, love your wives as Christ loved the Church and delivered himself for her . . ." (Eph 5:25). In other words, it is only by introducing a generous love into marriage, a love which participates in the very love of God and is therefore a sacrificial love, that marriage itself is introduced into the Christian mystery. It is then that marriage, with its whole reality, becomes a true realization in the existence of husband and wife of the very love of Christ and the Church, of God and his creation.

Conversely, the anointing of the sick is the sacrament not of fecundity but of weakness: it comes to consecrate illness, and illness unto death. But it consecrates it only with a view to healing—to immediate healing if such be the will of God, but in any case, to the final and total healing of human nature in the Resurrection.

The correlation of these two sacraments, then, illuminates very clearly the true sense of the Christian mystery. This mystery is that of the Cross, but the Cross has no other end than the definitive restoration of the creature corrupted by sin, the consecration of the creature to God in Christ for a literally divine fullness of life.

Let us carefully note that, if by the Cross we mean suffering and death, it is not the Christian mystery which has introduced them into human life: we find them there as an inexplicable enigma, an enigma with no solution. But the mystery, taking hold of suffering and death by the power of Christ, makes them into the Cross of the Savior, not for sight but for faith. It transforms them, that is, into an all-powerful means of abolishing sin, of conquering the powers of death, of accomplishing the reconciliation of the creature with its God, and so, finally, of bringing it back from death to life and to the fullness of life which is that of children of God.

In the same way, the various rites called "sacramentals," those, that is, which have to do with the blessing of one or another aspect of human life, without having been expressly instituted by the divine Word in Christ, simply extend to the whole of existence this presence of the Cross and its vivifying power.

Priestly Spirituality and Lay Spirituality

The preceding considerations should help us to see in its true light the problem of the relationships between priestly (or, more generally, clerical) spirituality and that of laypeople. Debate on this problem is, as everyone knows, more lively in our times than ever before. But it seems as if many of the attempts to clarify it go astray after dangerous will-o'-the-wisps or get inextricably entangled in contradictions.

When we see, however, that the whole sacramental mystery is organized about the Eucharistic sacrifice, and when we consider the final purpose of this sacrifice (the special *res tantum* of the sacrament), it is clear that all Christians are called to realize one and the same priestly spirituality. All are to come to offer themselves in this sacrifice to God revealed in Christ and to offer the whole universe together with themselves in the Eucharist of Christ. The ministerial (the ordained) priest has nothing to distinguish him, in this regard, from any one of the baptized, from any one of the faithful, from any layperson (that is, from any other member of the "laos," the People of God) except that he is the minister of this active presence of Christ which uses him to communicate and extend his unique priestly action. By this very fact, indeed, the priest is bound, with a very special urgency, to realize in his own love that "knowledge" of God which is the soul of the Eucharist. But all Christians, by the very fact that they are Christians, should similarly move toward the same knowledge, the same love which priests are entrusted with the task of awakening in them.

More precisely, every Christian priest should consecrate his entire life to the union of Christ and the Church in all his members. In his life, this is what should replace the various individual tasks undertaken by others in human society. And it is this consecration, exclusive and absorbing, which explains why the Church came very early to impose celibacy on bishops and even, in the West, to extend this requirement to priests of the second rank and even to deacons and, finally, to subdeacons.

Later on, we shall need to examine the meaning of monastic celibacy, but it is important at this point to see clearly that the meaning of clerical celibacy is not exactly the same. In renouncing family life (and many other things), the monk has no other purpose than that of freeing himself from the world in order to belong wholly to Christ. But the priest frees himself from belonging to a particular family in order to be "all things to all people," according to the word of St. Paul (cf. 1 Cor 9:22). In this regard, his celibacy, then, is not purely ascetic. In consequence, if it results in a merely negative attitude about the world, about people, about people's responsibilities in the world—which is perfectly legitimate, at least for a time, for monastic celibacy—the result is complete nonsense from the priestly point of view. The celibacy of the priest should rather be oriented, and immediately oriented, toward a limitless extension of the charity of God for men. Spiritual paternity is essential to the exercise of the priesthood. If a false or misplaced conception of priestly celibacy tends to render a priest incapable, or even less capable, of this paternity, it might be said that his celibacy ends by turning against its proper purpose.

In return, we can now understand the increasing strictness with which the Church, in the course of the centuries, has opposed the undertaking by priests of secular tasks: trade, political, or social responsibilities, etc. To say that it is possible to carry out the priestly work of Christ through tasks of this kind is to give a meaningless answer. It is precisely the layperson's role to extend the priestly work of Christ into such tasks. What distinguishes the vocation of the priest from the layperson's is this and this alone: the performing of priestly work *instead of* all other kinds of human work. Or, better, the ministerial priest abandons the different tasks apportioned to other men in order to initiate and to foster the accomplishment of the unique priestly work of Christ through all the tasks that other men are carrying out.

Occasionally, to be sure, the Church may allow priests to exercise a lay function, if circumstances are such that they could not materially exercise the priesthood without it, or even if their priestly witness, in a given society, needs must, for the moment, if it is to be made effective and understandable, be thus immersed in the forms of ordinary life.

This also explains why the Church, in particular cases, has allowed and still does allow priests to have a family and has sometimes allowed even bishops to do so. But these situations cannot be presented as normal, still less as the type of priestly life which is to be taken as the ideal. If the priest is not wholly given over to the work of preaching the Gospel and of carrying out the sacramental celebration, then the very reason why he was set apart from the assembly of the laity ceases to be manifest and runs the risk finally of disappearing. The priest who does not preach the Gospel, who does not celebrate Mass and the sacraments, or who does this only on the margin of his real life has been ordained for nothing. What he is then doing is what every lay Christian ought to be doing his proper task, which constitutes his proper vocation, is practically abolished.

Chapter 5

THE PRINCIPLES OF THE ASCETIC LIFE

The prayer of faith causes us to contemplate the Christian mystery and to adhere to it; prayer, that is, sets before our eyes the Cross of Christ and causes us to accept it. The sacramental life places this mystery within us. Christian asceticism, then, is simply the systematic adaptation of our whole life to this mystery which should become its soul. It is the effort to make life accord with faith.

The Christian Meaning of Asceticism

This recognition of the place of the Cross in our life, this deliberate seeking after the Cross, should not be interpreted wrongly. We must not see it as any misprizing of creation, as if any work of God could be evil. In particular, Christian asceticism implies no condemnation either of the material world or of our own body. In this respect, in spite of the existence of more or less analogous practices in very different religions—fasting, austerity,

abstention, and mortification of all kinds—we must be careful
not to confuse the motives which can impel Christians to the
practice of asceticism with those that move, for example, Bud-
dhists and Manichaeans.

For Buddhism, it is the individual existence which is evil.
In this sense, the whole world, as we see it today, in its many-
colored multiplicity ceaselessly reborn, is to be fled from, overcome, abolished. Buddhist asceticism is, therefore, an abstention
which becomes an end in itself, tending to the extinction in
us, not only of all desire but also of the will to live. To quietly
eliminate oneself as a distinct being by turning away from every
image, from every particular thought—this is the beatitude
toward which this asceticism is oriented. It is a nirvana which,
in practice, can be defined only in terms of annihilation.

Less universal but no less radical in its pessimism is Manicheism, the loyal heir of Mazdean dualism. Not all existence is
condemned here, only one aspect of it: its dark aspect, identified with matter, as opposed to the wholly spiritual, the wholly
luminous. In this perspective, it is only in so far as we are corporeal that we are fallen. Salvation will, then, consist entirely
in disengagement from the bonds of the body. It will, in fact,
be identified with death, considered as disincarnation. Yet, to
achieve this end, the spirit must have learned in the course of its
earthly life to detach itself from all its bonds, from all its carnal
appetites, so that death will be the fulfillment of all its desires
which have thus become purely spiritual.

In this view, there can be no question of any sanctification
of the body. Not only will marriage be condemned, but the stability of the marriage union and its fruitfulness will be regarded
with more horror than debauchery, considered merely a weakness, or than unnatural vice, which is necessarily unfruitful. . . .

Manicheism simply carries to an extreme a tendency underlying the majority of ancient spiritualities born in the near East.

Historians tend to place the origin of this tendency in Persia because there it was formulated most clearly in Mazdaism. But it is probable that its origin was more widespread. In any case, it passed on into the Greek world, in particular with the current of Orphism. It asserts itself in Plato, who uses the old pun on *soma* (the body) and *sema* (the tomb). He then opposes "heavenly love," attracted only by spiritual discarnate realities, to "earthly love," mere physical desire. The Neo-Platonism of Plotinus deduced all the consequences of these principles. Seeing in the soul a divine spark imprisoned in matter, he preached a salvation of the soul which would be nothing but its disengagement from the material and its return to the primordial, wholly spiritual One.

There is no doubt that Christian asceticism is always tempted to confuse its motivation with this view of things, the simplicity and logic of which seem so attractive. The confusion comes about from a mistaken identification of the Greek opposition between the body and the soul with the opposition made by St. Paul between what he calls "the flesh" and "the Spirit." But, for St. Paul, "the flesh" is not the body as such, which for him is the work of God, destined to become a "member of Christ" and "temple of the Spirit." The "flesh," as St. Paul means it, is what the whole human being, body and soul linked together inseparably, becomes when it is separated from God. For "the Spirit" is not the spirit of human beings, but the very Spirit of God who is to animate in man the only life worthy of the name, outside of which the whole human being sinks to the level of a corpse.

In the same way, the opposition made by St. John between "the world" and God should not be confused with the Buddhist opposition between the universe in its indefinitely renewed multiplicity and some immovable, indefinable, impersonal being, "inexistent" in the usual sense of the word. St. John's is the opposition between the God who is not only personal but suprapersonal (or, better, ultra-personal) and the world, not inasmuch as he is the Creator of it (which would be nonsense), but inasmuch as it has rebelled against him. And this rebellion, obviously, in the Christian view, is the act, not of wholly passive matter, but of the created spirit, insanely wishing to oppose, to be equal to, the Creator Spirit.

If there is a Christian dualism, in other words, it is a dualism of wills, one which is in no way metaphysical—between forms of beings in themselves irreconcilable, but historical—between free wills which could not oppose one another if there were not an indestructible relationship between them.

These principles having been clearly established, the undeniable fact remains that Christianity, like the other religions or religious philosophies of antiquity, preaches an asceticism which certainly (although not exclusively) includes corporal renunciations, even if these are here quite differently motivated. To discover the meaning of Christian asceticism, we must see how its motivations were clarified little by little in the history of the People of God, under the influence of the divine Word and of the providential experiences in which it engaged the people.

The Old Testament and Asceticism

From the first page of Genesis and throughout the whole account of creation, we are struck by the continual insistence on the fact that everything that exists is good in itself. Here, every existence appears as the work of God, a pure product of his good will alone. "And God saw what he had made, and it was all very good . . ." is, as it were, the leitmotif of the priestly account of creation (Gn 1).

The immediate consequence of this is that God's gift of the good things of creation to humanity is one with the divine blessing. In particular, there was a special blessing for man which crowned all the others: his fruitful union with his wife.

The Fall intervened. But the Fall changed nothing basic in this primal reality. The blessings of the patriarchs repeat those of creation (cf. Gn 49). And the Pasch, the first redemptive covenant with the People of God, was sealed by the gift of the promised land: the land "flowing with milk and honey" (Ex 13:5).

Yet the fact was that as soon as Israel was settled in the promised land, they forgot their God. More precisely, it became apparent that their allegiance was, as it were, divided between God himself and his gifts. The fundamental sin of the people showed itself as idolatry. That is, the people who had hitherto been nomads, living in a constant dependence on providence, in one motion, as it were, became settled, were initiated into agricultural ways and customs, and plunged into the vegetation cults common to the agricultural peoples of Canaan among whom they had come to live. For Israel, in other words, idolatry was one with an exploitation of the riches of the world by self-centered humanity, seeking, above all, to satisfy themselves, to assure their own tangible satisfactions. To the extent to which they do this, people forget God.

At the same time, moreover, the development of one's appetites, which increases as means of satisfying them become organized, plunges a person into injustice. The individual who is solidly established on this earth comes to consider his or her neighbor, his or her own brother, as an intruder or a competitor, as a rival to supplant or even as a slave to dominate.

In the eyes of the prophets, the sin of Israel primarily consisted of this complex of idolatry and injustice, closely associated as it was with the people's becoming settled and established in Canaan—even though Canaan was the promised land.

Hosea expresses this by the image of the adulterous woman applied to the unfaithful nation:

> "... She said: I will go after my lovers, who give me my bread and my water, my wool and my flax, my oil and my wine.
>
> "This is why I will block up her path with thorns: I will build a wall around her, she shall no longer be able to go out. She shall pursue her lovers without being able to rejoin them; she shall seek them without finding them. Then she will say: I will go back to my first husband, for I was happier then than I am now.
>
> "For she has not remembered that it was I who gave her her cheese, wine and oil, who gained her the silver and gold that have been devoted to Baal ..." (Hos 2:7–10).

Here we find for the first time, along with the renewed affirmation that all these things are good since they come from God, the new affirmation that humanity, being what it is, becomes stifled by the enjoyment of them. They forget that God is behind his gifts. Instead of God, they confect those false gods who are only the personification of their appetites, of their slavery to their own riches.

The only cure possible under these conditions is for God then to deprive man, for a while, of these good things. In this way, people will come to recognize once more that God is the sole source whence these things came to them. Hence the conclusion of the prophet: "This is why I will allure her, I will lead her into the desert, and there I will speak to her heart" (Hos 2:16).

Isaiah has us take a further step. He shows us how the wealth of the unjust causes their misfortune, turning them away from God at the same time as it sets them against their brothers and sisters. The prophet does not, therefore, hesitate to adopt a formula that is the exact opposite of the traditional one which blesses the rich for their riches; he says:

> "Woe to them who join house to house, who add field to field, until they remain alone in the midst of the land! . . .
>
> "Woe to them who call evil good, and good evil: who put darkness in place of light, and light in place of darkness; who take the bitter for the sweet and the sweet for the bitter! . . .
>
> "Woe to those who are wise in their own eyes and prudent according to their own beliefs! . . . because they have rejected the law of the God of hosts, they have misunderstood the word of the Holy One of Israel" (Is 5:8–24).

Thus Isaiah came to consider the rich far more cursed than blessed in their wealth. Jeremiah came near to a still greater paradox: that the poor could be blessed in their desolation. In his own life, he seemed the very example of the outcast: he had no wife, no children; his vocation had set him against his fellow citizens. But, considered as a traitor to his country, imprisoned, he found his security in God alone, and his fidelity to the call of God was his one consolation.

The truth, still implicit in the teaching of Jeremiah, became formally explicit in the Servant Songs, the jewels of the second part of the book of Isaiah, connected with the end of the Exile in Babylon. This is, as it were, the high point of revelation in the Old Testament. Here we see a man overwhelmed by every possible kind of anguish. He is poor, and, it seems, sick, rejected, despised by the rich and well-off. He is considered to be chastised, abandoned by God himself. And yet, it is he who is the only faithful servant of the Lord, the only one in whom God delights.

"We considered him as one chastised, struck by God, and afflicted. But he was wounded for our transgressions, bruised for our iniquities. The chastisement that gives us peace has fallen on him, and by his bruises we are healed" (Is 54:4–5).

Not only, then, can the sinner be afflicted by God for his or her own healing, but the suffering of the just person may acquire a redemptive meaning for others, for sinners. . . .

In the Wisdom writings, apparently at about the same period, the figure of Job comes to be set up as that of the man struck down, desolated, above all others. His friends, devout in the traditional fashion, cannot explain what seems to be an exceptional punishment except by an exceptional fault. But God intervenes in person to say, "No." He maintains, without thereby dissipating the mystery, that it is Job, in preference to his friends with their short-sighted piety, who is the only faithful servant of God and that God in return is his one true friend.

Along the same lines, many of the Psalms present the "poor man"—who no longer has anything in which to put his trust and his hope, except God alone—as being the faithful one, the only one whose faith God recognizes and accepts.

After this come the apocalyptic books, of which the first is the book of Daniel. Their common theme is that the world, though created by God, has fallen prey to the powers of darkness, to the spirits of evil and hatred, to the first and the greatest sinners at whose instigation humanity itself came to sin. Consequently, when we put our hope in this world, we enslave ourselves, not to the kingdom of God but to this ephemeral kingdom of the powers in revolt against him. Yet the coming of the divine kingdom is near at hand. It will denounce and overthrow the vain security of earthly kingdoms. If we are to be ready in view of this coming of the King of Ages, therefore, we must break all our ties with the powers that pretend to rule in his stead. This finally amounts to giving up all thoughts of establishing ourselves in "the present age."

It is not astonishing, therefore, that at the era in which the apocalyptic writings flourished, we see appearing in Israel communities of an entirely new kind. These were much more than sects; they were sketchy indications, at least, of what monastic life in the Church was to be. The members of these communities separated themselves from the general mass of people in order to live a life of strictest fidelity to God, a life in which voluntary renunciations and preparation for the trials to come in messianic times held an important place. Even though it is not certain that the Qumran community actually lived in the place where its Rule was rediscovered, the attraction of the desert is undeniable. Men buried themselves in it in order to anticipate the kingdom to come, which is "not of this world." For they knew that "the shape of this world passes away," and they therefore wished to have no other security than that afforded by faith in the kingdom and in the heavenly King who was to inaugurate it.

It seems clear that not only voluntary poverty, but also celibacy was common in this environment. From thence came forth the Baptist, living as an ascetic, crying out in the desert to the crowds who came to join him: ". . . the ax is already laid to the root of the tree" (Mt 3:10). He summoned men to *metanoia*, that is, to a complete transformation of their "mentality," to prepare themselves for those ways of God of which the prophet spoke, which are not our ways.

The Gospel and Asceticism

Finally, Jesus appears, first as following in the wake of the Baptist. He is the Son of a Virgin. It is not the rich and powerful who welcome him, but poor shepherds. The old Simeon, the prophetess Anna (a widow who never left the Temple) were his first heralds. When he opens his mouth to speak for the first time to the crowds, what does he say? "Blessed are the poor. . . . Cursed are the rich" (Lk 6). Later, he says bluntly, "If anyone wishes to come after me, let him renounce himself, let him take up his cross and follow me" (Mt 16:24). That this is no mere rhetorical figure, his own death soon proves.

When St. Paul wishes to give an explanation of the most profound meaning of the Cross of the Master, he writes, "Have in you that mind which was in Christ Jesus: he who, being the very image of God, did not consider seizing equality with God as if by robbery, but humbled [literally "emptied"] himself, taking the image of a slave, in the likeness of men, and, finding himself in our human condition, he humiliated himself . . . making himself obedient to death, and even to the death of the cross . . ." (Phil 2:5–8).

Behind this text, it would seem, is the parallel between Adam and Christ familiar to St. Paul (cf. Rom 5; 1 Cor 15). Adam had desired to seize equality with God as if by robbery. And thus he refused to be a servant, to humiliate himself, to obey. But, in so doing, he had drawn down on his race precisely the evils which were to be taken away from it by the humility, the obedience, the self-"emptying" of the faithful Servant.

Christ has thus opened the way for us to follow in his footsteps, as St. Peter says (1 Pt 2:21). It is by this way that we are to go forward toward the purification of the heart (literally, the circumcision of the heart) of which Jeremiah speaks, the refashioning of our heart of stone into a true heart of flesh—in which Ezekiel sees the essence of the new and eternal covenant promised by both prophets. It is by following on this way that *eros*, fallen human love, capable only of desiring and of taking everything for itself, can be dominated, subjugated by *agape*, that divine love which gives and which gives itself.

The motto of Christian asceticism is henceforth: "to follow Christ." And this is why the martyr is the first and lasting model of the Christian ascetic. The word "martyr," which means "witness," is applied in the Apocalypse of St. John to those who, giving up their lives in fidelity to Christ, witness by their death to the life-giving power of his Cross.

Asceticism and Martyrdom

The most striking "witness" of a martyr which we possess is certainly that of Ignatius of Antioch, whose letters open up to us his thoughts and feelings as he was taken from Asia Minor to Rome, there to be handed over to the beasts. The striking formula concerning the crucified "eros" is his, and we must connect this with his other phrase concerning the chalice of Christ's blood which represents for him, by contrast, the incorruptible *agape*.

His letter to the Romans shows us how the prospect of martyrdom could come to arouse a positive aspiration, an overwhelming ardor. This is the more striking because he evidences no trace of hatred, no misprizing of life or of creation. It is clear that he overflows with love, but that he has understood that love consists more in giving than in receiving and that herein also is true happiness. He will willingly die for Christ, simply because Christ died for him. He desires to carry his cross in order to follow him, or, as St. Ignatius himself says repeatedly, to attain him, to be found in him.

St. Ignatius has no slightest thought that suffering or death could be good or salutary in themselves. But he believes that the suffering and the death of Christ have become such. Thus it is only his faith in Christ that gives him in turn up to the Cross. More precisely, as he himself makes quite clear, it is his Eucharistic faith. In the Eucharist, he is nourished by the Body and the Blood of Christ, that blood which he calls "incorruptible love." He believes, therefore, that, in his own death, Christ will slay death and sin to communicate to him, in perfect identification with Christ, the fullness of life.

We see the result of such a vision in the martyrdom of that Polycarp who was the friend of Ignatius and who had gathered his letters together before following him to a similar trial. Here the martyr succeeds in making his own death a Eucharist. The prayer by which he there consecrates himself to God is simply an extension of the Eucharistic Prayer and, as the spectators of his death stated, they saw him on the pyre as a Eucharistic bread baked in the furnace of love. At the same time, they emphasize that, dying in this way, he seemed not so much to die as already to attain, in the Christ with whom he was identified, the life of the resurrection.

Later on, when persecution had ceased to rage even though new outbreaks were to be feared at any moment, the systematic practice of asceticism came into existence as preparation for the martyrdom that was always possible, just as earlier it had been a preparation for the imminent parousia: for the entrance of the heavenly King into his kingdom. Christians could not settle down in this world as if it should or could be their permanent dwelling place. Yet this was their temptation, as they knew well, as soon as the world relaxed its hostility. To fight against it, they freely exercised themselves in doing without what they might be called at any moment to leave for Christ. Already, however, the question arose: if, in the end, martyrdom is not imposed on those who are thus prepared for it, what use has this preparation been? Origen and others answer: if martyrdom is not to be the crown of asceticism, asceticism of itself, by itself, can constitute as it were an unbloody martyrdom. . . . Is its purpose not to free us to belong wholly to Christ, to the divine will, whatever it may be?

The Asceticism of Ancient Monasticism

A little later, when the Roman Empire had become at least nominally Christian, all at once persecution ceased. It was precisely at this moment that monasticism arose as a substitute for martyrdom. It might be said that as soon as the Church ceased to be forced by the world to live *in* the world without being *of* the world, she felt herself obliged to live in this way by her own choice. Now that the world was offering her its friendship, she seemed to fear being engulfed in it. Hence monasticism.

We should not forget also that, from its first beginnings, the primitive Church had developed along with the ideal of martyrdom, that of virginity consecrated to Christ.

While Christ himself had exalted the ideal of marriage as no one had done before him even in Israel, he who was born of a Virgin had, nevertheless, placed the family among the best of the good things that his disciples could be called upon, like himself, either to abandon or never to possess. In St. Paul's First Epistle to the Corinthians, he exalts celibacy as the means to a more direct or more complete fidelity to Christ. This implies no depreciation of marriage in his thought. Does not the same apostle exalt marriage as the image of, and an effective participation in, the love between Christ and the Church (cf. Eph 5)? Nonetheless, he observes, marriage involves new bonds with the world, our being established in it to a certain degree, and, to that extent, it diminishes our freedom to follow Christ. As St. Paul says, the married man is, or at least may be, divided between his desire to please Christ and his desire to please his wife (cf. 1 Cor 7:25 ff.).

All this shows us clearly that monasticism, like martyrdom, simply prolongs and deepens the piety of the "poor" of the Old Testament. Biblical, Christian asceticism cannot be a condemnation of the gifts of God. A preference is what motivates it, a preference for the Giver over any of his gifts. It seeks only to make us free: free to accept his love, free to give ourselves up to it.

It is in this perspective that we see the meaning of the three vows which, in the East as in the West, have come little by little to express the essence of the monastic life (or the "religious" life in the technical sense of the word, as applied to a life of special consecration to Christ). These three vows are simply a full acceptance of three permanent renunciations designed to put us integrally at the disposition of Christ.

Poverty always is basic. In a sense, it includes the three vows: they simply extend its application to the whole of life. Poverty in the narrower sense makes us free with regard to the world. Chastity makes us free with regard to the flesh. Obedience makes us free with regard to our will itself and its basic egoism.

It should be clearly understood that "the world" from which poverty frees us is not a mere synonym for creation. In the biblical sense, and particularly in the sense in which St. John ordinarily uses the word, it means the organization of all things, not in function of the plan of God but in consequence of the Fall of humanity (of humanity and of the spiritual powers beyond it). In the same way, the "flesh" in the sense of St. Paul is not the body as such: it is its disorganized instincts, maddened by man's disobedience to a higher law. And, finally, that will of one's own, that "myself" which we must renounce by religious obedience, is not our personality as God has willed it but that caricature of it which, as it were, has trammeled its true and healthy development.

The Developments of Medieval Asceticism

It is nonetheless undeniable that, in the historical development of Christian asceticism, the delicate balance between this fundamental optimism and conditional pessimism has not always been maintained. We must at least go through its history cursorily if we are to appreciate both the variety of its aspects and the threat of deformations always hanging over it.

The earliest monasticism, in which the harshest asceticism clearly had nothing in view other than freedom to follow Christ, was born in Egypt. It spread further very soon, first of all into Syria. In this second center of monastic asceticism, we see it taking on spectacular forms already somewhat removed from its primitive sobriety. Here the aspect of struggle against self became more exaggerated, in practices like those of the Stylites (religious who condemned themselves to immobility on an isolated rock or pillar), of those who were actually walled in while alive, or again, for example, of those who mortified themselves by such things as carrying enormous chains.

But it was above all when this asceticism was carried from Egypt and, even more, from Syria into the countries of the West that it began to take on new features which somewhat altered its significance. This took place in Celtic monasticism particularly. Merely transferring to a northern climate a way of life worked out in hot or temperate climates was enough to make many of the austerities of the early monks far more painful. To this must be added the fact that the Celtic temperament—imaginative, sensitive, introverted—would react to the same things quite differently from the Mediterranean.

When the heroic ascetics of ancient monasticism inflicted all kinds of harsh austerities on themselves, they knew quite well that these were painful, but it was not the pain that they were seeking; it was the freedom, or, at the most, the endurance necessary for self-mastery. But the monks of Ireland mortified themselves with the idea of making up by voluntary suffering for the unregulated pleasures to which they might previously have abandoned themselves. They did not seek merely to cut away paralyzing attachments but to undergo the sufferings their penances caused them as the punishment for attachments too willingly consented to. The penitential aspect had certainly never been absent from asceticism, since it would not be imposed at all were it not for sin, but this aspect now came to predominate. And further, penance came more and more to be conceived and even to be reckoned up as a certain sum of sufferings deliberately accepted.

Another step was taken with St. Peter Damien and his whole era (eleventh century). The religious soul then came to concentrate on the Cross, no longer as the instrument of our liberation or as a testimony of love but as a particularly impressive example of suffering deliberately accepted, even sought out. New mortifications of a directly punitive character, such as scourgings, came to be practiced in this spirit.

Thus the way opened out by the Irish monks led, toward the end of the Middle Ages, to an asceticism of compassion. Certain forms of Franciscanism, centered more on the stigmata of St. Francis than on his own spirituality, led in this direction. The theory was formulated clearly for the first time by the Dominican mystic of the fourteenth century Henry Suso. The objective the ascetic had in view was no longer so much to fight and overcome the power of sin through Christ and by his power; it was rather to suffer with him, as if to bring some alleviation to his suffering by taking a part of it on oneself. The beauty and especially the generosity of this ideal are beyond dispute. But it is also beyond dispute that this ideal tended to be formulated in a sentimental context far removed from the sobriety of primitive Christianity or of monasticism and not in accordance with the lines of a sane theology.

Developments of Modern Asceticism

What we have just said is still more true when we go from the asceticism of compassion to that of reparation. This made its appearance in the modern forms of devotion to the Sacred Heart more or less directly inspired by St. Margaret Mary Alacoque. To suffer in order to make up for the "sufferings" caused the sacred humanity of Christ by the unfaithfulness of Christians, particularly their infidelities concerning the Eucharistic Presence, may, certainly, express a profound impulse of love for the Savior. Yet it is not exactly true that Christ "suffers" today in the Eucharist. If the offering of the sacrifice of the Cross at Mass causes no detriment to the glory of Christ now risen from the dead and ascended into heaven, there is all the more reason why he cannot be "wounded," properly speaking, by the mediocre correspondence of Christians with the love he shows us in the Eucharist.

This being so, how can the sufferings that we inflict on ourselves compensate, make reparation, for those of the Savior?

Analogous and perhaps still more urgent questions must be raised with regard to the asceticism of substitution by which, in the course of the nineteenth century, attempts were made to extend these last developments still further. Pious souls, it was said, in inflicting voluntary sufferings on themselves in union with Christ, would, like him, be substituting themselves for the sinners whom punishment would otherwise strike down. Thus these pious souls would hold the divine judgments suspended over the world. The castigations with which innocent persons afflicted themselves would thereby be spared those who had deserved them. Everyone knows to what extremes such reasoning was carried: as if the mass of innocent persons suffering in the fire at the *Bazar de la Charité* were the counterweight needed to hold back the arm of God's justice, outraged by the infidelities of the times. . . .

These last developments, in which several sometimes too adventurous lay theologians, like Léon Bloy, took great pleasure, certainly betray what is at least questionable in the line of thought by which Christian asceticism came to justify itself during a recent period. If we were to draw it out to its logical conclusions, we should have a very strange idea of God, as far removed as possible from that of the Gospel: as if he required a strict ransom of suffering and blood for sin while having no concern whether it were the sinner or the innocent who paid it, provided only that it be paid exactly. Nothing is more contrary to the very idea of grace; nothing is less like the true countenance of the Christian God than that of the blind and even bloodthirsty Moloch which came thus to be superimposed on God's features.

A more or less explicit awareness of all this, along with a spontaneous disgust for the sentimental, perfervid atmosphere in which these themes were developed, explains the abrupt reaction that took place against them. A large part of the devotion to the Sacred Heart, formerly so flourishing, has come to share in the same disfavor. And any asceticism that is at all exacting and rigorous runs the risk of sharing in it also.

Yet it would be very superficial to stop short with the obvious defects that certain modern formulations manifest from the

point of view of the tradition of holy scripture and the Fathers.
We can only rightly criticize these formulations by bringing to
light the seed of truth they certainly contain, even if they did
not always convey it very happily—and by doing so better than
they themselves could have done.

The asceticism of compassion strives to do justice to a theme
which is essential to the thought of St. Paul, the theme which
he himself expresses in such formulae as "If we suffer with him,
we shall also reign with him" (2 Tm 2:12). In other words, there
is a participation in Christ's Cross which is the indispensable
way to participation in his glory, to life in him.

So, too, asceticism conceived as reparation should serve
immediately to dissipate the delusion of a salvation gained for
us without our having to pay for it in any way ourselves. On the
contrary, as the First Epistle of St. Peter says, it was in no way to
dispense us from suffering that Christ suffered in our stead: it
was "to leave us an example, so that we can follow his footsteps"
(2:21). What is more, since we should always conceive of and
detest sin as being, above all, an offense against divine love as
that love manifests itself on the Cross and as the Cross brings
it to us in the Eucharist, the effort of the ascetic should take on
the meaning of an adherence (which in this sense is actually a
kind of reparation) to this love which, saddened by our sins,
remains nonetheless itself the reparation of sin. When St. Paul
urges us not to "sadden the Spirit," is not this precisely what
he has in mind?

Finally, the idea of an asceticism of substitution gains an
authentic and certainly essential meaning if it is conceived as
consciously accepting and entering into that twofold solidarity with Christ and with our human brothers in him, which
unquestionably causes us to cooperate in the salvation of the
world as well as in our own, whenever by faith we unite our
sufferings with those of Calvary. Here is the deepest meaning of

that other phrase of the apostle's, "I carry out in my own flesh what remains to be suffered of the sufferings of Christ, for his Body, which is the Church" (Col 1:24).

Given their proper place in a fully scriptural and traditional perspective, the motives governing modern asceticism thus regain a meaning which goes far beyond the deficiencies and even the errors which certain of their formulations may have. In seed, all this is to be found in the Servant Songs of the second part of Isaiah—some of the most mysterious but most profound aspects of the Cross of Christ and of Christians, which were to be rediscovered and fully developed in the light of the Gospel.

Yet these analyses should at the same time remind us once again of the dangers of distortion and caricature to which the most vital Christian truths are exposed when, in meditating on them, sentimental imagination tends to outstrip faith. Christian asceticism can remain healthy only by remaining authentic. And it cannot remain authentic in any other way than by a continual reference, as explicit as possible, to the fundamental truth of faith: the revelation of the love of God—in its most transcendent, most "supernatural" aspect—through the mystery of the Cross.

When it is reestablished on this basis, Christian asceticism, far from involving us in any suspect kind of "dolorism," remains or again becomes what it always should be: an effort toward liberation, resulting directly from faith—liberation from this world for the sake of the world to come. . . . It is the work of faith if it causes us to take the cross as the cross *of Christ:* that is, a conflict with the world, the flesh, and, finally, perverse will; an effort not to reject the world, to kill the body, or to annihilate the will but rather to save the world from itself and to prepare for the resurrection of the body by regenerating the human will that has been mortally wounded by sin.

Chapter 6

CHRISTIAN ASCETICISM AND CHRISTIAN HUMANISM

The study of the origin and development of Christian asceticism has allowed us to estimate the complexity of the motives governing it and the delicacy of the equilibrium that must be maintained between them. All this might be summarized by saying that it presupposes, in the evaluation of the human condition which must be our starting point, both a metaphysical optimism and a historical pessimism. A metaphysical optimism since everything is good in itself—in our own nature and in the universe, our body as well as our soul, matter as well as spirit—for everything has been willed and created by God. A historical pessimism inasmuch as sin has vitiated the very conditions of our spiritual life, our natural relationships with things. But sin, in its source, does not belong to matter but to the created spirit: it is the willed revolt of an intelligence against its Creator. This revolt sets creation, as it were, against itself. The highest goods that it contains, instead of leading us beyond them to the Creator, screen him off from us. Necessarily, therefore, we must sooner or later break with these things if we are to return to him.

Yet this death, voluntarily accepted as a sign of his love newly recognized and welcomed in our hearts, is to become the principle of resurrection, that is, of an integral restoration of creation, once again brought into harmony with its Creator. But this cannot be done except *in Christ*, as St. Paul says. Death of itself has no saving power: it is nothing but the final product of sin, of separation from God. It becomes the way of salvation only when God joins us therein, through his Word made flesh. The cross is life-giving only if it becomes the Cross of Christ received through faith in Christ, the Son of God made man.

All this we must try to understand if we are to discern the concrete pattern of an asceticism that is truly and fully Christian. This requires first of all an examination of the anthropology, the idea of humanity, presupposed by Christian asceticism. Then we need to see exactly what sin is as well as the fallen state which it has meant for humanity and which must be our starting point. Then we shall be in a position to understand how the fundamental process of creation is interconnected with the process of redemption and how the latter, at first sight antagonistic to the former, is actually oriented only toward restoring its original design.

The Christian Teaching Concerning Humanity

The definitive formula of the biblical and Christian view of humanity is given us in a sentence of St. Paul's—one which also constitutes, as it were, a summary of all Christian spirituality: "May the God of peace himself sanctify you completely, and may he keep in wholeness your spirit, your soul, and your body without reproach at the parousia [literally, *in* the parousia] of our Lord Jesus Christ" (1 Thes 5:23).

In this formula, the spirit (*pneuma*) is or is not an integral part of human nature, according to the point of view. In itself, the Spirit is transcendent to human beings: it is, in God, the breath of God's own life. Yet since God made men and women only to adopt them, to make them his own sons and daughters, it is essential to his design to communicate the Spirit to them. Thus individuals are not wholly themselves unless they have in them the Spirit of God.

This Spirit does not simply dwell in humanity as in a temple. Or, to put it another way, since God's temple is a living one, it cannot contain the divine Spirit except by being animated by him. Thus the more the Spirit is integrated with a person, the more he or she may be said to become "spirit." As his or her soul (*psyche*) vivifies his or her body (*soma*), it is itself vivified by the Spirit; it becomes "spirit."

And this is not a kind of fortuitous accident. Certainly it is *the* grace above all others, the most completely gratuitous gift of God, the grace that could least of all be merited by humanity. But this does not alter the fact that God made human beings in order to give them his Spirit. In this regard, the "spirit" is not a part of the human soul (that would be nonsensical) but that toward which the human soul tends—that in which it will be perfected by going beyond itself.

The relationship of the body to the soul is somewhat analogous to that of the soul to the "spirit." The body, likewise, is only made for the soul, only lives in the soul the life for which it is destined. And, as the soul in turn lives only in the "spirit," the body itself, in the integral destiny of humanity, is to become "spirit."

In the order of principles, which is also the order of ends, the soul is to live for the Spirit in becoming "spirit," as the body is to live for the soul and be animated by it, in such a way that, finally, the whole person, body and soul, may become a child of God, a living temple, animated and made "spiritual" by his Spirit. In the order of actualization, as appears in the biblical account of creation, while the Spirit hovered over the primeval chaos, the divine Word drew from it more and more perfect bodies, until into the human body is breathed the living soul which proceeds from the divine Spirit and is constantly to be "inbreathed," inspired, by his actual presence.

Such a view of things differs sharply from that of Greek spirituality as this is formulated by Plato, for example. Here, by contrast, the soul (*psyche*) conceived above all as intelligence, as *nous*, is in direct opposition to the body. To repeat: for the soul, its *soma*, its body, is a tomb (*sema*) into which it has fallen and from which it can only aspire to free itself. Conversely, when it has done so, it finds itself divine in itself. Is it not a heavenly spark which has only to be extricated from its shell of clay to shine out with a fire which can be hidden but which cannot, of itself, undergo any change?

In the Neo-Platonism of Plotinus, this view is made even more explicit. God is unity itself, the One. But, inasmuch as he "thinks" the universe, he manifests himself as Intelligence, *Nous*. And in the multiplicity of the universe itself, he retains, as it were, a shadow of his essential unity by means of the *Psyche*, the Spirit of which our souls are only little parts. In extricating itself from matter, the soul becomes once more pure intelligence. It has to do nothing more than to become unified in itself in order once more to become God, or rather to become again in fact what it has never ceased to be in principle: the One, the Only True Being: *Theon genomenon, mallon de onta;* "Becoming, or rather being God" (VI Ennead).

According to this view, the return to God (which is the same thing as absorption in him) is effected simply by purification.

The soul has only to renounce what is foreign to itself to become God again in again becoming itself.

Thus the outline of the Platonic and Neo-Platonic view of humanity differs from that of the Bible and Christianity in a whole series of points, which it is important to pin down precisely.

In the Greek scheme, the divine transcendence is much less sharply brought out than in the biblical. The personality of God is nonexistent. Moreover, the personality of humanity is only provisional. More generally, the process of creation (if one can still use the word here) is indistinguishable from the process of disintegration, from the Fall. It follows then that return to God, "conversion," must simply be the inverse of "emanation."

It cannot be said that, in such a conception, matter is as clearly *the* evil as it is in Manicheism. Matter is only a limit toward which the process of emanation from the One tends in its progressive degradation. But it could be said that, for the soul, evil consists in being immersed, swallowed up, in matter. More generally, evil is any attachment to distinct existence, any refusal to let oneself be reabsorbed in the One.

On all these points, the Christian view is quite different. God is personal, supremely personal. And humanity, inasmuch as it comes from God, as it tends toward him, is also personal. There can be no question of individuals losing themselves in God, in the sense of losing their distinct existence in him. . . . This individual existence has been willed by God and willed without reserve. Union with God, far from reabsorbing this human existence in God, serves on the contrary to open it out. And this is true of the whole of humanity. For God has created person's body as well as his or her soul. More generally, God is the Creator of matter as well as of created "spirit." Bodies and the world of bodies are not the final product of a disintegration of being; rather, they are, as it were, the permanent basis for the creation of humanity.

Salvation, therefore, does not consist in the extrication and purification of one part of humanity from the other: the soul from the body, the *nous* from matter. Salvation consists in the restoring of the relationships originally willed by God: of the body to the soul, of the soul to the Spirit.

In contrast to a fundamentally static universe in which all movement, all impulse can only be a degradation, the biblical universe seems moved by a basic dynamism, behind which can be discerned the dynamism of the divine life itself. In such a context, the relationships of beings to one another take on an importance that has no analog in other systems of thought. The body cannot be understood except in its relationship to the soul nor the soul except in its relationship to the divine Spirit. In both cases, the inferior does not tend toward the superior in order to disappear in it but in order to be fully itself in escaping from a suffocating imprisonment, a deathly paralysis. This opening out, this transcending of itself on the part of the inferior corresponds to an understanding, a generosity, on the part of the superior—a condescension, if you will, but one which implies nothing of a fall nor of a dethronement.

Along with these different views of humanity, of the world, and of God, there goes an equally different view of the divine image in every person. The idea of the image of God is not absent from the vision that may be called Hellenic. But here it is as though humanity were a microcosm, the reduction of a macrocosm: the grand whole in which the divine and the earthly form one sole being. In this case, the divine image in humanity is limited to the spirit, that is, to the *nous*, the fine point of the intelligence. This image, however, is not so much an image as a spark of the divine fire. The effort of purification, freeing this spark from its shell of matter, tends to reintegrate it with this fire from which it came.

In the biblical vision, on the contrary, the image really is an image: it is not a little bit of the model; it cannot be confused with the model even though it came from it. The perfection of this image requires both the active presence of the model within it and that it should always be something distinct from the model. It is an image like that of the sun in a mirror: it would disappear if anything were to come between the mirror and the source of light, but it exists as an image only because the mirror exists as essentially different from the sun, although turned toward it.

Then, too, the image is not something of the soul only but of the whole person, indissolubly body and soul. This must be emphasized: it was Adam made from the earth whom God, in Genesis, made "to his image and likeness." And conversely, Ezekiel saw the God who dwells in inaccessible light "as the likeness of the figure of a man" (Ez 1:26). The image of God in his creature is, in fact, this living kinship with him which subsists only in the living relationship which he himself arouses, when this relationship is accepted. This is why we can equally well say that the divine image in humanity is changed, effaced by sin, and that it cannot be lost; for the individual, whatever he or she may do, exists and is maintained in existence by God only as being capable of the living filial relationship with him which is adoption. This is what is meant by some of the Fathers when they say that people can lose their living likeness to God but not the very image according to which they were made and without which they would no longer have existence.

These contrasts between the Greek and the Christian views of humanity lead to a further contrast which has not always been pointed out since it is expressed in two formulae which are so symmetrical as to be confusing, although they are completely antithetical. The Platonic or Neo-Platonic spiritual ideal consists in restoring the resemblance of God in ourselves so as to know him, since like is known only by like. The spiritual ideal first of Judaism and then of Christianity is to know God, by means of his own revelation, so as to come to resemble him. On the one hand, there is a growing resemblance of which the self is the author, which causes one to know God in knowing oneself perfectly in one's essential being. On the other hand, there is a growing resemblance of which God is the author, which causes us to resemble him to the degree to which he makes himself known to us in what he has that most completely transcends us: his creative love, *agape*.

Greek Formulae as Used in Christian Spirituality

Yet in spite of all the above contrasts, the fact is that Christian spirituality since the Fathers of the Church has made abundant use of the formulae of Greek anthropology, notably of Neo-Platonism. Before condemning this practice altogether and stating, as some people have done, that it meant an adulteration of Christianity, we must take the trouble to understand why it came about. Then we may, perhaps, be in a position to discover its exact import and, particularly, to observe that it meant a refashioning and adapting of the original Greek conceptions far more than their supplanting any properly Christian ideas.

The first point to be noted is that while Christian spirituality could not adopt the dualistic metaphysics implicit in Platonic or Neo-Platonic conceptions, it had no reason to reject the psychological observations on which this metaphysics was founded—even though Christian faith was obliged to criticize the metaphysical doctrines themselves. For what cannot be admitted as a definition of human nature may correspond to concrete observations of this nature in the actual conditions in which we find it today. These observations certainly lacked the indispensable background which only divine revelation could have provided. But this does not prevent their being well-founded to the extent that they are empirical.

For the Greek opposing of the body to the soul goes along with an over-systematized presentation, and so a crystallization, of factual observations which the divine Word does not deny even when it illuminates them in a totally unexpected way. The fact that, according to the Bible, the body was made for the soul in no way prevents us from recognizing that, today, in the concrete condition of humanity as it is, the body is a drag on the soul. Consequently, although the soul deceives itself in believing that it will find God in simply rediscovering itself, it is no less true that it will not find God and it will not rediscover itself without a certain liberation from the chains by which the body, and the world along with that body, hold it down—even though it is also quite true that these chains have been forged by the soul itself.

The Bible, for its part, asserts that the soul which has withdrawn itself from subjection to the divine Spirit, far from ruling its body the more perfectly and raising it the more completely to its own level, gives it over to confusion and, in so doing, is drowned in the maelstrom of instincts which it has set loose. So, too, when the soul does not orient toward God the organization of the world as it ascends toward him within humanity itself, then the individual tries to organize the world *against* God and, in so doing, becomes its prisoner.

What Christian spirituality could not accept as a complete description of the world and of humanity as the creation of God, it could, then, accept as a description of the appearances presented by the world and humans today, following the Fall.

It is in this sense that, with the Alexandrian school and Origen in particular, Christian spirituality adopted many Platonic and Neo-Platonic conceptions, although not without correcting them and, above all, not without modifying their basic intent. The boldest along these lines among the thinkers and spiritual writers of the East was Evagrius Ponticus. And, in the West, the most steadfast in the adopting of the framework of Neo-Platonism was St. Augustine, though here his own retractions have not always been given sufficient weight.

For Evagrius, man's soul (*psyche*) is the link between his spirit (*nous*) and his body (*soma*). Depending on the soul's inclining toward one or the other of these poles which attract it, it conforms to God or to the devil. The *nous*, as he conceived it, is not so much a part of the soul as the image of God within it: more precisely, "the place of his presence," as Evagrius expresses it. This place is "carved out" to his likeness by the very action of God, when the soul wholly tends toward him. But when, by means of the *pathe*, the sensible impressions received by the soul from the body, it turns its back on him and thinks only of its body, then the enemy of God, the devil, enchains it in an idolatrous servitude, rendering it unfit for *agape* and for any knowledge of God.

The soul must, therefore, free itself from the body, or, more precisely, from the *pathe* emanating from the body which have enslaved the soul. In achieving *apatheia*, that is, freedom from these bonds, it is thereby made fit to receive anew "the love of God poured out in our hearts by his Spirit" (Rom 5:5), and thus to "know God." Evagrius himself, however, is the first to emphasize that we are not to wait for the "knowledge of God" simply to be produced in the soul after it has attained *apatheia* by its own efforts. On the contrary, we attain *apatheia* as the fruit of our own efforts, together with the *agape* which is its positive counterpart, only in and by means of the "knowledge of God" which remains his wholly free gift.

The Augustinian synthesis is simpler. Immersed in the world by its senses, the soul must begin by withdrawing itself from the world, by re-entering into itself, and thus rediscovering itself. Thus it will rediscover the image of God to which it was made. But God is not his image; he is the model of it. And so, having re-entered into itself, the soul must still go beyond itself in order to find him. Yet it cannot accomplish this return except by hearing the Word of God which made all things and which, by the Incarnation, now resounds in this world where the soul has forgotten him in forgetting itself. Thereby the soul is recalled from lust ("the love of self carried to contempt of God") to charity ("the love of God carried to contempt of self"). . . .

These two syntheses, profoundly different in detail but parallel in inspiration, have largely dominated the spiritualities of the East and West, respectively. But, in both the one and the other tradition, the tendency toward a one-sided spiritualism was effectively restrained by opposing factors which never let themselves be completely eliminated.

In the East, alongside the Evagrian tradition and interwoven with it, a more popular line of spirituality was maintained which found its first great expression in the body of writings called "Macarian," that is, attributed to the Macarius of Egypt who was the master of Evagrius himself in the monastic life.

Here, according to a theory entirely biblical in inspiration, the soul is not centered in the *nous* ("the intelligence") but rather in "the heart": understood as the focus, at once (and inseparably) intellectual and voluntary, spiritual and sensible, of the human person as an integral whole, including explicitly his or her body and its life. Sanctification is not conceived, therefore, as a mere liberation with regard to the body, restoring the divine image in the highest point of the soul; it is understood rather as an effort to "draw Jesus into the heart"—that is, to bring the incarnate God (not God as pure "spirit") into the focal point of the whole human being, indivisibly both body and soul. And this is to be carried out by means of a mastery of the body which subjugates it to grace and thus regenerates it, however mortifying this process may be, rather than by a weakening which would reduce it to nothingness so that the soul might escape from it.

Still another line of Eastern spirituality, connected with the writings of the Areopagite, brought a correction or a decisive complement to Evagrian spirituality, not so much with regard to the human aspect of it as the divine. Substituted for or superimposed on the image of the soul as entering into itself, becoming itself again in becoming *apathes*, and then gathering everything up into the *nous* ("pure" intelligence), the Dionysian writings give the image of the necessary exodus of the soul, its "ecstasy" not only outside itself but outside everything created or creatable, in order to find God.

Again, in the West, the Augustinian idea of charity, in which love of self is not so much renounced or transcended as purified by again becoming love of self as the image of God, was categorically opposed by St. Gregory the Great. He maintained that charity always presupposes a necessary going out from oneself toward an Other who is not simply "more intimate to us than we are to ourselves" but who is still more, and above all, the "wholly Other": the divine Other. *Numquam caritas potest esse nisi inter duos*, he says: "There can be no charity except between two distinct beings." But thanks to the Aristotelian renewal, it was St. Thomas who, without breaking with the tradition of borrowing from Hellenism and without breaking even with the Christian Platonism of Augustine, nonetheless by the orientation of his Neo-Aristotelianism brought about a decisive return to the Pauline view of humanity.

For Aristotle had ceased to conceive of the soul as some-how paralleling the body in a superior world, separated from the body although weighed down by it. He made the soul the proper "entelechy" of the body, that is, as it were, the directive idea intimately determining all its development. His successors, however, had interpreted this in a purely materialistic sense, as if the soul had no distinct existence apart from the body, and it is not impossible that Aristotle himself actually thought of it in this way. His teaching on this point, therefore, had seemed irreconcilable with Christian doctrine. Nonetheless St. Thomas took it up again and, by somewhat "re-Platonizing" it, made it much more satisfactory from the Christian point of view than any form of Platonism or Neo-Platonism. For, like Plato, he saw the soul as a form—and, moreover, a substantial form—endowed with its own spiritual being, in itself indestructible. But he saw it nonetheless, as did Aristotle, as the form of *the body*, and of one particular body, determined by its insertion into the material world. The unity of the human person, body and soul, is thus restored, in harmony with the biblical view—restored, that is, in a spiritual dynamism which causes the body to be unified and perfected in itself in and through the soul.

The soul, in turn, in accordance with the way in which St. Thomas thought of grace, is perfected and exceeds itself in God. In contradiction to Peter Lombard, St. Thomas did not accept the idea that grace is purely and simply the gift of the Holy Spirit, of the Third Person of the Holy Trinity as he is in himself. It seemed to him that, in this case, the individual would indeed be the temple of the Spirit, but not his living temple, vivified by the presence of its Guest, assimilating our life to his own life. The uncreated grace of the gift of the Spirit, therefore, according to Thomas, is extended in the soul itself by a created grace, that is, by a divine quality making the soul like to God, causing it to participate in his own life.

This teaching was frequently misunderstood later on to the point of being interpreted in an exactly opposite sense. The characterizing of grace as created was taken as a pretext for representing it as a second nature, a "supernature" superimposed on our original nature. Nothing could be more contrary to the profound thought of St. Thomas. If grace, as he conceived it, is created, it is in the soul that it is so; he says expressly that it is not a superior and distinct nature added to the soul like a mere garment but a quality infused into it. While grace is supernatural in the basic sense that it is superior to any created nature or to any that could be created, it is in no way a "supernature." It is, as it were, a new "accident" inserted into the substance of the soul, fitting it as a soul to live the very life of God, wholly divine.

No theological notion, certainly, is more mysterious than this idea of grace which is created but in such a way as to render a creature whom it recreates, without changing or destroying it, "a participant in the divine nature," according to the phrase used in the Second Epistle of St. Peter (1:4). How can a created reality cause us to participate in the uncreated? Yet the paradox is simply that of a reality actually inserted in us to the point of being wholly our own, without ceasing nonetheless to be in itself divine. This is the paradox of that Spirit who is the Spirit of God but who makes himself the "spirit" of the soul. It is the summit and the crown of that dynamic vision of a creation adopted by its Creator; it is the perfection of that life of relatedness, of one being's reference to another, which is the basis of the biblical universe. And here this universe most completely transcends the highest of purely human visions of the world, even those developed among the most religious of Greek thinkers.

About a century after the Thomistic synthesis, the East saw another at once deeply traditional and strongly original, take form along its own lines. This is the synthesis of the Bishop of Thessalonia known to Byzantine and Russian Christians as St. Gregory Palamas. It seems at first sight to be opposed point by point to that of St. Thomas. In reality, it was almost precisely the same spiritual preoccupations which motivated it and to which it wished to do justice. Yet its metaphysical presuppositions are different, although they are not so completely contradictory to those of St. Thomas as they might appear.

For Palamas, the living God who offers us his grace remains at once absolutely transcendent and yet very really communicated to his creatures. He expresses this in a line of thought which, by way of the Greek Fathers and especially St. Gregory Nazianzen and the other Cappadocians, unquestionably goes back to a Judaism of purest biblical inspiration. As the rabbis distinguished between, without separating, God in his inaccessibility to the creature and the face (or the angel) of God in which he really communicates himself, so Palamas distinguishes between the divine essence, totally incommunicable, in which neither humans nor any other creature can participate either in this life or even in eternal life, and the divine "energies," in which God actually condescends to his creatures. In contrast to the divine essence, these energies can be participated in, while they yet remain uncreated and wholly divine. They are the life of God inasmuch as he wishes to communicate it, a life inseparable from his essence and from the three persons who are one with that essence but distinct from them to the point of being capable of being participated in by created persons.

What is more, since the human person is inseparably body and soul, the divine energies in permeating the soul transfigure even the body of flesh: this is the light of Tabor, the light shining from the face of Christ at the Transfiguration, as it had once been reflected from the face of Moses at Sinai and as it snatched away the prophet Elijah in the fiery chariot. This light, which not only illuminates the soul but also transfigures the body, is nonetheless called "uncreated" for the reason that it is the product, the immediate activity of the divine energies in us.

If we wish to indicate the points of contrast between St. Thomas and Palamas, we can pick them out easily. On the one hand, absolute simplicity of the divine essence, in which grace already allows us to participate and which we shall see without any intermediary in the eternity of the blessed. On the other hand, division—or at least real distinction—between the divine essence and the "energies" so that, in grace, the energies act directly within our whole being, while the essence itself, in this life and the next, remains impenetrable and inaccessible to us.

On the one hand, again, created grace, but one which assures our participation in the very essence of God. On the other, uncreated grace, but one which causes us to participate only in the energies radiating from the essence.

Although St. Gregory Palamas was as persuaded as was Thomas himself of the necessity for realistic thinking and for a realism which should be critical and therefore nourished by Aristotle rather than by Plato—though by an Aristotle rectified by the Bible and the tradition of the Fathers—he was certainly a less rigorous philosopher. His concern was directly spiritual, and he wished to be a theologian only to defend the spirituality which seemed to him traditional, not to speculate for the sake of speculating. It is, therefore, an easy game to criticize, from a strictly philosophical point of view, the real distinction he made between the divine essence and the divine energies.

The fact remains that the same contradiction encountered here is at least latent in the Thomistic theological conception of a grace which is created even though it causes us to participate in the divine nature itself. For on the one hand as on the other, we run into the unheard-of paradox of biblical faith, the paradox that no Greek concept could include: the transcendent God who yet communicates himself and who really communicates himself, without—for all that—absorbing his creature, much less being dissolved in it.

Furthermore, we must not be deceived by some of his expressions. While Gregory Palamas speaks of the divine essence as unpartakable, unknowable, this must be understood, as with the Cappadocians, in the sense of an adequate knowledge or of a participation which would make us divine persons. Conversely, the participation which St. Thomas envisages is only an analogical participation and the vision necessarily not comprehensive. Under one formulation as under the other, what is meant is a communication of the divine life which is authentic, and which becomes authentically our own, without implying any pantheistic immanence or any form of externalism.

Moreover, the notion, which at first sight seems so disturbing, of an "uncreated" light which yet can be seen even by the eyes of the body simply synthesizes this life of the body in the soul and the life of the soul in God by grace, which is the ideal of humanity as Thomism itself conceives it. There is no doubt that, in Thomistic thought, the transfiguration of the body at the resurrection, however mysterious it remains, will be the effect of its receiving the radiation of the beatific vision as it takes possession of the soul in its entirety—a soul to which, let us remember, it is essential to be the form of a body.

In spite of the apparent conflict between Thomism and Palamism, we should, therefore, recognize in both systems, from the viewpoint of spirituality, the final triumph of the biblical idea of humanity over all the dangers of warping which the usage of terms or ideas borrowed from the Hellenistic idea of humanity might have involved.

Nevertheless, we cannot draw the consequences which follow for spirituality from the fact that the biblical idea of humanity is in no way static but, on the contrary, eminently dynamic, unless we see how the different elements concerned play their harmonious—or, on the other hand, discordant—roles in human history.

The Fall and the State of Fallen Nature

The teaching of the divine Word concerning the Fall is given us in the third chapter of Genesis in the second account of creation. But we need to fill out the data furnished by this first account with those of two other texts, and profoundly mysterious ones, from the same book: the account of the fall of the "sons of the Elohim" by committing fornication with the daughters of men (chapter 6) and that of the tower of Babel (chapter 11).

The first account shows us the Fall of humanity as taking place in the very heart of the intimate relationship uniting Adam and his wife, through the diabolic suggestion which disturbed this fundamental harmony and, at the same time, the harmony of humanity with God. The second account presents almost the same elements, but here their order is reversed: the demons' fall and solicitation come into the foreground, but it is in a perversion of sexual relationships that humankind is drawn into it. And the third account brings human society on the scene and shows us, in its own disintegration, the effect of its coalition against God.

Let us take up these elements one after the other. There is no question, according to the third chapter of Genesis, of seeing in sexual relations as such the original sin, as some heretics have thought. On the contrary, Genesis states as categorically as possible that the normal relationship of a man with his wife, including their common fruitfulness, is blessed by God and is even the supreme blessing given to man in his creation. This does not preclude the fact—and all the Fathers of the Church are in agreement on this point—that the first sin was introduced within their relation with one another. The insistent mention of the fact that before they sinned they were naked and felt no shame, that their nakedness then became shameful, and the serpent coming between them being described as "the most naked of living things"—which, due to an ambiguity of the Hebrew language, can also, and in this case certainly does mean "the most wicked"—all leave no room for doubt.

To ask what precise sin is indicated here is futile. The symbolic form of the account baffles such infantile curiosity. What it is meant to tell us is (1) that humanity fell by listening to the suggestion of the devil "You will not die . . . you will be like gods" rather than to the divine Word; (2) that this suggestion led humanity to prefer immediate sensible appearances to the still-hidden realities of faith; and (3) that this call to put sensual pleasure above everything else was echoed, listened to, within the relationship between man and wife.

It should be noted that the blessing of human sexuality is, for all that, not withdrawn but now, as it were, matched with a curse. Woman will be saved, as the apostle says, by the fruitfulness subsistent in her relations with man, but this fruitfulness itself will become painful, just as man, in all the activities by which he maintains the life of the family, must now toil laboriously. Besides, the powerful attraction which binds them together is changed into a slavery. More precisely, woman tends to sink from the role of man's companion and complement to the humiliated and humiliating role of a mere plaything of his desires—of the desires which he himself cannot or can hardly overcome, still less elevate.

When we go on to the strange account of the "sons of the Elohim" (understood as angels) enraptured with the daughters of men because of their beauty and making them their wives, from whom is born a monstrous race of wicked giants, it is evident that symbolism (and one very hard for us to decipher) plays an even greater part here than in the preceding account.

This symbolism becomes clearer, however, when we remember that idolatrous cults were always treated by the prophets as "fornication" and that this fornication was not simply spiritual since in Canaan these cults included the practice of all forms of "sacred" prostitution. In other words: (1) the Fall of humanity, here more explicitly than in chapter 3, is only a repercussion of a previous fall of angels, of "pure" spirits; (2) this fall of the angels, insofar as we can have any idea of it, came from their determining to take hold of and turn to their own profit the earthly and human creation. With this creation, as we know from the prophets, God wished to have relationships which would be, as it were, the ideal model of the relationships between husband and wife. But, instead, there came about a fornication and even a prostitution, in which sensual perversion went along with a false spirituality; (3) idolatry is actually a worship of the created "powers," of what there is of spirituality immanent in physical nature itself but as dissociated from its Creator; and (4) this "vain," that is to say empty, worship is nonetheless not without fruit, but its fruit, grandiose in appearance, is unhealthy: a monstrous humanity whose very grandeur is intrinsically perverted.

This last point brings us forthwith to the third of our three accounts, that of the tower of Babel. It is obvious that it describes the beginnings of what we call civilization. People join together and unite their efforts to build themselves a city. But they themselves plan their common work in a spirit of rivalry with the power of God, from which they intend to free themselves or, better perhaps, which they hope to seize for their own profit. The result is that their alliance disintegrates, while their work never becomes anything but a ruin, unfinished and unfinishable.

When all the complementary data resulting from these three texts are thus brought together, it is striking what a rich and coherent whole begins to emerge. The first point is that sin is both what is, in a sense, most personal and yet also something which cannot be reduced to an individual act nor to a sum or collection of individual acts. In all sin, from the first on, is involved the tendency toward the other person which characterizes the whole life and the whole being of the individual. Man sins in that relationship with himself which is inseparable from his relationship with her who is "bone of his bone" and "flesh of his flesh." But, at the same time, every social relationship is changed. And, behind all this and behind even the most apparently material aspects of sin, there prevails a spiritual collusion with perverted spirits, in which the whole relationship of humanity to the universe and to what is beyond it appears as corrupted.

But if we try to plumb the essence of sin, we ascertain that, with the angels, it would seem, it is a form of possessive pride: wishing to put themselves in the place of God, they wished to possess his creation as their own, by evicting him from it. With humanity, on the contrary, it is the aspect of egotistical desire, and of sensual lust, that predominates. But, behind this, pride again is the moving force: the will to be free of God, to put oneself in his place. More precisely, we find in humanity a will for immediate enjoyment—enjoyment detached from any other consideration, stifling faith—faith in the divine Word imposed as a transcendent obligation but giving promises for the future which are eclipsed by the immediateness of sensuous enjoyment.

Yet, in its very sin, humanity cannot make itself really irreligious, still less areligious. Human beings only transpose their religion from the Creator to the creature. If idolatry is the supreme sin, in other words, then all sin is idolatry in embryo, implicit idolatry. Whence in fallen humanity the chaos of exaggerated desire, out of proportion to its limited object. Whence the enslavement of humanity to the "powers" which rule them by the intermediary of their sensual satisfactions, never really satisfying them in their alienation from the true God. Whence the instability of social ties, which turn to the exploitation of individuals by one another, in their common revolt against the only One who could bring them together in common faithfulness to the grace they have refused.

These views may furnish at least a sketch of the situation in which humanity finds itself when now it again wishes to seek God, who has never ceased to call individuals back to himself.

Fallen Humanity's Search for God

In their Fall, men and women remain nonetheless the creatures of God, in a world also created by him and, more precisely, created by his Word, even if that Word is now obscured.

Humanity's deepest life, in other words, continues to awaken in its first contact with the universe in which it is immersed, from whence it proceeds, to which it belongs by reason of the human body. Thus a person's first perception of the sacred comes about through his or her perception of the goodness, the beauty of the world. . . . But individuals tend, as by an invincible inclination, to make of this world—of that about it which satisfies their immediate appetites and of that about it which, at the same time, awakens in them a confused response, a resonance to deeper calls—their first, their basic idol. They divinize the immediate satisfying of their needs by the powers of nature; and the highest level they can attain is to divinize the world itself because of that impression of sacredness which its beauty continues to make on them, although they are no longer capable of piercing the denseness of what transmits this impression to them.

Nearer to themselves and, as it were, within themselves, the attraction that the opposite sex holds for them causes them to discover that self-fulfillment and union with another person are inseparable, or, rather, that the only completion possible is in another. But the opposite sex becomes simply one more idol for them, in which it is actually their own sensual passion that they idolize, in such a way that, far from truly placing their companion on a pedestal, they bring him or her down to the level of an anonymous and delusive mechanism for ensuring their pleasure.

All around, society develops a person's mind and furnishes him or her with objects ready for the individual to act on. But, at the same time, it walls a person up in neglect of God, in false domestication of a universe which has ceased to be a sanctuary only to become a prison—for humanity only rearranges it to make it more and more completely the instrument of its self-oriented desires. All this, furthermore, burdens with sorrows, with increasingly frustrating contradictions, a life embittered by the search for self-centered pleasure alone. Such a life, by its very development, tends toward death. Because of its basic refusal to sacrifice immediate enjoyment—the sacrifice implied in any going out from self—it turns in on a "self" which is no longer understood except as radically isolated, and so tends toward the immobility of death.

Yet the divine Word does not cease trying to pierce through this crust, this shell of indifference, of willed ignorance in which men and women have, as it were, secluded themselves, of which they can no longer rid themselves.

And the divine Word succeeds in reaching them by way of this very orientation to suffering, to inaccessibility to oneself,

which continually threatens their life as now constituted, in its
unconscious but ineluctable tendency toward death.

The Word of God in no way brought either suffering or
death into the human world. It finds them there, as the certain,
the unavoidable consequence of sin. But it gives them the possibility of a new meaning. Let humanity accept in faith the rend-
ing detachment made inevitable by its impassioned attachment
to itself, to its most superficial self, and the individual could be
given back to love, to the *agape* of self-giving, which is a man
or woman's only real possibility of becoming, not the equal of
God but his living image, his child.

Yet, for this to come about, the love which the Word proclaims to individuals must be brought to them by that Word,
brought to them even in the depth of the abyss of refusing to
love opened up by sin in a world self-enclosed but parched by its
break with the living wellspring. The cross on which humanity
has crucified itself by its own sin would never save men and
women if Christ had not made it *his* Cross.

But now, by him, in him, the cross becomes for humanity
the only possible way out of these stifling cells in which its various idolatries have imprisoned it: out of the "flesh" in which
men and women are held fast by their idolatry of members of
the opposite gender (or rather of sex in the increasingly limited
sense in which fallen humanity tends to understand it); out of
the human city, which is nothing but the Babel of a will to power
reduced to a will to mutual enslavement; out of the "world," the
first and last idol which, while it seems to offer humanity everything, separates it from "the one thing necessary. . . ."

We see, therefore, that the choice is not between asceticism and humanism, between the cross of the Christian and
humanity's self-development. Humanity's self-development,
in the actual conditions in which its sin has placed it, of itself
leads men and women toward an inevitable confrontation with

suffering and death. And to sinful people left to themselves, as the literature which the divine Word has not illuminated unanimously testifies, this confrontation appears under a purely negative and therefore hopeless aspect. Whatever of good people discover in themselves and in the universe seems as if undermined by suffering, annihilated by death. The best that an individual can do, in religious philosophies such as Stoicism, is to resign himself or herself to what appears to be inevitable, feeling in a confused way that the root of all these evils consists in a mad and foolish opposition to the obscure but sovereignly good will that moves the universe.

The Word of God, once again, has in no way brought suffering and death into the world darkened by sin, the world in which it resounds anew, no longer as the creative Word but as the redeeming Word, the Word that sets free. It has found suffering and death in the world, and these are precisely the only fruits sin can produce. But it makes use of them as the seeds made ready by creative providence for the repairing of sin. It makes them love's ways of access—and it was by losing love that we were lost—to human beings who had closed themselves to love by closing in on themselves.

Chapter 7

THE ASCETICISM OF THE CROSS
AND THE DIFFERENT CHRISTIAN
VOCATIONS: LAY SPIRITUALITY

Our human condition is substantially the same for all—the condition of humans fallen by sin and raised up again by the grace brought to him by the divine Word. The ways of returning to God are, therefore, not only convergent but also analogous, even though they may not be exactly alike in every detail.

Yet to the diversity of persons and their situations correspond different types of vocations, different forms of life proposed by the same grace to one and another for the same purpose. It might even be said that every vocation is, in a sense, individual, as every person, every human destiny, is unique and irreplaceable. There are, nonetheless, different families of "charisms," different fundamental forms which grace may come to take among human beings, by which the same Spirit works differently in all the members for the good of the one body which they form together in the whole Christ. It is these different vocations, and the different concrete realizations by which the same redeeming grace carves out its ways in human life, which we now need to study.

The most serious error we could make here would be to imagine that there might be some ways of Christian life in which the cross would be present and even overwhelming, and others in which it would have little or no place. If we were to believe a certain school of thought—which has more and more adherents today, it would seem—while God sets apart certain persons to come to him by way of a negative, crucifying asceticism, He allows the great majority, on the contrary, to join him by way of a positive asceticism of self-development. . . . Such a supposition is based on a complete misunderstanding of what was explained in the previous chapter: that creation itself, inasmuch as it is fallen, makes the cross inevitable, and that the cross, in Christ, becomes salvation, the only possible salvation of creation. There cannot, then, be any "creative" vocations as opposed to "redemptive" ones. Every vocation is at the same time a vocation to the cross and a vocation to the resurrection, to the restoration of what God created good in the beginning and which must become so once again at the end. The cross must, therefore, be present equally in every form the Christian life can take. But there are many different ways in which the cross may be brought in.

The Various Christian Vocations

The great majority of men are certainly called to a certain provisional settling-down in the present world, through the accept acceptance of some task in the earthly city, the establishment of a family and, throughout all this, a free development of their natural abilities. At the other end of the scale, it would seem, is the vocation of the monk: of the man who has broken his bonds with the world by poverty, severed them, as it were, in his own flesh by celibacy, and renounced himself, his own will, by obedience. Yet, sooner or later, every man must abandon his goods, his family and the freedom to dispose of himself: the sufferings, the defeats inevitable in every life drive us closer and closer to this abandonment; and death sooner or later enforces it. Conversely, the monk renounces himself only to become himself, even here below, in a better sense and one which anticipates the resurrection. In the same way, his renouncement of earthly marriage allows him to anticipate the eschatological reality of the "marriage-feast of the Lamb," and his voluntary poverty renders him fit, as no one else here on earth, to be "an heir of God, co-heir with Christ."

The clerical and, in particular, the priestly vocation, engages a man in a paradoxical going and coming between what might be called the common lay vocation and that relatively exceptional lay vocation, the monastic. Like the layman who is not a monk, the priest, the cleric and anyone who has a special responsibility for the Church (by actively engaging in Catholic action), continues to live in the world; even though he is not called to marriage, he is called to the spiritual paternity which is quite as absorbing as (and perhaps even more absorbing than) natural fatherhood. Yet this implies requirements of detachment and personal purification as pre-requisite to its exercise— requirements which in their way are no less rigorous and may seem even more rigorous than those of the monk.

It is this that explains what is called the "religious" vocation in its various active rather than contemplative forms—in any case, its non-monastic forms. The great renunciations of the religious life are adopted, not directly for the sake of the spiritual welfare of the man who vows himself to them, but rather for the apostolate to which he feels himself called.

Nevertheless, the contrast should not be carried too far—and here least of all: for there is no fruitful apostolate without the personal sanctification of the one who devotes himself or herself to it, nor any true sanctification which does not put us at the service of other people, and, in particular, at the service of the Gospel which is addressed to them.

The Lay Vocation as the Vocation of the Baptized

The layman, in the true sense of the term as used in the Church, is not profane, un-sacred. On the contrary, he is one of the faithful: a person who, by his faith, has pledged himself in Baptism to the basic Christian requirements, common to all. At a second stage, it will be specified in each Christian life whether the individual's vocation does or does not involve the special realizations of the common Christian ideal which constitute the monastic life, the clerical life, or the different forms of the apostolic religious life. If, at this point, the answer to these various possibilities is in the negative, the counterpart will be a positive enhancement of the values of certain tasks which, for anyone not a Christian, might be called profane, but which, for the Christian, can no longer be such. This is true above all of the task of marriage which presents itself to him as the sacrament of the very mystery of Christ in the form which his life is called to take.

We need, therefore, first to examine the vocation of the layman in what it has in common with that of the monk, the priest, the religious—since this is and remains the foundation of everything that the layman who is simply a layman can further accomplish, just as it is and remains the basis for more specialized vocations. Then, and on this basis, the secondary elements of the lay vocation—those which would seem profane were he not also one of the faithful—will be seen in his case themselves to have become sacred.

The fundamental lay vocation, taking this in the sense of the vocation to be one of the people (*laos*) of God, is, then, the vocation common to all the baptized. Like every Christian vocation, this has a positive aspect: commitment to Christ, which inevitably (under pain of complete unreality) goes along with a negative aspect: renunciation of Satan. It must be noted that here, as in the vocations which seem more ascetic, renunciation comes first as the necessary pre-requisite to positive commitment. A person cannot belong to Christ if he or she continues to belong to Satan. True enough, Christ alone can free us from Satan finally and completely, but he will never free us unless we first consent to abandon Satan and to pay the price necessary to do so.

To clarify this still further, we need to remember that the traditional formula of renunciation applies to "the devil, and all his works and all his pomps."

To renounce Satan is to renounce the very principle of sin: adherence given to the suggestion of Satan, that is, to prideful revolt for the sake of satisfying material lusts erected into an absolute, with a rejection of the faith that would have us go beyond the sensible and immediate by obedience to the divine Word. To renounce Satan's works is to renounce particular sins, all the partial disobediences which follow on this original and generalized disobedience.

And to renounce what lies between these two, Satan's "pomps," is to renounce all the things, good in themselves, which he has managed to make into a trap, or, rather, into bait for the trap of disobedient unbelief in which he wishes to ensnare us and in which we have been ensnared. This renunciation means breaking with "the flesh," inasmuch as its disoriented

instincts fascinate us and desensitize us to the call of the divine
"Spirit." It means to break with the "world" inasmuch as its
organization is set up in secret or open opposition to the kingdom of God. In a word, it means to renounce every partial good
to the extent to which it has become, or tends to become, an
"idol" taking the place in our heart reserved for the only "good,"
the essential Good, who is God himself. . . .

The baptismal renunciation is thus an acceptance of the
cross, an acceptance which will henceforth mark our whole
life, whatever may be the particular mode it will take later on.

But this acceptance of the cross is simply the pre-condition
for the positive commitment to Christ which gives it its meaning by giving it its purpose.

In the commitment to Christ, we recognize afresh, in the
faith we give to the divine Word made flesh, the revelation of
the divine love that is seeking us, the love that was from the
beginning behind all these partial good things which have been
displaced, so to speak, so far as we are concerned, by the fraud
of the devil. The whole world should, then, once more become
the primary sign of the love which created us and which now
saves us, and the instrument of our glorification of God, of
the "thanks giving" which recognizes this love in all things and
which surrenders us to it in obedient faith. At the same time,
our body becomes once more the Temple of the Spirit. And
human society is here reborn, from the "mass of perdition" in
which it tends to coagulate, into the Church, the extension of
the society of the Trinity gathering together in the love which
is its proper life the common life of all created persons. The
elemental society of man and wife, in particular, and the family
which is its fruit, are revealed as the image of the union between
Christ and the Church and of its supernatural fruitfulness, and
more than an image—the providential way opened out from the

first design of creation to the supreme design of the redeeming and reconciling covenant.

Here it should clearly be noted that there is no question of contrasting renunciation of Satan with commitment to Christ as if they were two sets of realities which could be associated while remaining heterogeneous. Commitment to Christ, with all that it implies, will not be concretely realized except in and by real renunciation in act of Satan, his works and his pomps. And, equally, this renunciation is not possible except by reason of this commitment. It is in dying to self, to the "old man" of Adam's humanity, hardened in his sin, that the new man is born who is "Christ in us, the hope of glory." But if there were no new man, the death of the "old man" would be without hope: to seek it, to anticipate it would be nothing but senseless suicide.

The Lay Vocation as Vocation to Life "in the World"

If the layman, when he arrives at the age in which the possibilities open to him must be made specific in a series of choices defining his particular vocation, is led neither to the monastic vocation, nor to the clerical, nor to any of the forms of the apostolic religious vocation, then the choice of a profession and the commitment to the bonds of marriage, and so of a new family, should take on for him a positively Christian meaning.

Let us note, to begin with, that the determination of our place in existence is always made by the intersection, as it were, of one line which is the resultant of the external circumstances in which we find ourselves placed, with another line which is the resultant of our personal maturation in its most interior aspect, the most irreducible to any external determination—which is not to say (quite the opposite) that it does not have its own proper coherence and logic. For the Christian, the circumstances in which he finds himself placed become a sign of the will of God as this is clarified by the teaching of the Gospel. And his most personal attractions are seen as transposed and transfigured by the influence of the Holy Spirit established in the most intimate depth of his "heart," in the biblical sense of the word.

Work

Whether his vocation is intellectual or manual, whether he is inclined toward tasks of directing or of executing, or toward the most disinterested kinds of cultural work, he must, therefore, see his work as being ultimately the special form that "faith working through love" is to take in him. This means that he should make of the work for which he feels himself more and more particularly destined his own special way of living charity, that he should make it his self-gift to the creative, the generous design of God himself which at the same time is being opened out to him by this faith. This should take on a twofold meaning for him, subjective and objective, which cannot be divided in the concrete without thereby making charity unreal.

Under one aspect, each person's work should be for him his special opportunity to live in all his activities that charity which results from faith, arousing in us an act of thanks giving in which the whole being gives itself to God recognized in Christ. Under the other aspect, which cannot in practice be separated from the first, his task is to introduce this charity, from the point of his own insertion in the world, into the life of other men.

Under this aspect, everything that he does, in the most seemingly "profane" orders of activity, must be done in such a way as to break up the present organization of the world in view of the satisfaction of egotistic lusts which cannot help secretly warring against one another even when they provisionally aid one another. For the Christian, on the contrary, even through the very conflicts in which his fidelity to his faith will necessarily involve him with those who refuse it, his whole activity has no final purpose other than that of gathering all men, in so far as this depends on him, into the communion of God's charity. It is by giving this meaning, this ultimate purpose, to all his activities, it is in carrying them out concretely always in the light of this finality, that the Christian will make all his works an achievement of the charity which should be reigning first of all in his own heart.

If this is to be possible, it presupposes that the activity to which he devotes himself will be one that can be "supernatural-ized." Any activity, that is, which in itself involves sin or which leads to it as if inevitably, the Christian must ruthlessly avoid. But those which he may make his own can be consecrated in two different ways. They can be consecrated positively, in their positive human value: the enrichment that they can give, along their own proper lines, to his capacity and to the capacity of others to conceive and to carry out their vocation as children of God, called to live in the presence of the Father in a continual and total "act of thanksgiving." And they can also be consecrated negatively, simply by the abnegation they require, and so by the witness given to the cross, to its fruitfulness "in Christ": a wit-ness which they provide the Christian the opportunity to render by providing him with a cross which is peculiarly his own.

But when we leave the abstract order and come to con-sider particular cases, we see that in every Christian's activity these two possibilities are always as it were very closely overlaid. Experience shows that the activities which are the most positive from the first viewpoint, such as the loftiest cultural pursuits, are endowed with a fearsome tendency to turn themselves into come kind of idol-making. Thus, for the faithful Christian, they cause an internal tension perhaps more painful than any bitterness that might be connected with humbler kinds of work. And, consequently, they involve him in conflicts, in particularly tragic ruptures with those who are pursuing the same tasks without the same faith. . . .

On the other hand, there are servile forms of work which seem at first sight to have nothing but a trial of faith to offer the one who devotes himself or herself to them, so barren are they of positive human satisfaction. And yet frequently they may afford him or her opportunities for generous contact with others, so clear that faith and its witness can as it were already gain in them some foretaste of the eternal reward. The poor person who gives a cup of water to another poor person may find therein an immediate recompense, of a fullness (because of a purity) certainly surpassing those that the Christian artist, and still more the Christian politician, can find in any of his or her achievements.

More simply still, the more the horizons of any truly creative work are extended and broadened, the more it requires us continually to go beyond what we have already seen and achieved—a requirement which is without doubt one of the most crucifying forms that the cross can take on in our human life. The most ambitious, the grandest human works are those the achievement of which, even when relatively successful, and in proportion to their success, is the most unsatisfying, if not delusive. For the Christian who measures the always painful hiatus that separates every partial incarnation of creative charity from its absolute realization, and who knows further that his loftiest achievements, which are at best only provisional, can be changed into even more redoubtable obstacles in the path of the final realization of charity—this experience of the cross within human creativity knows no limits. . . .

Conversely, for the same Christian who knows the transcendent value of the "love of God poured out in our hearts by the Holy Spirit," the work most unrewarding from the human viewpoint, when it is the occasion for an act of pure charity, may perhaps become more luminous than the most glorious human achievements.

Whatever the task at which he labors, the Christian "in the world" must, therefore, believe that he is collaborating in the coming of the kingdom of God. But he must believe at the same time that the achievements which at first seem the most brilliant may reveal themselves as the most fragile and even the most deceptive, just as he must be convinced that the failures which seem the most irremediable enter into the plan of God and its infallible realization. It is here that he finds his cross, the cross which is his own: not aside from his work, but deeply within it.

Marriage

This paradox is, if possible, still more marked in the marriage of a Christian. For marriage, more than any of his professional tasks, consolidates his settling down in the world, and yet, if it is a Christian marriage, more than anything else it opens him out, while in this present world, to the world which is to come.

In marriage, the whole personality, indissolubly body and soul, perfects itself, completes itself, and so should here find its final unity, in another being. If it is successful, marriage is nothing at first sight but development. Yet the self-development of one of the participants in a marriage cannot be authentic unless it takes place concurrently with that of the other. And hereby the cross is more than ever brought into this very development.

For, if marriage is to be more than the superficial and basically discordant association of two egoisms, there must be

included in the possession of the other person, a radical dispossession of self. For a man thus to unite his life, his being,
to another life, to another being, is to communicate all that he
has, all that he is. The giving up of all one's goods, of one's own
body and, finally, of one's own will, which is at the basis of the
monastic profession is, in a certain way, equally at the basis of
the marriage pact. The husband who understands this Christian
meaning of his marriage—which is simply the supernatural
fulfillment of that toward which the natural reality of the union
of the sexes tends—knows well that he no longer has anything
which he can call exclusively his own. Another person possesses
together with him all that is his. He can dispose freely of none
of his goods—material, cultural or even spiritual. His own body
is no longer his own; he cannot expect to receive even those
joys to which marriage gives him full right unless he also gives
them; and he cannot claim them in the name of his personal
desire without making sure that his wife at the same moment
can yield whole-heartedly to that desire. More generally, he can
no longer dispose of his existence, his time, he can no longer
choose any of his occupations merely in respect to his own
will: at every moment this will must go out of itself, so to say,
renounce itself, make room in itself (and a determining one)
for the will of another person. . . .

Thus even on the hypothesis, humanly speaking chimerical, of a harmony as constant and close as can be imagined,
every generous marriage, and still more every Christian marriage formally established on the faith and lived in the charity
of Christ, requires a continual self-renouncement, a continual
relinquishing of self.

Obviously, this requirement will he increased by the inevitable imperfections of each of the two persons, the dissonances
which cannot help entering into their most profound harmony.
Even when you love and are loved as greatly as you wish, the

other person remains other. This is enough to impose an unre-
mitting sacrifice of self to the person to whom you are bound.
Furthermore, in the conditions in which sinful humanity finds
itself, otherness is inevitably colored with some hostility. There
is no union so well-matched as not to include many conflicts
about details, many unresolved and probably unresolvable ten-
sions, and, finally, a greater or lesser degree of mutual incom-
prehension, of mutual dissatisfaction. Unless this is to lead to a
break-up—or to a settling down in failure in which an interior
break-up is poorly concealed under the preservation of external
bonds—you must know how to accept all this, to integrate it
positively in your union, into your very life. What more abundant source of ever new sacrifices?

To those men and women who are most profound both in
the human reality of their earthly love and in the supernatural
reality of their life of faith, a community of life like that of marriage brings with it a cross that is still more intimately painful,
still more penetrating. This is the discovery that they make,
as they can make it nowhere else, of their own insufficiency.
We have to love another being more than ourselves to discover
painfully our own incapacity to love as we should love. Perhaps
no revelation of our insufficiency is more humiliating, more
desolating than the realization of the awkwardness, the mean-
nesses, even of the grossness, or simply of the painful emptiness
of the best of whatever we do (or believe that we do) in order to
prove, to express the generosity of our love. . . .

It is by reason of all this that marriage lends itself to being
a school of faith and charity which, if we have the humility to
accept all its teachings, can certainly lead to holiness. And it
is because of all this that the human reality of marriage is not
truly attainable except in the sacrament. For this is what makes
possible that faith—which must sometimes be heroic—in the
other person, that unreserved gift of self, which are the radical

requirements of every union which is ultimately to be for the good of those who have contracted it. For the sacrament of marriage makes this mutual faith a participation in faith in Christ and a concrete realization of this faith.

In all truth, in Christian marriage, to the eyes of faith the husband is Christ, the wife is the Church: that is, they give one another the strength continually to go beyond the inadequate appearance, the deceptive realization, of what they ought to be. And thus it is that the husband comes to love his wife as Christ loved the Church, in renouncing himself, in giving his whole life, day after day, ever anew, for her—just as the wife gives herself to her husband, lives only in him and in his life, as the Church lives in Christ. And this is not simply an "as if"; for those whom the sacrament has joined together, this is henceforth the basic means of realizing charity, "the love of God poured out in our hearts by the Holy Spirit."

All this finds, as it were, a supreme development, a decisive elevation, when the mutual love of marriage fructifies in a common love for the children.

Fatherhood and Motherhood

Fatherhood and motherhood are so essential to human development that, as we said earlier, in contrast to married love, they cannot, properly speaking, be sacrificed. Those who, in following a vocation that presupposes celibacy, renounce married love cannot for all that renounce fatherhood or motherhood. They are simply called thereby to undertake a higher form of parenthood, one not limited to the narrow circle of one particular family, but open to everyone.

What is certainly the most remarkable—and can become the most sanctifying—characteristic of marriage is the spontaneous way in which the exclusiveness, the essential single-mindedness of the affection it presupposes is of its nature called to open out. It must expand in the community of a new love, detached from the outset from those who are the subjects of it, and leading them to greater and greater detachments.

Certainly there are few experiences more exalting for a man than to see his own life in some way separating itself from him and, under his very eyes, taking on a life of its own—and even more so for a couple thus to project and incarnate their love. Yet this separation, this projection, are also the seed of greater sacrifices.

The husband and wife who have become parents find themselves, from the very beginning, drawn by force of circumstances more and more to transpose their love for one another into a common detachment. What unites them henceforth are cares, shared indeed, but cares of which the couple are no longer themselves the objects. That life in the other person, for the other person, which they had previously experienced separately, they must now come to experience together for one, for several third parties. They must, as it has been said, stop looking in one another's eyes so as to look together at what has become a separate reality from them.

But this is as nothing compared with the inevitable crisis brought on by the children's growing up. It is then, at the very moment when they see before them the finished product of their common efforts and anxieties, and at the moment also, ordinarily, when, as life wanes, the emotions have a tendency to become disturbed and so the more passionate—it is then that the parents must know how, through love, together to detach themselves from that object, those objects, on which all their best affections have been centered. To accept the fact that their child is himself and belongs to himself: that he no longer belongs to them—that he is arranging his life to suit himself, that he has his own loves in which his parents have no place, and, above: all, perhaps, that he no longer is *them*—that he has a moral character which undoubtedly proceeds from theirs, but which also radically escapes them, is different from them: this is perhaps the cross that is hardest to accept. But it is also the most necessary, if life is to attain its true maturity.

Death

Yet all these crosses of the layman who lives "in the world" without being of the world are only sketches, rough drafts, of the final, total, cross to which he must inevitably come at last—death.

Everything that the monk has renounced, the layperson must one day renounce, and everything the layperson has possessed that the monk has not will be the object of a sacrifice to that extent the greater and more painful. "One always dies alone," says Pascal. This is true, in a sense. But the one who has contracted earthly ties can, in another sense, no longer die alone, and he or she must die more than once.

The death of the person with whom we make but one single being is perhaps a more searching experience of death than the direct experience of it. It is like a living death: a death which we must carry in our own life, that we feel to the very depths since we feel it while still living. And, reciprocally, to die when it means leaving those whom we love, is to die in them as much and more than in ourselves. . . .

Furthermore, to the one who has labored in this world, death in some way anticipates the death of the universe: every work you have done now leaves you and you experience its dissolution, even though it will in fact continue to exist for some time after you are gone. For the one who is dying, this relative kind of survival, in one's work or in one's children—which affords some consolation, doubtless, to the one who is only, thinking about death in the future—now has no value. On the contrary, he or she dies only the more completely since all this, which was wholly his or her own but which can henceforth be nothing to him or her, is to survive. . . . For the lucid and faithful believer, this moment of death, or this moment when death is for the first time seen as imminent, is the moment of a sacrifice which, in purity and intensity, can be that of a martyr: it is, as it were, the entrance into that monastery of agony to which we are all called, the rigor of which no one else knows.

This wholly natural way in which the cross can be introduced, and is in fact introduced, into every Christian life pursued in the world should not make us suppose that such a life can do without voluntary asceticism. It must rather be said that the cross imposed by the natural course of events, on us as on Christ, only becomes a sanctifying, life-giving cross, to the extent to which it is freely accepted. This freedom of acceptance always makes some systematic asceticism necessary, and there can be no Christian life, in the world or relatively out of the world, which can dispense with it.

In the Gospel as in Judaism, the asceticism of the layman is made concrete in three practices, already formally grouped together in the book of Tobias and taken and illuminated by the Sermon on the Mount. These are: almsgiving, prayer, and fasting—three practices necessary to every faithful life, of which the practices of the monastic life might be considered as only the development and the deepening.

Almsgiving

Almsgiving, understood in the widest sense, comes first. No Christian life, whether of an individual or a family, can be pursued in a closed circle, or as if in a hermetically sealed jar. The life of the Christian family, like that of the individual Christian, should open out to the whole world, to all humanity. It should be poured out, as it were, in an overflowing of pure generosity, which will necessarily take the form of a renouncement, of a sacrifice with no immediate return. This is almsgiving: for there is no Christian, nor group of Christians, who can live within themselves, ignoring the rest of the Church, of the universe, or not concerning themselves with it. What seem, at first sight, the best of families may, if they fall into the delusion that they can be self-sufficient, and particularly the delusion that charity can be practised merely within the ambit of the family circle, become dried up, suffer a kind of sclerosis, a hardening: they suffocate their own members, and the love which seems to reign within them insidiously turns into a kind of monstrous collective egoism.

To reduce Christian charity to almsgiving alone, as is done in our way of speaking today, is certainly an abuse. Yet it contains at least a dim perception of the fact that there is no authentic charity where almsgiving is not practised. Still, we need to understand exactly what Christian almsgiving really means.

According to the Gospel, it must not, obviously, look for any publicity, or even for any gratitude. Still more should it be exempt from any "paternalism," from any tendency to bribe, even morally, those who are its beneficiaries.

Primarily, almsgiving should undermine and finally destroy the notion that we are the masters of our resources, even though we have produced them by our own work. Through continually influencing the use that we make of our money, almsgiving—whatever its extent or its mode—keeps us from putting our trust in what we possess, by keeping us from ever considering it as exclusively and thus entirely our own.

It does all this by obliging us always to live for others—in principle for all others, known or unknown, near or far—as well as for ourselves.

Almsgiving cannot be efficacious if it is limited to what we have over and above what we need. It must constitute a continually renewed occasion for real privations, which are felt as such. Only in this way can it keep us from ever putting our hope in our possessions—this, again, through forbidding us ever to consider them as our own.

It is also quite true that the "materiality" of our almsgiving must be only part of a true gift of self. This is the reason why almsgiving, since early Christian times and before that in Judaism, has been almost synonymous with the formula of St. James: "To visit widows and orphans in their affliction" (Jas 1:27). This is also why neither the progress of organized welfare-work nor even of "social security" can take the place of almsgiving, even though these may lead to some changes in the way it is to be carried out. So long as there are Christians in the world, they must open their hearts to the sufferings and needs of others, and they must spend themselves personally for others, showing by their deeds that they think of their goods as not only their own property, but as that of other people as well.

Prayer and Keeping Watch

If the love of God "whom we do not see," as St. John says, must, for the Christian in the world, find its permanent witness in a love for "his brother whom he does see" (Jn 4:20), a love

which costs him something, then this love must find in intimate
dialogue with God both its source and its direct manifestation.

We do not need, in this connection, to go over once again
the content and the forms of Christian prayer. But we need to
point out what an effort to recollect himself, to extricate himself
from the sea of the world, this prayer demands of anyone who
is immersed in that sea. Under the pretext that the ideal of the
Christian in the world should be to pray everywhere and in
everything that he does, some people have thought that they
could dispense themselves from the special times of prayer of
"professional" religious. There could be no grosser misunderstanding. It is the life in which everything is organized in function of prayer which can, if absolutely necessary, do without
moments especially consecrated to it. But the more a man is
engaged in the life of the world, the more imperious is his need
to leave that life at regular intervals, if he is not to be drowned
in it. And it is during these intervals that he must systematically
renew the sources of the life of prayer which, tacitly or more
or less explicitly according to circumstances, should tend to
permeate all the occupations, all the thoughts that these circumstances give rise to. His capacity to tend toward this ideal
will be in proportion to the regularity of his spiritual renewals,
and of the depth of his breathing in, his calling on, the Spirit
in these renewals.

Whence that insistence of ancient Christians writers such as
Tertullian on the obligation imposed on every Christian to take
at least a few minutes every night from the hours of sleep—to
escape the torpor of a soul too used to this world, wrapped up
in its work or buried in its repose.

Such a "vigil" has a symbolic value, and one that is far more
than symbolic, by reason of the effort it requires to rise at regular intervals above the sea of occupations and distractions,
to escape from being drawn into the ways of the world, from

being fascinated by its slogans. No practice is more essential, perhaps—although very few prove more difficult to carry out—than the keeping up, day after day, of these escapes to God, to his Word, than these periodic enterings "into our own room" where our heavenly Father is the only One to see us, and which alone permit us to see him.

The regularity, as well as the fruitfulness of these hours—or at least these moments—of "vigil" in which faith is renewed at its source, will be assured by the practice of making a retreat. If the person who devotes himself or herself to the work of this world feels a great need for physical and psychological vacations, should not a Christian feel a still greater need for such spiritual vacations? Seen in this light, the respect due to Sunday, the "day of the Lord," takes on its full meaning. Each Sunday should be the occasion for some brief recollection, linked up with the continuous chain of daily prayer, between the few days (as many as possible) of annual retreat, taken if possible, in complete solitude and quiet.

Fasting and Continence

Prayer is connected with fasting by Christ himself. For it seems that there must be a certain privation with regard to physical repletion in order to be disposed for spiritual food.

Today we are almost completely unused to fasting. We tend, unquestionably, in harmony with the cult of comfort in which our whole era involves us, not even to see the sense of fasting. And yet, to remain hungry from time to time and, more generally, to deprive oneself not only of what is superfluous, but even, for the moment, of a little of what seems necessary—this is, without any doubt, a practice essential for that liberation, that stripping of oneself without which we cannot give a certain degree of attention to God.

Thus fasting is especially connected with periods particularly sacred to prayer, such as Lent, and it is even more closely connected with the practice of almsgiving. St. Leo the Great, in his Lenten homilies, has brought this out with his own special clarity: what is given to our neighbor in alms should be taken from our own self-satisfaction by fasting. True almsgiving and realistic fasting should be simply two inseparable aspects of one and the same ascetic practice, in which charity is nourished by renunciation There is no Christian almsgiving, no sacrifice for others, which is, as it should be, a sacrifice of charity, unless its converse is some privation consented to, accepted joyfully. And, equally, what takes away from fasting the appearance of gratuitous mortification is to have as the immediate reason for denying ourselves the carrying out of some precise and, as far as possible, personalized act of generosity. It might even be said that the purifying efficacy of the mortification of fasting, and the impetus it gives to our prayer will be in function of the very concrete preoccupation with our neighbor and his needs that goes along with it.

Fasting itself is only an elementary form of that doing without, that abstinence which should hold in check the continually threatening unruliness of our desires; it should habitually cut down the idolatry with which all our pleasures, even the most legitimate, are fraught. We need, unwearyingly, to undo that accommodation to the world which here ensnares us and would speedily, if we yielded to it without resistance, stupefy us spiritually. The constraints proper to work of all kinds are particularly effective here (getting up at a regular time early in the morning, general self-discipline in the use of time, the greater or lesser impossibility of being one's own master in professional life, and still more, perhaps, especially for the mother, in family life, etc.). These, nevertheless, are not enough, particularly to counterbalance the softening effects of comfort and, more generally, of the pervasive sensuality in which contemporary civilization bathes us.

Yet we should also give this civilization due credit for the manful habits which it has brought back, to which we can give Christian meaning and value—for example, physical hygiene and exercise.

Water as a form of therapy—and particularly the generous employment of cold water—is for children, perhaps, the best and most natural means of initiation into asceticism. A well-regulated use of it can do great good to adults also, becoming a more healthy and efficacious practice than all sorts of artificial mortifications. The mystical wisdom of St. Teresa was quite down-to-earth enough to realize this fact.

More generally, the practice of some form of physical exercise, austere in itself and involving us in all kinds of effort and inconveniences, can provide material for self-discipline that is properly ascetic, in the sense that the word has taken on in spirituality.

Is it necessary, in this connection, to denounce the false asceticism (actually the routine and, to tell the whole truth, "bourgeois" sloth) which, in too many "religious" and clerical circles dresses up in empty formulae a simple lack of virility? There are too many communities in which the belief is still current that one unused or unusable bathroom is an indication of spirituality, too many seminaries in which it would seem as if the preparation for a self-sacrificing priesthood could take place only in an atmosphere of ammonia!

It goes without saying, however, (or it should) that the abstentions, the self-disciplining practised by every Christian are no less important in the field of sexuality than in that of comfort or food. To say this—contrary to what many people today tend to believe, thus artificially prolonging an adolescent kind of eroticism throughout their lives—is not to imply any condemnation of sexuality as such. Quite the opposite. The particular necessity for everyone, married or not, of sexual asceticism has been made the more imperative with the modern rediscovery of the centrality of sexuality in human sensibility (and in much more than sensibility alone). To the eighteenth and nineteenth centuries, which tended to see in sexual relations no more than a physical pleasure, in itself inconsequential, the unruliness of the sexual instinct might well seem of little importance. But to us, to whom depth-psychology has revealed the human fullness of every sexual experience, the traditional Christian statement of the case should no longer cause any difficulty.

In fact, while an asceticism of sensual privations is obviously imposed on those vowed to celibacy by their vocation, it would be naive to think that it is not needed by married people as well. From the moment that we admit what is at the basis not only of every Christian marriage but of every marriage that wishes to be fully human—that each person must find self-fulfillment in and by the fulfillment of the other—an asceticism of this kind is imposed. Each person's desires or inclinations must necessarily be kept well in hand and therefore restrained at certain times, out of respect for the desires and inclinations of the other. If one or the other does not know how to abstain at certain moments, then there will necessarily be the tendency to seek egotistical enjoyment, first apart from the joy of the other, then contrary to it.

It should also be noted, that the unruliness of all our desires, which is the consequence of sin, manifests itself in the field of sexuality particularly through the relative anonymity, the impersonality of desire. Fidelity to husband or wife cannot, therefore, be preserved without the disciplining of desire, and this cannot be acquired or retained without a certain practice of deliberate abstinence. The person who is accustomed to give in immediately to any desire, even one which is in principle legitimate, will one day, almost inevitably, come to give in also to illegitimate desire.

And, finally, it is indisputable that, among all our activities, spiritual as well as physical, sexual love is one of the most absorbing in our whole psychology. This is in no way to condemn it, but rather to recognize what constitutes its grandeur and, at the same time, its danger for the sinful beings we are; it will in no way spoil or paralyze the healthy and pure exuberance of married love if husband and wife deprive themselves of its natural manifestations from time to time, by mutual consent. On the contrary, as having become the object of a truly free consent, of a personality which has achieved self-mastery, such deprivation cannot but bring to the affection of husband and wife a new depth, a more integrally human beauty, and so a new worth.

This particular kind of fasting, while it will give to married persons the opportunity of coming nearer to God in that solitude which is the condition *sine qua non* of a deepening of prayer, will give them at the same time a new power of spiritualizing their union itself. This is not to say, however, that it should necessarily tend to become discarnate in order to progress and be deepened. But there is no doubt that what is of the flesh must, if it is to acquire the spiritualization of which it is capable, first be mastered, rather than be allowed to enslave everything in the marriage relationship.

Moderation in Self-Discipline

Whatever be the form of asceticism that one has in mind, it must never be forgotten that it always remains a means in the

service of an end: the domination of our lusts, disordered by
egotism, in the service of charity, of generous love. Consequently, it is not the number of ascetic practices, still less their
obviousness, nor even their difficulty, that is important in the
Christian life. It is the clear-sighted generosity with which they
are used, always regulated by the end we have in view. Here
there is no general law. Each person must test himself, little by
little, must come to know the disciplines which are effective for
him, and the rhythm of applying them which is best adapted
to further his own spiritual progress, and act accordingly. Not
the least gain from his efforts, furthermore, will be the practical
knowledge of himself which he will attain by the constant, but
never strained, concern to find this personal balance and ceaselessly to reestablish it. For all the ancient ascetic writers, "discretion"—that is, discernment in the application of asceticism
to one's own life—is in this regard at once the key and the test.

For married people and, more generally, for all those whose
life is closely bound up with that of others, it goes without
saying that the inevitable repercussion on these other persons
of what we ourselves practice must always be taken into consideration, and even to a determining extent. Abstention, even
of a kind which might be beneficial for us under other circumstances, can never be so if it becomes for other people a
frustration of what they need, or, quite simply, of what they
have a right to. And still more, any asceticism will turn into
pharisaical hypocrisy if it expresses itself by positively incon-
veniencing others. Certain "saints" in embryo who candidly
believe that the perfume of their virtues is ascending to heaven
would do well first to make sure that it does not seem a stench
to their neighbors!

Chapter 8

THE ASCETICISM OF THE CROSS
AND THE DIFFERENT CHRISTIAN
VOCATIONS: MONASTIC
SPIRITUALITY

The monastic vocation is understood only in part or not at all by most Christians today. Even so, a renewal of monasticism has become evident in the Church during recent years, while Christians in greater and greater numbers, even in countries like the United States in which such a phenomenon would seem unlikely, often feel themselves irresistibly attracted by an ideal of which they often have only a very confused notion.

This situation has a number of causes. Obviously, the materialism of our civilization tends both to becloud for the great mass of Christians the sense of what a monastic vocation represents, and to revive the need for it among the best Christians. It should be added that in the West, at least since the high Middle Ages, the variety of "religious" vocations has grown greater and greater, with the result that there has been a tendency to lose sight of the monastic vocation as such. The modern Code of Canon Law reflects this situation: while there is abundant mention in it of "religious" in general, there is not one single prescription, not even a definition, that applies to the monk in particular.

Yet it would be quite extreme, not to say erroneous, to conclude from this that the Church in the West has lost all appreciation of the values proper to the monastic life. A papal document such as the Bull *Umbratilis*, addressed by Pius XI to the Carthusians, is sufficient to show that this is not so.

It should be added that, if the Christian East has preserved even to our times a much more precise sense of the monastic life than the one current in the West, nevertheless the reality of monasticism, during the last two or three generations, has been threatened by almost complete disappearance. Even more than has been the case with Catholic Action movements in the West, the movements of apostolic renewal in the East have had the unfortunate consequence of eclipsing, in the eyes of the most fervent young Christians of these countries, the prestige—so long unequalled—of the monastic life. The holy Mount of Athos has been depopulated with a frightening rapidity during the last decades. Other monasteries, and those the most fervent, find themselves rent by the more or less activist aspirations of some of the religious. . . . But, in return, the secret maintenance and, later, the resurrection of monasticism in Russia is a striking phenomenon. The same thing must be said of a renaissance proclaimed in Romania, in Lebanon and among the Copts of Egypt. . . . It is amazing to see, wherever traditional monasticism is reborn in these countries which first saw its birth, common aspirations arising throughout, which are also those permeating the monastic revival in the West, among the Benedictines as well as the Cistercians.

Everywhere, in fact, monasticism's self-rediscovery is being carried out by way of a "return to the sources" that refocuses attention on the essentials.

Flight from the World and the Salvation of the World

What certainly makes it difficult for many Christians today, even very fervent Christians, to appreciate monasticism is that it is without any question a flight from the world. Is this not opposed to the Christian ideal of saving the world? Others go further and say that behind monasticism lies a hatred of the world opposed to the love (so fundamentally biblical) of the world as a divine creation. And thence it is only a step to maintaining or suspecting that monasticism involves, if not a more or less hidden Manicheism, at least a conception that is more Platonic (or Neo-Platonic) than Christian. . . .

What we have already said about the indubitably biblical and Gospel sources of all Christian asceticism should suffice to dissipate such harmful simplifications. To choose, or to believe that we have to choose, between love of the world and hatred of the world is to have no understanding of the paradox inherent in the Gospel. St. John expresses it more frankly than anyone else when he says: "Do not love the world, nor anything that is found in it . . ." with this explanation: "The whole world is in the power of the Evil One," while he also states explicitly: "God so loved the world that He gave his only Son, so that anyone who believes in him will never perish but will have everlasting life" (1 Jn 2:15 and 5:19; Jn 3:16).

This means that our attitude toward the world cannot be a simple one, for, according to the point of view from which it is considered, it appears to Christians under two aspects, not only different, but completely contrary. If we consider the world as it was in the beginning and as it is to become, it goes without saying that it is God's creation, that it is good in itself, and that we should love it as does God himself to the point of sacrificing ourselves for it. But if we consider the world as it has become in consequence of sin—not in the least the world God willed nor the one He made, but the one we have made by our sin—we must recognize that it is the enemy of God and so our enemy, and that I it must, as such, be overcome by the victory which St. John also speaks of, the victory which is our faith (1 Jn 5:4–5).

Since the world is organized against God, it imprisons us within the circle of its disobedience. We must begin then by breaking out of this circle in order once more to find God. In other words, we must not only flee the world but conquer the world in order to free ourselves. It is when we have thus conquered it, when we are no longer enchanted by it, that we can effectively concern ourselves with freeing it. Therefore, far from opposing the flight from the world to the salvation of the world, we must begin by fleeing it, by keeping our distance from it, to be in a position to work at saving it. We do not love the world with a truly realistic love unless we begin by hating it: we must hate the world as it is precisely because we must love the world as God willed it. Only thus can we give it the witness of that saving, re-creating love with which God has never ceased to love it. The slaves of the world, by their love which is mere spineless adulation, can only complete its ruin. Those who are free of the world, and they alone, can contribute to its salvation.

Every Christian should, therefore, at once work to free himself from the world and to save the world from itself. In spite of appearances, the two, far from contradicting one another, must go together. But everyone is not called to break off all his ties with the world at the outset, even though everyone must dissolve them sooner or later.

This is the difference between the properly monastic vocation and the general Christian vocation. We cannot even say that the one consents to renouncements which the other can avoid, for the monastic vocation consents from the outset to the renouncements to which every faithful Christian must sooner or later come.

We should recall that, in the earliest ascetic writings, asceticism in general appeared as a preparation for martyrdom. One renounced certain things freely in order to be able to renounce everything when necessary. Thus the monk advances the moment of making the great renouncements to which death will bring us all. And again we should add that he only anticipates death by faith so as equally to anticipate, so far as possible, the resurrection. The essential complement of the monastic renunciations, of anticipating one's liberation from the bonds of the world, is actually the possibility of attaining—also and to the same extent by anticipation—a foretaste of eternal life. For every Christian, it might be said, the degree of his effective participation in the cross during the present life is also the degree of his experience of the life of the Spirit, and thus a real anticipation of the life of the resurrection. This is what puts him in a position to collaborate effectively with the Risen Christ in the diffusion of the Spirit throughout the world, and so to contribute to its salvation.

Counsels and Precepts

But before all these perspectives are opened out we need to go more deeply into the distinction between the counsels and the precepts which is at the base of the monastic as of every religious vocation. Although this distinction was clearly defined only during the Middle Ages, it was nevertheless clearly perceived by the ancient monastic writers. It can, in fact, be deduced from the evidence of the Gospel itself.

Jesus proclaimed "Blessed are the poor," but He clearly did not prescribe total destitution. He did, however, actually ask this of certain men. To the rich young man, who had practised, or who believed himself to have practised, all the commandments since his youth (let us say that he had not positively transgressed them), Jesus said: "One thing is lacking to you: go, sell all that you have and give it to the poor: you will have treasure in heaven; then come and follow me . . ." (Lk 18:22). Again, St. Matthew's Gospel does not hesitate to have him say: "There are those who have made themselves eunuchs for sake of the kingdom of Heaven. He who can understand this, let him understand" (Mt 19:12). And just previously He had said: "All will not understand this word, but only those to whom it is given" (v. 11).

A little further on, the same evangelist also relates the story of the rich young man. But, while Jesus had preceded the recalling of the commandments, negative and positive (including "thou shalt love thy neighbor as thyself") with the phrase: "If you wish to enter into life," He said "If you wish to be perfect . . ." before his demand for renouncement (Mt 19:17 and 21).

How shall we understand these different texts?

There is a simple explanation, a first sketch of which can be found in the *De officiis* of St. Ambrose. He compares these two series of Gospel requirements with the Stoic distinction between *kathekon* and *kathorthoma*. On the one hand, the *officium medium* represents the strict minimum without which we are excluded from everlasting life. On the other, it is the *officium perfectum* which leads to the fullness of that life.

This line of reasoning runs the risk of actually ending up in a two-level morality: one reserved for the great mass, condemned to stagnate forever in a radical inferiority; the other reserved for an elite, who practice a superior kind of morality and so have a right to superior rewards. And, let us not forget, the Church will never agree to canonize such a distinction, which too closely resembles that made by the Gnostic sects between the merely "psychic" and the truly "spiritual" Christians.

The fact is that, since the Sermon on the Mount, the search for perfection cannot be facultative. It belongs to the very essence of the commandment as it is revealed not to be limited to "thou shalt not kill," etc., but to include both the interior obligation and the positive call to love God above all things. Thus not to concern oneself with perfection is not to concern oneself with the commandments themselves.

Here is the first point which must be clearly brought out: the practice of what we have come to call the evangelical "counsels" is not ordered to a "perfection" of a higher order than that to which the "precepts" themselves are ordered. It is ordered precisely to the perfection *of the precepts*, and, we must add, this "perfection" flows in principle from the precept itself, is included in its requirements.

If this be the case, the question might be asked; why are not the counsels imposed on everyone? Two things are to be said in answer. The first is that the "counsels" belong to the order of means and not to that of ends. The precept is established in reference to the end, and the means is included in it only indirectly and secondarily—supposing that the precept were carried out to perfection without the use of the counsel, the perfection achieved would be thereby no less perfect (as, conversely, a use of the means which in fact did not lead nearer to this perfection would have no value).

The second point is that the "counsels" are not applicable always and by everyone, any more than they are, of themselves, infallible in achieving the end. To live one's whole life in continence or in strict poverty is a gift not given to everyone. And, furthermore, to live in this way is not sanctifying of itself and by itself. The will must also be applied clear-sightedly and perseveringly to the end which it had in view in taking this means. And, equally, the married person or wealthy person who achieves the perfection of charity through the circumstances of his or her own life, is, *ipso facto*, far closer to God than the monk who does not.

But to achieve this perfection, such a person must actually have followed, as is commonly said, if not the letter, at least the spirit of the counsels. Yet we should dwell a little on the legitimate meaning of this expression which is sometimes used in an entirely equivocal and deceptive sense. When St. Paul himself speaks of "using the world as if one did not use it," he is not proposing a "purely spiritual" asceticism as opposed to a "material" one. To renounce "in spirit" something which one does not in some way or other renounce in fact is actually only a delusion. There is nothing purely "spiritual" in man, and nothing about him can be less "purely spiritual" than his asceticism, because the necessity for it follows precisely from this indivisibly material and spiritual life of ours with the added factor of the relative immersion of the "spiritual" in a disoriented "material" which is the always present consequence of the fall.

Consequently, the layman will not practise "the spirit of the counsels" by practising them "spiritually," which means nothing, but rather by practising them from time to time instead of practising them all the time. He will give alms, he will keep vigil, he will fast, he will impose on himself periods of sexual abstinence; above all, perhaps, he will often do the will of those with whom he is concerned rather than doing his own, even though he remains in principle the master of his life and goods and has a wife and children.

What distinguishes the monastic life from ordinary lay life is not, therefore, even the practice of the counsels, but is a commitment to a constant practice of them, at least of those which can be the object of a lasting promise: poverty, chastity carried out by celibacy, obedience. But, for the monk himself, the counsels are only a means, and it is in view of the perfection of the precepts that he uses the counsels; lacking this, the practice of them would lose all its Christian sense.

In return, even when a Christian is not pledged to a way of life which presupposes the constant practice of certain of the counsels, it is still necessary for him to practise them to the extent to which it is evident, *hic et nunc*, that this is imposed in order that his search for the perfection of the precepts—a search imposed on all by the Sermon on the Mount—may not be a sham. For all men must tend with all their strength to love God above all things and their neighbor as themselves, and this is impossible unless, at least at certain times and under certain circumstances, we follow the counsels to the letter.

The Monastic Way of Life: the Monastic Vocation

Yet we have not got to the root of the matter if we make the monastic way of life consist only in the adoption of what is called pre-eminently "the way of the counsels," that is, the continual practice of effective poverty, of strict chastity, of obedience. This "way of the counsels" actually applies just as much to the various forms of the religious life which successively appeared during the Middle Ages in the West, as to the monastic life. Conversely, this life existed and even had perhaps its most perfect flowering, not, certainly, before the three great counsels had been practised in this way, but well before they had been isolated, considered apart from all the rest of the ascetic life.

For the ancient monks, the monastic way of life certainly implied irrevocable self-commitment to the constant and strict practice of the three counsels, but also and primarily it implied something both vaster and simpler. The monastic way was defined by a radical application to the whole of existence of the statement of the Epistle to the Hebrews that here below we are "strangers and pilgrims . . . having no abiding city, but seeking that which is to come" (Heb 2:13, 13:14). Hence, even if the monk is in fact fixed by the vow of stability in a monastery chosen once for all (as in the Benedictine Rule), his is to be a nomadic existence, and one of eagerness for the desert—which makes it almost the exact opposite of such a life as found in a world that tends with all its weight toward settling down, becoming established. The life of a nomad, or, if you prefer, of detachment from everything that tends to root one down, and the correlative attraction of the desert, the only place in which, by definition, nothing is fixed and settled because no one can settle down in it—this is the impulse which is at the basis of every monastic vocation. And the properly monastic way of life is defined, concretized, by everything that makes for encouraging and satisfying this aspiration.

It is also necessary, obviously, that this nomadism have the motivation given it in the Epistle to the Hebrews, the search for "the city whose foundations are eternal"—in other words, faith, in the sense of that Epistle. This is perfectly illustrated by the teaching of Cassian, who makes the monastic life consist in the progressive realization of a threefold detachment. The first, the initial detachment, is from all our possessions, from all the attachments which, once again, not only fix us but root us in the present world. The second, which gives the first its purpose and its immediate justification, is detachment from the whole egoistic, sensual, proud life which is that of sin. The third, in which the first and the second are developed together, is a supreme detachment from everything which is not God and his kingdom, in order to attain the one and the other as speedily as possible.

In other words, as Cassian affirms along with the whole monastic tradition (remarkably formulated and explained before Cassian with regard to this point by Gregory Nazianzen), the monk is he who continues that wandering which began with the call of Abraham (Gn 12), was carried on by the Exodus of the Hebrew people from Egypt, and then by the Babylonian exile. He makes his own the new and supreme "Exodus" of Christ in his death on the cross (cf. Lk 9:31) which must mean, finally, according to the Epistle to the Hebrews, our abandonment of the earthly Jerusalem, as of every earthly city, to join Christ on the cross "outside the walls" and, going with him beyond the very limits of the world—those *flammantia mænia mundi*, the flaming walls of the world, of which the Latin poet speaks—to attain the heavenly sanctuary, the very presence of the Father.

Within the Constantinian Church, which had (at least apparently) made peace with the world, the monks, as St. Gregory Nazianzen emphasizes, were like the Recabites, the sons of Jonadab, who did not consent to become sedentary, to settle down, even in the promised land, but who, in their intransigent fidelity to the imageless God who had first of all been the God of the desert, never ceased to live in their tents.

The text of Cassian just mentioned leads us also to an important distinction with regard to that anticipated death which is the monastic life. Actually, the monk does not, properly speaking, anticipate death. What he can anticipate, so that death when it comes will not be a defeat, and an irremediable one, but the victorious liberation which immediately prepares for the resurrection—what he can voluntarily anticipate are the detachments that death will require of us and that it will accomplish with a thoroughness that can only be approximated here below:

detachment with regard to the world, with regard to one's own flesh, with regard to oneself (the egotistic and pleasure-seeking "I," taken captive as it is by the pride of the rebel "powers").

These detachments called for by faith put us in a position to overcome the power of sin within us by "the love of God poured out in our hearts by the Holy Spirit" (Rom 5:5). And then this life, of which *agape* has taken complete possession, which death will only consummate in *agape*, anticipates the resurrection itself in its intimacy with God.

As the rule of St. Benedict so forcefully emphasizes, it is finally, the search for God—seeking to meet God and to meet him immediately—taking hold of everything in us and doing away with everything else for us: this search and this alone constitutes the meaning of the monastic life and justifies its renouncements. Certainly, every Christian must seek God. But the monk is he who is possessed by the desire to find him and with so great an urgency that he abandons everything else for its sake: he no longer seeks him, as we must inevitably begin by doing, in and through his creatures, but, to the extent that is possible in this life, beyond his creatures and in himself.

Let us make it clear once again that this abandonment of all things is only provisional: in seeking the King, we cannot help also seeking his kingdom, his universal kingdom. But, because the shortest way to the kingdom is the way leading straight to the King, the abandonment of the fallen world is also the most direct way to the world that has been saved.

The Monastic Vocation
and the Common Vocation

Yet how can it be that certain persons are called to this short and narrow way, while God leaves the multitude to travel a road which is slower and less difficult (at least in its first stages)? Two determining motivations for a monastic vocation can be distinguished. They may be perceived separately, sometimes one and sometimes the other consciously predominating. But, in the depths of the soul, the two are always connected.

In the first place, there are those whole-hearted persons— passionate if you will—who have found out from experience that they cannot attempt to "use the world as if they did not use it" without being consumed in it. It becomes clear to them sooner or later that the monastic vocation is simply the form which the Christian vocation itself must necessarily take in their case. St. Bernard is, perhaps, an eminent example. It is impossible to imagine him married, the father of a family, a saint in the world along the lines of St. Louis, nor even, perhaps, what is called "a good Christian." Impassioned, looking for integration by instinct, he could not have bound himself to beings of flesh and blood without making idols of them. For him, the cloister was the same thing as salvation.

This is what explains the question: "What does one have to do to be saved?", so common among the early monks, as if this were the unique purpose of the monastic life (which is quite different from saying that the monastic life is the only means of being saved).

But there is another motivation for the monastic vocation, no less ancient than the preceding, and this was given as a justification of asceticism, particularly by Origen, even before the existence of monasticism. This is the direct call to contribute to the salvation of the world, to its deliverance from the rule of the Evil One, by delivering oneself from his rule. In strict fidelity to the Gospel accounts of the temptation of Christ in the desert, this appeal becomes concrete in the idea strongly inculcated by Origen that: each demon overcome by a particular ascetic is thereby deprived of his power to disturb other men. Put in this way, the idea may seem very strange. But it only expresses the assurance—profoundly mysterious but absolutely certain, according to the Scriptures (confirmed, moreover by the deepest spiritual experience)—that there is a rigorous solidarity in the spiritual life of all humanity. If the dogma of original sin affirms this with regard to sin, the dogma of the mystical Body affirms it still more strongly with regard to holiness.

Even more profoundly, it can be said that notwithstanding the existence of personal freedom and responsibility, the whole spiritual universe is ruled by this mysterious solidarity. Nothing happens in the most secret places of any conscience which does not have its repercussion on all other consciences. And we are even to think that our exterior apostolic activities only touch the consciences of others as it were from without, while our most interior spiritual struggle aids them mysteriously but very really from within: in opening them and aiding them to open themselves out, as if by the spontaneous sympathy of the *agape* poured out in our hearts, to the Spirit from on high who alone can drive out the spirit of evil.

Thus St. Thérèse of Lisieux, who expresses with such vigorous clarity the missionary sense of her penitential and contemplative vocation as an unknown Carmelite, only faithfully echoes that Christian instinct already formulated by Origen, in quite a different way, but with the same decisiveness.

But, to repeat, in every case these two motivations for the monastic vocation are more or less closely associated. It is because a man understands that he requires a life of detachment in order to come near to God that he feels called in this way invisibly to come near to other men. And, conversely if the concern for his own salvation, to be attained cost what it may, makes a man indifferent to the salvation of others, he has completely misunderstood the nature of Christian salvation.

But, above all, let us repeat, in every authentic monastic vocation, the search for God—seeking him as a Person, at the price of all the sacrifices which He may ask and which one believes that He now does ask—is behind the search for salvation, for oneself and for other men. There is no true monk who is such only in order that he himself will be saved sooner or later, or in order that others will be saved at last. On the contrary, it is of the essence of the monastic vocation that it be a desire to meet God, not only later on but from now on, and in consequence, whether one knows it or not, to hasten as it were the outpouring of the Spirit upon the whole world.

And this is where another motive appears that underlies the vocation to the monastery like the vocation to martyrdom: the precise call to give witness. The monk, like the martyr, is a witness and, like the martyr, it is not by his word that he gives his witness except in exceptional cases: it is by his life, his whole life. He witnesses, for the Church and in the world, to the reality, and the present reality, of the Spirit. Committing himself wholly to, sacrificing everything for this reality, this actuality, he witnesses to its supreme value in a world that does not understand it. And, for the Church, he is the anticipation here below of what she is tending toward in eternity. Without the monastic vocation, without the monastic life lived under their eyes, without the possibility of visiting monasteries and of immersing themselves therein from time to time, the Christians who live in the world would infallibly be absorbed therein. If the Church did not have the monastery within her, it would be as though the apostolic community of Pentecost had not had

Mary in its midst; the Church would be seized by the spirit of the world, would forget to seek and to call without ceasing on the Spirit of God, would forget that the life of the Spirit can and should be a reality for us here and now, the life in which the eschatological life of the kingdom is as it were anticipated.

One more question arises: how does a monastic vocation actually reveal itself? We can answer this question by recalling what was said about every particular Christian vocation. It is always made by the intersection of motivations that are purely interior, spontaneous, resulting from our deepest freedom restored by the contact of the Spirit with the most intimate depths of our soul, with motivations springing from the circumstances by which divine providence itself is guiding us. There are cases in which one or the other of these aspects predominates.

Some persons, even before they knew that such things as monasteries existed or exactly what they were, felt an irresistible attraction toward the life of dispossession, toward intimacy with God. Others, by contrast, who at first seem avid for life and for everything that draws us to it, through the very events of their lives are as it were irresistibly guided toward the cloister. If the romantic vision of the monk who has become such out of disappointed love is an over-simplified caricature, it is quite true that certain people need as it were actually to have experienced the vanity of the idols we fashion for ourselves if they are to realize the unique value of God alone. Of others, on the contrary, it might be said that it is the very purity of an affection denied by circumstances or destroyed by death which leads them to go beyond it, perhaps when they are threatened by despair. And still others, without seeing so clearly, are led by indubitable indications to accept a way of life where nothing, humanly speaking, attracts them, in the conviction, slowly imposed, that this is the only path on which God awaits them. . . .

Continence and the
Awakening of the Soul

Seen in these their proper perspectives, monastic poverty, chastity and obedience provide as it were the scaffolding or the armature of a life ruled by continence *(enkrateia)* in the ancient meaning of the word. This should be understood in the most general sense of resistance to the exaggerated desires of fallen human nature, so as to regain the dominion of the spirit within us (the Spirit of God taking possession of our spirit) over the sensible impressions (the *pathe,* or the "passions" in the sense that the seventeenth century still gave to this word).

The *enkrateia* of the monk, as the early writers say, should result in *apatheia.* This, in the sense given to it in monastic literature and especially in Evagrius, is by no means insensibility. On the contrary, it is the mastery of our sensibility by charity, *agape*, in a soul given up in complete obedience to the demands of faith. Such a soul henceforth, instead of being the plaything of its greedy sensibility, is wholly subject to divine love and has brought even its body into such subjection. It has not, for all that, arrived at some unthinkable state of impeccability, but it knows better than anyone else that it subsists only in and by the grace of God, to the degree to which its faith working through charity has effectively given up to love everything within it.

Enkrateia, consequently, is applied systematically to all the ways by which the *pathe,* the sensible impressions, which, in the man who simply lets himself live, rule his egotistic will and reinforce it, or rather stiffen it more and more. Poverty brings the monk back to the satisfaction simply of his elementary needs, and these are held in check and still more tightly reined in by the practice of fasting. Chastity, or rather complete continence, disengages his will from burial in carnal pleasure. This goes together with vigilance, understood in the strictest sense of the term: struggle against the propensity to stifle conscience in a sleep where, in a voluptuous impulse to dissolution, it abandons all its cares, all its disturbing aspirations, for the sake of the false peace of the carnal person here also buried in sleep. The ascetic is, and seeks to be, a person fundamentally awake (*neptikos*), one whose conscience has been rescued from forgetfulness, from the true death of the spirit in which we are buried by life in this world. It goes without saying that such vigils are wholly taken up with reading and meditation of the divine Word: the monk only detaches himself from, he only divests himself of, these heavy grave-cloths in which he has been wrapped up by the world and the flesh, in order to listen anew, with a free and docile heart, to the divine voice which does not cease to call even the man who has become insensible to its appeals.

This is why the final foundation of *enkrateia*, of self-mastery, consists in the self-abandonment—the loss of self assured by obedience. Man wished to be wholly his own master, and became in fact the slave of the flesh and of the world—that is, of the devil, of sin, of death. He cannot be given back to himself, to his true self which is the divine image within him, except by submitting himself once more to the constraining hand of God upon him. But in order to reach a man where he is buried in the creatures which he no longer encounters except under the aspects that flatter his pleasure-seeking egoism, God will make himself heard only through the medium of those who are his witnesses in this world: those prophetic voices which speak of the one who has imposed himself on them, first in spite of themselves and then within the most intimate depths of their hearts, just as now he is to speak and impose himself on this man. A living obedience to the tradition of the spiritual masters who, in the Church, are keeping the divine Word living and present, must, then, go together with faithful meditation on that Word, in the watchfulness which rescues us from this world asleep in the depths of its enervating pleasures, and the detachment which frees us from its service which is slavery.

The first form of monastic obedience was, in fact, this docility (again spoken of by Cassian) in following the teachings of the ancients, that is, in applying the divine Word to one's own life in living conformity with the example and the teaching of tested "spiritual men." This was very early more strictly defined as consisting in recourse to a spiritual Father, to a monk who was himself fully formed, fully given up to the Spirit of God. For the spiritual Father—whatever may be the authority, in principle absolute, with which, it is said, the religious novice should submit himself to him—never seeks to make his disciple his possession. He simply guides the neophyte toward the "discernment of spirits" to which he himself has been guided by his own effort of faithful obedience. He teaches him to distinguish the attractions which really come from the divine Spirit from the subtle temptations of the demon, or simply from the hypocritical assertions of his own will. The formation by obedience, the crucifixion of self-will in which obedience consists, has no other purpose, therefore, but the restoration of true freedom, the freedom of those immediately led by the Spirit of God. We shall return later to this most important point when we come to speak of progress in the spiritual life.

To conclude for the moment, let us emphasize that all the detachments, all the self-liberation of the monk are ordered thus to awaken in him that higher consciousness, that depth or high point of the soul by which God holds him, but from which he has been estranged by his disordered desires, benumbing him, enfeebling him, with the mirage of satisfaction ceaselessly deferred. . . . This is the meaning of the essentially uncomfortable, continually poised, kind of life which the monk requires himself to live: not to sleep, not to fall asleep again, and, even at the price of a painful vigil, to revivify and ceaselessly to keep awake the heavy and hardened heart which the heart of humankind born of Adam has become.

The Spiritual Combat and Interior Peace (*Hesychia*)

Already in St. Paul, the effort of the ascetic is presented as a perpetual combat. Or, to be more precise, asceticism is the spiritual exercise, the gymnastics, which train and harden us for the spiritual combat. In this combat of the "new man" to overcome the "old man" and take his place, as St. Paul again says, "Our struggle is not with flesh and blood, but with the principalities, the powers, the rulers of this world of darkness, the spirits of wickedness that are in the high places" (Eph 6:12).

In antiquity, this aspect of struggle with the forces of evil was the essential aspect of the cross of Christ. And so it is also the deepest aspect of asceticism, and particularly of monastic asceticism. In all its hardships, in its sufferings generously undergone, in the real death to the world and to self that it implies, it is wholly oriented toward the spiritual combat. And we must understand this phrase in the fullness of its primitive meaning. "Spiritual combat" does not mean simply "interior combat"; the question is one of warfare against spiritual enemies, or, still better, of warfare between two spirits in which the stake is ourselves, but in which we cannot remain passive: the warfare waged within us by the Spirit of God against the spirit of evil.

We cannot pass rapidly over this last point. For it is one of the characteristics by which the true monk, in contrast to one who is still only a novice, is distinguished from the ordinary Christian. The latter also struggles against the devil, but the devil does not usually fight against him openly. The ascetic, the monk, on the contrary, forces the devil to unmask himself. Thereby he carries the struggle to a depth within himself which the layman knows nothing of, and which it is doubtless better that he should not know, for it would fill him with a vertigo against which he would have no effective defense.

Against the monk as against everyone else, the devil certainly uses all the weapons, or rather the intermediaries, which are familiar to him and by means of which he overcame humans in the beginning, These are: the world (in St. John's sense), the flesh (in St. Paul's sense) and, finally, man himself: that false "I," that artificial but usurping "I" which people have created for themselves by sins and which is pledged to death. But the great renouncements of asceticism and the entrance into *xeniteia*, the "nomadic" life without ties to, or stake in, this world to which these renouncements are the means, and finally, the entrance into the desert—all this causes these masks of the power of sin to fall away. Little by little, to the extent to which the ascetic makes progress, sin reveals itself to him in its basically spiritual reality, but of a spirituality gone astray. It is only then that it can be cut off at the roots and finally uprooted, attacked and destroyed in its source.

Too frequently we remain the victims of infantile imagery and discard the thought of the demon as being merely a childish phantasm. In reality, the statement of our captivity to the demon, so evident throughout the whole Gospel, far from being something childish, when properly understood is revealed as the only fully mature view of the present condition of sinful man, the condition from which the asceticism of faith is to free him. Although it is generally manifested on the level where the human spirit emerges in the senses, it nonetheless remains wholly spiritual. For there is no sin where there is no consciousness. It is the perversion of consciousness, and nothing else, that finally causes sin. Yet sin does not proceed simply from our human consciousness. It is born in a consciousness far more "spiritual" than our own: spiritual to the extent that it could, without absurdity, be tempted to make itself equal with God.

We do not sin, we do not live far from God, therefore, simply because we are ensnared in the senses. It is much more, and more deeply, because we have been taken captive by a perverted spirituality, even though it is one that in its "spiritualness" is a whole abyss beyond us. If this has taken possession of us by means of the senses, it is because it knows too well the complexity of our nature and plays on it like a virtuoso to keep us well in hand. This does not prevent the fact that our sin, even when it is carried out at the level of the senses and by means of our immersion in the impressions that they make on us, is spiritual in its final substance, both in ourselves and as it wholly precedes from a "pure" spirit—perhaps the purest (in this sense) of all created spirits. As Evagrius says, if it is the *pathe*, sensible impressions, that subjugate us, it is spiritual intelligences that make use of these impressions to enslave our intelligence, our *nous*, and keep it away from the divine Spirit.

This is why the spiritual combat—making use of all the Weapons of various physical austerities but making still greater use of prayer, of increasing meditation on the divine Word, and relying, through the sacramental life, upon "Christ in us, the hope of glory," is primarily a matter of faith. Properly speaking, it is the struggle of faith in us against everything that hinders it.

For we should note again, as we saw in the account of the temptation in Genesis, that faith is always a victory of faithfulness to the divine Word, to a requirement which is immediately costly, in favor of a promise at present invisible. Faith, then, is only exercised in overcoming the attraction of the sensible and the immediate. And, in turn, it is faith alone which can make us engage in the struggle and carry off the victory, because faith has us look beyond the visible: has us glimpse, together with the unperceived slavery in which we are held, the equally unseen Deliverer.

Yet no war is waged except in view of peace: a stable and, if possible, final peace, in place of one that is superficial and therefore precarious. Thus the spiritual combat of its nature tends toward interior peace: toward that perfect tranquility of the flesh and the spirit which the ancients called *hesychia*—whence the name of *hesychasts* given in the East to monks who are such not only according to man (as Evagrius says), that is, according to exterior practices, but according to the Spirit.

The peace, the *hesychia* of the "awakened" soul—in contrast to the false peace of the soul asleep in the torpor of the world and the flesh—is not merely negative. Its negative aspect, if it must be called so, is the *apatheia*, dominion over the *pathe*, disordered sensible impressions, and so over the perverse spiritual suggestions of which they are the instruments. But its positive aspect is the reign of charity in us; that "knowledge of God" which is not simply a vision of the spirit nor even a contemplation from afar, but restoration to the image of God according to which we were made to begin with, which is re-established only because we have again become the temple of God, the place of his presence, a place that this presence has itself carved out to its own likeness.

If, under a preliminary aspect, the quieting of the soul, consequent on its purification, is produced only by virtue of the ascetic effort, the *ponos*, under a deeper aspect, only mystical contemplation, the knowledge of God uniting us to him, completes our purification and causes us to enter into that "peace which surpasses all understanding," into that *hesychia* which is the repose, the Sabbath of God, into which He desires to bring all his people.

The Attraction of the Desert, and the Spirit

In freeing us who are in the world from the world itself and in preparing for our liberation from the flesh and from our corrupt selves, the spiritual combat prepares us for the migration to the desert: for that entering into the depths of solitude in which, the flesh being crucified with its lusts, the self can be wrested from Satan in order to be restored to the Spirit. For this is the motivation given by all the early monks for burying themselves in the desert: they went there to confront Satan and conquer him in his last hiding-places. No other motive is given in early monastic literature for becoming an anchorite, for fleeing (and not only-separating oneself) from the world.

The origin of this idea which disconcerts us, at first sight, is to be found in the synoptic Gospels. For these agree in telling us, as St. Mark says in so many words, that Jesus, after his Baptism, was "driven into the desert by the Spirit" which He had just received, there to be "tempted" (more precisely, "put to the test"—*peirasmos*) "by the devil" (Mk 1:12–13; cf. the parallels: Mt 4:1 and Lk 4:1–2).

Behind the Gospel text, as behind other monastic texts, is the conviction that the desert is the dwelling-place of demons. Why so? Doubtless because man, according to the traditional Jewish view expressed in the first chapters of Genesis, was brought into the world to confront the Prince of this world, the Angel fallen before the fall of man, and to drive him out of the world. Thus the devil is incontestably the ruler of the desert, untrodden by human feet, while he asserts his victorious presence in tombs where he has succeeded in doing away with humans through death (this explains why we find in the *Life of St. Antony* and many other monastic writings that ascetics, before going deep into the desert, often prepared themselves by spending some time at the entrances to tombs).

If such objectifying of the demon's presence seems fantastic, we should realize that in many respects it is only the projection of a very profound spiritual experience. And this lies in the discovery that the desert, solitude, is the most terrible of trials for sinful man, the trial which reveals to him all the demons he bears within himself. For, however strongly we may be tempted in the world and by the world, here the temptation—even with the too easy complicity it finds within our own flesh—comes at us from without.

But anyone would be extremely naive if he thought that entering into solitude would do away with all this! Quite the contrary, in solitude not only in most cases does his flesh begin by arousing within him a host of phantasms the existence of which he had never suspected because hitherto external distractions had served more or less to repress them, but also the depths of his own soul are only then opened out to him. And they reveal themselves to be as it were haunted, or, if you prefer, possessed. We discover in ourselves, that is, abysses of folly, and, quite simply, a void, a dizzying agony which the screen of other creatures had hidden from us. We now discover that, according to the phrase of Stoic philosophy, "we are never less alone than when we are alone": but first in a tragic sense. In fact, when we perhaps believe ourselves most completely our own masters, then we finally perceive that we are not so at all: that the powers of darkness hold us captive, powers which allow themselves to be seen or divined only when the intermediaries which they ordinarily use to enslave us have all departed.

This is precisely why the early monks emphasize the fact that the novice should not rush precipitately into solitude; he could not endure it. Or, and this comes to the same thing, God does not wish to reveal to him prematurely his captivity to the devil because, far from being able to escape from it, he would be overwhelmed by it.

But, to the ascetic already trained and hardened for spiritual warfare, solitude affords the occasion for the supreme battle, and the only one that can be truly decisive. All the pretences, all the false trappings of demi-virtues in which he placed his trust, now fall away in a flash. He must see himself, recognize himself for what he is. He must transfer the struggle from the superficial levels of his being, from the mirages of the world or the phantoms of the flesh, to the darkened abysses of his own will which is only a will enslaved. Then each man finds revealed to him that the strength of God is fulfilled in our weakness, that his grace is sufficient to us, that it is when we are weakest that we are strong, provided that, at this moment, faith does not weaken. . . . Solitude, indeed, is the great trial of faith. It is only when a man has gone through this trial that he can say with more than his lips, "It is no longer I who live; it is Christ who lives in me" (2 Cor 12:9 and 10; Gal 2:20; all these texts are quoted in the *Life of St. Antony* to make us understand the meaning of the trial he went out to meet in going to live in the desert).

It is at the end of this trial that the monk is truly possessed by the Spirit of God and unreservedly so. For solitude, where faith is stripped bare but affirmed without alloy, should cause us to pass on (and it alone can make us do so) from the terrible experience of our initial possession by the spirit of evil to the radiant and life-giving experience of the Holy Spirit. Not that the Spirit had been absent hitherto. But now it is revealed that the Spirit, in the very depths of our darkness, fights within us against "the power of darkness." Now that He has put this power to flight by the living and heroically militant faith which He inspired in us, He can inundate the soul with his light.

As Diadocus of Photike puts it, before Baptism the spirit of evil lies in wait in the depths of the soul and from all sides, as it were, the Spirit of God calls to it in vain. After Baptism and the gift of faith, the Spirit of God drives out the spirit of evil and takes his place. Then it is the turn of the spirit of evil to attack us from without and to plunge his tentacles into us, reaching up toward that summit, now inaccessible to him so long as we hold to faith, where the Spirit of God now dwells. And the whole purpose of the spiritual combat is to have the Spirit take more and more complete possession of us, from the intimate depths of the heart to our whole soul, with our sensibility and even our body given up to his influence so that finally He comes to shine out through us victoriously upon the world.

Thus the whole meaning of the anchoritic life, of the most radical, the apparently most inhuman and deathly separations that monastic asceticism can impose, is to make us in all truth the living temples of the Spirit.

The *Life of St. Antony* describes the effect of this reconquest by showing us the human nature of the ascetic perfected by solitude as having again become fully "natural" and "rational," or, more precisely, "logical." These two adjectives may well seem paradoxical unless we understand the very special but also very profound sense in which they are used.

To say that the life of the ascetic who has arrived at full docility to the Spirit is "natural," to say that it is indeed the only truly "natural" life, does not mean that it is not essentially "supernatural" in the sense in which we use this word today, that is, pre-eminently the gift of God. But it does mean that, far from being an artificial, inhuman life, it represents our attaining, so far as this is possible here below, the life for which God made us. This is truly paradise regained; the life that God intended to give us at our creation, the immediate realization of which has been prevented and hindered by sin alone. When sin has been conquered, this life, this fullness of human life but the life of a person as the child of God and the temple of his Spirit, can finally flow freely.

This life is eminently "rational," "logical," because it is the only life conformed to true reason, the image and echo in us of God's own thought, which makes us spiritual beings in the true, the integral sense. This life is, again, "logical," because it is life in the "logos," in the Word of God made flesh, the life which in us, by our "divinization," corresponds to his incarnation. As the Son was made man, taking on our humanity in the condition to which sin has reduced it, now we are made sons, co-heirs with the Son, heirs of God himself, in that exalted condition of heavenly humanity in which the Risen Christ appeared and in which He is to manifest himself at the end of time to gather us all together in himself. . . .

The Cenobitic and Anchoritic Life

What has just been said is enough to show how the anchoritic life, the "flight of the alone to the Alone"—to use (but in a very different sense) the phrase of Plotinus—is essential to the monastic way. "I will attract her to the desert, and there I will speak to her heart" (Hos 2:10): this phrase of the prophet Hosea is as it were the key to every monastic vocation. And primitive monasticism actually was simply the eremitic life: the attraction to the desert, to solitude.

Yet in historical fact, for pure eremitic life, for radical anchoritism was very soon substituted, at least partially, the cenobitic life: led apart, but by a whole group in common. And in a certain way, especially under the influence of St. Basil, cenobitism came to react so strongly against eremiticism that it supplanted it in practice and even succeeded in condemning it in theory.

This came about by a gradual process which we need to follow step by step. We should note first of all that, as the *Life of St. Antony* testifies, even at the time when the preparation for the anchoritic life consisted in discipleship to an "ancient," in docility to the teachings of the "fathers," primitive anchoritism always included, at least in theory, an initial phase, a "school of the service of God" as St. Benedict was to say later on. And during this phase, far from being alone, the disciple trained himself to live in the most strict dependence on, in fullest submission to the teachings of a Master and to the example of all those who had preceded him in the anchoritic way.

Later on, taught by much deeply pondered experience, the best interpreters, such as Cassian, of the most fully matured monastic tradition, say that we cannot commit ourselves, according to the formula of St. John, to "love God whom we cannot see" without first being trained, in a life necessarily led in common, to "love our brother whom we do see." The apprenticeship of fraternal charity is thus considered to be the necessary prelude to the lonely flight to the Alone, to the solitary entrance into the desert.

Yet, if we can judge by the life of St. Pachomius, creator of cenobitism, that is, the monastic life led in common, it was practical considerations that first led to his instituting it. Pachomius observed that, for many men and even perhaps the majority, life in complete solitude, far from automatically freeing a person from the cares which hinder him in the search for God, may imperil him by drowning him in them. The need to provide, entirely on his own, for shelter, clothing, subsistence, threatens to overwhelm the solitary. And so Pachomius tried to organize a colony of solitaries who would lend one another mutual support.

But the experience gained in this attempt showed him that, without strict discipline, this living and working together would end in disaster. More deeply, this experience made him put his finger, as it were, on the dangers of entering into solitude without having gone through a discipline both strict and enlightened. Lacking such discipline, solitude is only anarchy, and, far from destroying self-will, affords it the opportunity to act freely, without restraint, not being judged or bridled by anything or anyone.

Thus the cenobitism of Pachomius, wholly empirical in its development, combined a materially prudent organization of the monastic society with a formation of the monks by the discipline of an obedience which, henceforth, would encompass their whole existence.

A little later, St. Basil made this new organization the object of a systematic development. In the name of charity, which should be exercised concordantly toward men as our brothers and toward God as our Father, he rejected the solitary life as an aberration pure and simple. For him, the monk ought not to leave the society of men for solitude, but should rather leave a society corrupt in its very principle for a society rescued from corruption by asceticism pursued in common, the community of charity. It is life in such a community and our adaptation to this new type of common life, which are now to be considered sanctifying. And the highest earthly development of this sanctification must, conversely, be nothing other than an increasingly perfect realization of the common life as the life of all in one single love.

This also led to a reduction in the size of monastic communities. Instead of the monastic garrisons, not to say colonies, of Pachomius, St. Basil desired less populous communities, in which all the monks could know and love one another as brothers, and, particularly, could be known and understood by the superior who became the father of all. In reacting further against Pachomius whose colonies dwelt in the depths of the deserts where the single anchorites had buried themselves, St. Basil led his monks back into the cities. The monastery as he conceived it was to be, as it were, a focus of the life of the Church. It was to be a kind of nursery for the different sacred orders, the center of all the charitable and educational works of the Church. . . .

The practical rules of St. Basil for community life were followed very widely by reason of their admirable spiritual good sense. But his system, opposing cenobitism to anchoritism, was never accepted in the East, and took root in the West only with all kinds of reservations. The cenobitic life was very soon seen to be the preparation and, as it were, the seminary for integral monastic vocations, that is, eremitical ones. And for the monks who were to pass their whole lives in cenobitism, the monastic society continued to be thought of as a society apart that leads and sustains all its members in an ultimately individual, personal work of sanctification. Whatever help this work may receive from the community, it cannot be perfected except in a solitude which is at least interior, safeguarded from all promiscuity by the relative separation of each individual from the others in the very heart of their common life. Various mitigated forms were later developed, such as the lauras of Palestine, villages or free groupings of ascetics who live in isolation during the week and, on Sundays and feast-days, gather together in a church or central refectory. And, also, there is the *scete*, where a very small group of companions live under the guidance of a spiritual master.

In the medieval West, the great monasteries usually included, within their cloister or nearby, a certain number of permanent or temporary hermits who, having come out of the community, still preserved some material connection with it and the uninterrupted exchange of spiritual goods.

Anchoritism and Spiritual Fatherhood

The choice between fraternal charity and solitude is, in actual fact, an artificial one. It can be proposed and required only so long as the dynamism inherent in every authentic monastic life is misunderstood. Once again, we do not leave the world to abandon our brothers but to give ourselves wholly to God. In other words, we do not leave world for the sake of leaving it, but for the sake of finding what it prevents us from finding.

When we have found this, we need not hesitate to return to the world, or, still better, like the Baptist, we draw the world irresistibly to the desert.

For the anchorite finds the goal of his anchoritism in the life of the Spirit. And the divine Spirit cannot take possession of him in solitude without making him into a "spiritual father." Then the anchorite no longer needs to fear contact with the world. Within him, henceforth, faith has "overcome the world." If the world rejoins him, "He who is in him is stronger than he who is in the world" (cf. 1 Jn 4:4).

Spiritual fatherhood, according to ancient monastic literature, is exercised primarily in two ways: by the word of counsel which plumbs the depths of hearts and enlightens them as to what they must do—and by the transforming action which the monk, by the sole fact of his presence, carries out and exercises on the life of those who come near him. This *dynamis*, this spiritual power, as it is called, can go so far as to work miracles in the literal sense of the word. But it is primarily capable of the moral miracle consisting in the influence of a saint on those who meet him: afterwards they are never exactly the same persons as they were before.

To a monk who has arrived at these heights are offered possibilities of acting on his fellows incomparably greater than those available to the most zealous apostle who has not gone through the same experience. For this action of the spiritual person seems to have become equally interior and exterior. One word, one look, from him is enough to set in motion effects unobtainable by the most fiery preaching, the works most overflowing with zeal. Nay, even without any perceptible contact with those he influences, the prayer of such a monk, the clairvoyance frequently accompanying it, the supernatural effectiveness which has become as it were normal to him, will work conversions, healings of soul and body, which, from a human point of view, are beyond hoping for.

For the monk who has arrived at such a point, the priesthood would seem to be unquestionably indicated, to crown his personal charisms with the gift that transcends all personality, but which a personality completely reforged in the furnace of the Spirit could, obviously, turn to the best possible account.

Chapter 9

The Various Apostolic Vocations: The Priestly Vocation and the "Religious" Vocations

The Apostolic Vocations

The various apostolic vocations (in the sense given to the word "apostolic" today, that is, a vocation to an active religious work in the Church) share both in the characteristics we have defined as being those of the lay vocations and in the characteristics proper to the monastic vocation. The vocations called "religious" are particularly close to the latter by the practice and the vows of poverty, chastity and obedience. Yet, even so, they are still closer to the lay vocations in that a particular task is what specifies them, in such a way that positive consecration to Christ is carried out both by means of this task and for the sake of it. Nonetheless they differ from lay vocations because the task in view is no longer a task by nature profane which the Christian is to consecrate, but one which is directly religious.

The primary apostolic vocation is that of the priesthood, which has come in fact, particularly in the West, practically to absorb the whole range of clerical vocations. This comes from the fact that, for many centuries, the lesser orders have no longer been conferred except as stepping-stones to the priesthood. And also, since for many centuries priests have come to be associated with all the tasks formerly reserved to the bishops whose "co-workers" they are, according to the formula of the Roman Pontifical—regular preaching, presiding at the Eucharistic celebration, and discharging almost all pastoral responsibilities—it has become difficult to make any radical distinction between the priestly and the properly episcopal vocation.

We shall begin, therefore, by considering the priestly vocation as a whole. We shall nonetheless specify certain characteristics proper to the vocation—in general today always conferred on a priest of the second rank—to the full priestly function of the episcopate. Then we shall examine what the diaconal vocation could become in the West and what it still is today in the Eastern Church, and also the vocation to other clerical tasks. From there, we shall go on to the apostolic vocations which, from the view point of Orders, do not affect a person's status as a layman as this term is understood in our times. Finally, we shall consider the active religious vocations, priestly or clerical as well as lay. We shall devote special attention to the emergence of secular institutes and other forms of religious vocations which seek to immerse themselves in the world as completely as possible.

The Priestly Vocation

Until the 17th century, the existence of a priestly vocation was minimized or sometimes frankly denied, if by this is understood a vocation to the diocesan priesthood. This situation, which seems hardly credible to us today, on the one hand reflected an archaic state of affairs in which priests *(presbyteri)* were actually only the advisors of bishops: assistant administrators of the Church, more or less infrequently delegated to carry out the sacred functions, which it was certainly admitted that they had the power to perform, but the regular exercise of which the bishops still actually retained. That such a views of things, corresponding to a situation long since gone by, could have been held for such a length of time is doubtless explained in part, for the West, by the development of clerical, and particularly of priestly, religious vocations. At least since the time of St. Augustine, it had been the tendency to think that every priest aware of his obligations ought to adopt the "religious life," characterized by the three vows. Since such a practice could never be made universal, it came about that the fullness of the priestly ideal was reserved to priest-religious, leaving other priests more or less under the impression that they were merely priestly unskilled labor, so to speak, and as such deprived of any spirituality of their own.

In the 17th century, the effort toward a reform and a renewal of the spirit of the secular clergy led toward a spirituality which would be, on the contrary, specifically sacerdotal, capable of rivaling (and, if possible, of successfully rivaling) the various "religious" spiritualities. The nearer we come to modern times, the more this spirituality "of the diocesan clergy" as it now came to be called, tended to be defined as a distinct species, the equivalent of the "particular religious spiritualities" developed during the nineteenth century in the strictly specialized forms these have known ever since.

As we have said already and will say again later, to push so far the specialization of "religious spiritualities" does not seem to be such a good thing as it has sometimes been thought to be. With even more reason, we do not think that the secular clergy, and the priests of this clergy in particular, have to follow an analogous path, nor even that in seeking their proper perfection, they should thus imitate in any detailed way the religious as such.

To begin with, let us recall what was said at the beginning of our consideration of the spirituality of the laity. This is in no way basically a "profane spirituality"—a concept which would be a contradiction in terms. The spirituality of the layperson—that is, of a member of the People of God—is in itself a sacral and even a priestly spirituality in the sense that it is a spirituality of association with the being and with the life of Christ, who, in his person and in all his Work, is the very consecration of humankind to God. In this sense, the monastic life itself can be nothing other than a development of the "lay" life, understood as the life of a member of the priestly people—a development brought about by the adoption of an ascetic mode of life which brings detachment with regard to the "present world" in view of the "world to come" to the maximum degree of realization possible in this life.

In the same way, the life of the ministerial priesthood is distinguished from the life of the laity in general only by its acceptance of the responsibility to furnish that life with its indispensable sources. In other words, what the priest possesses spiritually to distinguish him from the layman who is only a layman is the duty of providing others with what he himself should be living together with them. More precisely, this is what takes the place in his life of the particular task to which the ordinary layman is pledged. And this again is why the Church in the West, without wishing to impose the "religious" life on all its priests, has at least made it obligatory for them to give to the Church herself, in which and for which they are working, the place in their affections and preoccupations that other men give to their family and their home.

This leads us, then, to examine first the requirements implied by the tasks of the ministerial priesthood, and then the more particular requirements resulting in the West from the fact that, in view of these very tasks, the Church has imposed on her priests a life of celibacy.

The Work of the Priesthood

The primary task of the priest is to proclaim the Word of God. From this flows the sacramental celebration, and, above all, the liturgical celebration, in which he shows himself the "dispenser of the mysteries" proclaimed by the Word, all concentrated in the supreme Mystery, "Christ in you, the hope of glory," as St. Paul says. In these two actions, closely coordinated with one another, consists the "liturgy" in the etymological sense of the word—that is, the public service—of the apostolic minister in the assembly of the People of God, in the Mass.

As we have already said, these two actions themselves are the source of the three actions that specify the active participation of the laity and of the whole people of God in the holy action which Christ, by the medium of the ministers He has chosen, renders not only perpetually present but perpetually capable of participation. These three actions, let us repeat, are: the prayer which is essentially response to the Word of God; the offering by which (under the species of bread and wine) it is human life itself in its source which gives itself back to God through Christ;

and communion, in which this gift (consecrated by the priestly Eucharist) is given back to us, become the body of Christ himself, our incorporation into which is to be ceaselessly renewed.

The priest, who by his ministry in the name of the Head makes possible these three actions of the whole Body, should be the first to carry them out. Proclaiming the Word of God, he should have made this Word his own in a prayer which, while becoming fully his, will be fully the prayer of the Church. And, equally, he should be the first to offer himself to the consecrating power of the Eucharist of which he is the visible agent; he should be the first not only to communicate in fact, but to realize in his whole existence the meaning of communion.

Under these conditions, it is clear that the essentially pastoral role of the priest, for the sake of which he has been entrusted with the power to teach and the power to consecrate, imposes on him, above all, a very special duty personally to assimilate the holy realities of which he is to be not only the guardian but the transmitter. Charged with proclaiming the Word, more than anyone else he must have begun by examining it, penetrating it, making it his own. Charged with dispensing the mysteries of Christ, he must have begun by the first to live them.

This makes us understand how it is that to confer the priesthood on a monk who has attained the full development of his ascetic life can in many respects be considered as the ideal. Thus the Church in the East was led to give the fullness of the priesthood by episcopal consecration only to monks and, as far as possible, to monks already advanced in the monastic life and formed in its best traditions (for a long time, Russia recruited a great part of its episcopate from among the monks of Athos). This also explains why the West throughout the Middle Ages multiplied attempts to bring the clergy as a whole to lead a life which would come as near as possible to the monastic life.

We can synthesize these different facts, so remarkably convergent, by recalling the scholastic definitions concerning the states of life represented respectively by the "religious" life and the episcopate. While the episcopate, as the fullness of the ministerial priesthood, is here defined as the state of "perfection as acquired," the religious life is defined as the state of "perfection as to be acquired," or "as being acquired." The *perfectio acquirenda* thus appears as the most normal way toward the state which should be that of *perfectio acquisita*. For a state which, by reason of the responsibilities it implies, constitutes a demand for achieved perfection, would seem to be best prepared for by previous entrance into a state in which everything is actually designed to lead toward this Christian perfection.

Nevertheless, it is not without profound significance that the Eastern Church, which has imposed the anterior practice of monasticism on candidates for the episcopacy, has never imposed anything of the kind on its priests—only forbidding them to marry again, but allowing them, if they were already married before ordination, to continue in this state. And not less enlightening is the fact that, in the West, while celibacy has been imposed on all priests (and even on sub-deacons), the whole sum of the obligations called "religious" has never been imposed even on bishops.

The reason for this discretion, no doubt, lies in the fact that pastoral responsibilities cannot be effectively exercised by men, however saintly they may be, unless they have a minimum of contact, of possibilities of intelligent sympathy, with the problems of the great mass of men, married, living in the world.

Doubtless, in the ideal situation, the perfected monk who has become a true saint, whatever his austerities may have been and may still be, would see humanity in himself restored as well as purified by grace. The gift of the Spirit would give him something of the divine sympathy by which God, in spite of his inaccessible holiness, is nearer to men than anyone, more able to understand them—even sinners. But, precisely because this situation is ideal, because it is pre-eminently the product of a grace of which God remains the sole master so far as its daily distribution is concerned, it would be presumptuous on our part to institutionalize in any way the permanent possibility of such a situation.

In actual fact, by force of circumstances, the very conditions of a monastic vocation isolate a person from the world, cut him off from its problems. Except in exceptional happy cases, even very excellent monks who, as priests, could exercise the most elevating influence on the laity, usually could not with the right sureness of touch guide them from day to day in the whole of their existence. The Church has therefore judged it necessary to have, along with a "regular" clergy—one made up of "religious," that is, but living in the world—a "secular" clergy, close enough to those whom they are to lead, to lead them effectively.

Certainly their exclusive consecration to sacred tasks, and, quite simply, the very devotedness of their charity which should make them "all things to all men," to use the phrase of the apostle demand certain renouncements of this clergy, which fact explains why the Church, in the West at least, has not feared to impose celibacy on all her sacred ministers. But if certain ascetical separations were carried out by all priests and, in particular, by all those who have the permanent care of souls—all the pastors in the most exact sense of the word—it might well be feared that an unbridgeable gulf would appear between the life in which they should guide others and the life which is their own. To define as clearly as possible the very special character and the inevitable limits of the asceticism required of priests and, more precisely, of those who directly exercise pastoral charges, is, therefore, the best way to go about defining priestly spirituality as such.

The Particular Characteristics
of Pastoral Asceticism

For the sake of clarity, we need first of all to dispel certain over-simplified ideas which have recently come to light but which have been latent at least since the time of the Renaissance. Some theorists of the modern apostolate, of a truly apostolic priestly spirituality, have come to oppose it more or less radically to monastic spirituality. More generally, this tendency and these attempts are found in the context of a vast effort to oppose a spirituality of adherence to the world to one of flight from the world, a lay (understood in the sense of profane) spirituality to a sacral spirituality.

In this perspective, the spirituality to be proposed to priests, to leaders of Catholic Action, and to all the laity as well, would be one not of separation, but of presence; not centered on contemplation, but plunged in action; not a negative spirituality of renouncement, but a positive spirituality of consecration, etc.

It must be stated plainly that all these alternatives are factitious. To define a spirituality for apostolic priests, for militant Catholics, for laypeople, from such a starting-point, therefore means either to rest content with empty words, or else—(and most frequently under cover of such words) to fall into extremely harmful errors.

To summarize, or to resummarize: the Christian is not offered such a possibility of choosing between an asceticism of the cross and an asceticism of creation. Every kind of Christian asceticism, of the layman or of the priest as well as the monk, is an asceticism of the cross. But the cross rightly understand can never have any meaning other than the salvation of the world.

Consequently—we have said this already, but there is no harm in touching on it again—for the layman as for the monk, even though in a different way, the cross must be at the center of existence. And for the layman as for the monk, the cross which must be taken up when it comes at the appointed hour must be prepared for by renouncements and separations which have been freely willed and positively sought out. And this is all the more true of the priest.

Whoever prays in this world, whoever thus offers (offers himself) and "communicates in Christ and his cross, must first make a place in" his life for recollection, for silence, and so for solitude. The statement that the layman or the apostolic priest can, and therefore should, pray on the street, in the hubbub of conversation, or in the midst of very absorbing occupations, just as the monk prays in his cell, if taken strictly results in complete absurdity. Of course, the ideal of perfection is to arrive at such a point, and this is the ideal pursued by the monk himself. He does not bury himself in the desert because of any particular taste for the desert. He buries himself there to overcome his demons and be possessed by the Spirit. And, once the Spirit has in fact driven the demons away and taken their place in his heart, the monk has no further need of the desert. He can return to the world if the Spirit impels him to return there, or, still better, the Spirit himself will draw the crowds to him in the desert, and his solitude will be peopled with a true city of God.

But to suppose that from the outset one can pray in the *tohu-bohu*, in a chaotic hurly-burly, as well as one can in silent solitude, and that the vocation of the priest-apostle or the layman is to do this, is complete nonsense. It was not to the monk, in contrast to the layman or the priest, that Christ said: "When you pray, go into your room, shut the door . . .": it was to every Christian and, quite simply, to every man. A life that does not resolutely make room for silence and recollection (necessarily; solitary) cannot be a Christian life, for it cannot be a spiritual life; in fact, it cannot even be a human life worthy of the name.

The prayer of all places and all circumstances (toward which, certainly, we must tend) is not to be opposed to the prayer made at a determined time, under the most favorable possible conditions for recollection: the latter is the only source of, the only way that can lead to, the former. To refuse it, to turn away from it consistently under pretext of finding the other at the outset, is simply to be satisfied with words.

What is true of the asceticism of prayer is equally true of all the rest. We cannot offer ourselves to the divine demands, we cannot receive the divine promises that prayer has caused us to discover in the divine Word and to apply to ourselves, without all kinds of renouncements. We must begin by ceasing to belong to ourselves, to that false self which is ours at present, turned back on its greedy egoism, swollen with pride, in order to belong to God, to be capable of receiving the gift that He wishes to make us of his love. This is imposed on all, and this is particularly imposed on the apostle, who, let us repeat, is distinguished from the ordinary layman (as well as from the monk) by the fact that he not only has to receive the gift of God, but also to transmit it. His special problem entirely consists in how he is to practise the necessary renouncement in such a way that, instead of making this transmission more difficult for him, it will facilitate it.

Mark it well: if this transmission, as emphasized, presupposes a previous and particularly effective reception of the divine gifts, it must also presuppose a certain practice, if only temporary, of a monastic or at least a quasi-monastic life. He who wishes to be particularly consecrated to the "affairs of God" must begin by placing himself, at least for a time, outside of the world and its ways. This *xeniteia*, this life of "a pilgrim and a wanderer" to "which the monk commits himself unreservedly, should be" lived by the candidate for the priesthood at least temporarily. And, further, we should not hesitate to say that every Christian, to some degree, must have taken the same path if his Christianity has any depth. This, in early times, was the meaning of the Lenten initiation for candidates for Baptism. And this for seminarians, is the meaning of their years in the seminary.

Again, this period of lengthy initiation should have many renewals throughout the course of every Christian life in the world and especially every priestly life, and this is the meaning of those periodic retreats, the necessity of which for everyone we have already pointed out.

At a time when certain people would like, under the pretext of opening up the seminaries to life in order to prepare future priests more directly for their apostolic priesthood, to make a complete break with the kind of life traditionally led in seminaries, it is important to reassert all this in the most categorical fashion possible. A man cannot be, nor will he ever be able to be a priest who can hand on what he has first received without a prolonged period in which initiation into the sacred sciences goes along with a profound initiation into prayer, in a climate of detachment from the world and renouncement of self. Whoever refuses this admits thereby that he is unfit for the priesthood, and is indeed hardly capable of responding to what are simply the universal requirements of the Gospel.

The whole point is that this formation, once again, should not render a man unfit to resume effective contact with the world—a contact which will not only permit him to give that witness which every monk, every trained religious should be giving in one way or another, but also precisely to exercise pastoral responsibilities, with all that these imply.

Here comes in, not the choice between practising ascetical renouncements or rejecting them, but the far more delicate and subtle choice between different ways of practising and even, to a certain extent, of understanding these renouncements.

The distinction can most easily be made concrete by carefully considering the qualities of the celibacy imposed by the Western Church on her priests and all her sacred ministers, as against the qualities of the celibacy which is properly monastic.

Clerical Celibacy

Under one aspect, we have no hesitation in saying, the adoption of celibacy alone, inspired by an ascetic motivation of more complete consecration to Christ, constitutes an adoption, as it were, of the essence of the monastic life. For if the necessity for asceticism was first imposed in the Old Testament under the general form of poverty, one of the newest characteristics of the New Testament as compared with the Old is the transfer of the center of gravity of the ascetic life from poverty to continence, and particularly to voluntary virginity.

This is not to ignore the fact that, from the time of the Old Testament and especially in the last period of Judaism, virginity appeared as a particularly strict form of the poverty of the faithful who made their whole life a waiting for the kingdom. Already Jeremiah had had neither wife nor children (16:1–4). In the Jewish communities contemporary with the Christian era, the least that can be said is that the practice does not seem to have been exceptional. St. John the Baptist, like the Essenes with whom he may perhaps have been connected, was not married. The resolve, transparent through the Gospel of St. Luke, that led Mary to dedicate herself to a virgin life even before the Annunciation in spite of her betrothal to Joseph, makes us see in her piety the flower of the piety of Israel.

Yet, as the Christian treatises on virginity emphasize, and that of St. Gregory of Nyssa more clearly than any other (which is particularly interesting since its author had lived in the married state), it was the Gospel alone that fully brought out the positive significance of virginity consecrated to God in Christ. In relation to poverty, even as understood in the very interiorized sense already given it among the *anawim* of Israel, virginity voluntarily preserved represents a transfer from the giving up of our exterior goods to the giving up of ourselves, and thanks to this transfer, this renunciation now becomes the center of asceticism.

It is remarkable, furthermore, that this transfer took place, not in consequence of any depreciation of marriage, but rather of its exaltation. St. Paul, like Christ himself, far from setting up the ideal of consecrated virginity against that of Christian marriage, exalts them both together, and, even more, exalts the one by the other. For they propose a view of marriage in which the union of bodies, without being debased in any way, is nevertheless surpassed by the profound union of souls, and, more generally, of the whole of life. More precisely, the union of bodies is consecrated as the basis and means of expressing and realizing a total union, itself the anticipated image of the union of Christ with the Church.

It is under these conditions that the renunciation of marriage itself can become the sacrifice of an indirect and limited realization for the sake of a realization that is direct and total. The dignity of marriage is fully revealed in the possibility it presents of sketching out something of the very reality of the union of Christ with the Church, and, in this union, of the union of God with each soul. The sacrifice which renounces marriage in order to consecrate oneself exclusively to the superior union typified by marriage, therefore, only renounces it in a way that implies for marriage the supreme consecration.

Understood in this way, virginity, even better than poverty, leads, beyond the giving up of one's possessions, beyond the giving up of one's own body, to giving up oneself into the hands of God, through Christ, in the Church.

In this perspective, we can see very clearly how the personal renunciation of marriage is in no way a renunciation of what makes the whole "mystery" of marriage according to St. Paul (Eph 5), but, on the contrary, is a very special consecration, at once more immediate and more complete, to the union of Christ and the Church. But, at the same time, we see no less clearly the very important shade of difference that distinguishes ecclesiastical, (and particularly sacerdotal) celibacy. It goes without saying that in every case, the union of Christ and the Church is realized in the union of each soul with God through Christ. But, in the case of the monk, it is this latter union which is directly envisioned through his use of asceticism. In the case of the priest (or cleric), on the contrary, it is the union of Christ with the Church which is to predominate. Still more precisely, in the case of the priest more or less permanently entrusted with the care of souls, with a pastoral task in the full sense, it is the union of Christ with this more or less strictly defined concrete realization of the Church constituted by the group of souls entrusted to him: his parish in particular (his diocese, for a bishop; the whole Christian world for the pope . . .).

The monk, in becoming a monk, can have no immediate objective other than his complete liberation from all earthly ties to be wholly Christ's. The priest, in accepting the priesthood and more particularly the charge of souls, equally consecrates himself wholly to Christ, but, directly and by that very fact, to Christ in his brothers and especially in those to whom he is sent. His celibacy, with all that it implies and that extends it, should therefore be not only a celibacy in view of intimacy with God, but a celibacy in view of being, as the apostle says, "all things to all men for Christ." Doubtless, for the monk also, the consecration to God in Christ implies a consecration to the Church in her union with Christ. But the consecration of the monk in itself consecrates him in a unique way to this union inasmuch as it is first to be realized in each of us. The consecration of the priest, of the sacred minister of any kind, consecrates him to this union inasmuch as it is to be realized also and at the same time in other men.

In this way, we can unhesitatingly say, ecclesiastical celibacy is like, and even perhaps more like, the consecration of the married layman to his family than it is like the consecration of the monk to intimacy with God alone.

Once again, this is not to say that the priest does not also, in his own way, have to enter into intimacy with God. Every Christian, monk or not, must enter therein, and not only at the end of his life on earth but already here and now—in that whole part of his life which is, in each person, to be given over to seclusion, to retreat in the widest possible sense of the word. How, then, could this not be eminently true of the priest, who has not only to enter here himself but to draw others as well?

Yet, in spite of the initial distance which the priest must keep between himself and the world and his own flesh, and which he must ceaselessly strive to maintain, he can never, either in his preparation for the priesthood and still less in its exercise, make a complete break with the world as the monk can and should do as soon as he has resolved to answer the divine call to enter the desert.

In other words, the call and the consecration to the priesthood are an immediate call and consecration to spiritual fatherhood under the particular form of pastoral responsibilities, with the functions of preaching and celebrating the sacraments attached thereto. It is in view of this precise call, in view of this definite consecration, that the priest is required to renounce the marriage and the fatherhood of this earth. It is not purely and simply in view of taking up his cross and following the crucified

Christ. It is the business of the preparation for, and the exercise of, the priesthood fully to equip the priest for that to which he is called, that for which he is to be consecrated. And it is his business not to withdraw his interest purely and simply from the world for the sake of the things of God, but to withdraw his interest in a family life like that of the ordinary Christian for the sake of that family life, wholly supernatural in its principle, of the Church of God on earth—and of that special portion of the Church which will be entrusted to him.

The priest should, then (first of all in his studies) continue positively to concern himself with a great many things which are of no further concern to the monk, simply because they arc essential to the life, inseparably human and supernatural, of those to whom God and the Church wish to send him. All kinds of political, social, cultural and moral problems should attract his attention, which should not do so were he vowed only to that "search for God" (as immediate as possible in the attainment of its end, as radical as possible in the use of the means) to which the monk is consecrated.

Doubtless, the absence of a calling to any simply human task (which is correlative to his vocation to the tasks of the sacred ministry) and, above all, the renunciation of all personal family life, should separate him, like the monk, from the world in order to belong more completely to God. But the vocation to work among men for sacred ends and for these directly, with the vocation to devote himself to this work among a concrete group of men, should involve in his very celibacy (and not simply in the exercise of his ministry) a preoccupation of devotedness to others that has no immediate place in the monastic novitiate and consecration.

This is not to say (and it would be particularly dangerous to believe) that the priest can consecrate himself to the human beings who are or who will be entrusted to him as the married layman consecrates himself to his wife. He must never forget that, in relation to them, he is, like the Baptist, not the Bridegroom but simply the friend of the Bridegroom. His consecration to others, in other words, can never have as its counterpart, as it does in marriage, any possession of others. It should be far more closely related to that height of paternal (or maternal) experience at the time of the children's reaching maturity which, as we said earlier, constitutes the final consecration of parenthood in accepting detachment from their children. To make ourselves "all things to all men" and especially, as a spiritual father, to make ourselves all things to those who have been particularly entrusted to us, means by this very fact to renounce making them our own, and the more so the more we make ourselves theirs, so that in them we may be wholly Christ's and they themselves may be wholly Christ's, thanks to us.

The disinterestedness of the priest—not only carnal, which goes without saying, but also spiritual—in his devotion to his priestly tasks, and more especially to the souls entrusted to him in the exercise of these tasks, should, then, be complete. This is why he has need, more than any other Christian living in the world, of a continually renewed recourse to an asceticism of detachment, of self-abandonment, which, as to its basic principles, unceasingly rejoins monastic asceticism itself.

But, through this very disinterestedness, he must no less positively concern himself not only with what he is doing, but with those for whom he is doing it. In this sense, he must make his own all their legitimate preoccupations, he must understand their positive aspirations, their difficulties, their joys, and their sorrows. He can never let himself become absorbed in them, but still less must he ever turn away from them or gaze at them only from afar and above.

This "disinterested interest" is certainly the great difficulty, as it is the very special obligation, of the priestly life, inasmuch as this implies pastoral responsibility. We can attain it only by a ceaselessly renewed and particularly profound renewal of those detachments freely accepted at determined times which, as we have said, are essential even to the life of the layman, preparing for and fructifying the detachment from activity in and by activity itself, which as we have also seen, the lay life of its nature imposes. It is here that the effort—the particularly difficult effort, certainly—of maintaining virginity of soul as well as of body in the midst of the world is particularly beneficial for the priest so that he may be truly the spiritual father of his flock. And this is why the Church, in the West, has come to impose celibacy on all her priests, while in the East, without imposing it, she recommends it for all.

In return, it is quite true that the exercise of this paternity, the more it is deepened, facilitates the practise of this virginity by giving it a meaning—precisely as the ultimate development of natural paternity in the acceptance of the fact that the children, having grown up, are now themselves, facilitates the transcending of sexuality in the narrow sense to which every human being is sooner or later called. . . .

All this will be given various supplementary explanations when we come to study the development and the rhythms of every authentic spiritual life.

The Priestly Vocation and the Episcopate

A particular problem which has been raised in recent years is that of the forms under which the priestly vocation manifests itself to the person concerned. By analogy with the "religious" vocation in general, there has been a tendency, at least since the seventeenth century, to emphasize the subjective attraction felt by the person concerned, since to enter the priesthood without this attraction would be to risk, on the one hand, personal disaster in the Christian life and, on the other hand, devaluating the exercise of priestly functions, the reduction of the priesthood to the level of an ordinary career.

In reaction against a perhaps too one-sided emphasis on this spiritual point of view, certain more recent writers have insisted on the objective criteria of which the hierarchy is finally the sole judge. In this perspective, the "priestly vocation" properly speaking, would and could only be the positive call issued by the bishop to the candidate, after an examination of his qualifications, to present himself for ordination. This position in turn has aroused quite lively reactions and, in fact, has not been accepted as such by authority, as is indicated in quite a variety of documents issued on the subject by the Holy See during the last thirty years.

The truth contained in this point of view is that since the priestly vocation, in contrast to the monastic, does not have in view directly (still less, solely) the spiritual good of the subject, but rather the service of the Church, it can have no substance until the moment when the Church, by means of the responsible authorities, has made a judgment not only as to the attraction that may impel a man toward that vocation but also as to the means he possesses of corresponding to it. Nevertheless, there seems to be no doubt that these means themselves could not be effective unless an interior attraction were united with them—an attraction which, furthermore, can take many different forms psychologically. It is in this sense that the objective judgment of those responsible (the bishop or his representatives) is determining, not because it excludes or minimizes the importance of the personal factor, but because it belongs to this judgment, in the final analysis, to evaluate the authenticity of the personal attraction.

Yet the theory of the objectivity of the priestly vocation assumes its full value, it would seem, in connection with promotion to the fullness of the priesthood in the episcopacy. For the bishop as such is responsible (not only so far as he himself is concerned but also his whole clergy) for teaching revealed truth, for carrying out the sacred rites, and, through all this, for the accomplishment of the pastoral task entrusted by Christ to his Church, and this in a direct and absolute way. Priests teach only as he delegates them to do so; they preside at the Eucharistic celebration only in his name and under his authority; they feed the flock entrusted to them (even when they are theoretically "immovable" pastors) only in dependence on him. No one could, then, without grave fault, have the presumption to exercise the functions of a bishop unless, together with fullness of sound doctrine, he possessed the holiness of life, the superior wisdom presupposed by the functions of high priest and pastor. But who could believe himself to have attained such a height? It is therefore without question fitting that promotion from the subordinate priesthood to the major priesthood of the episcopacy should not be the object of any "candidacy." It must result solely from an appreciation on the part of the competent authorities of the way in which apostolic tasks and responsibilities have already been exercised in an essentially subordinate position. And this is what the Church tries to realize by means of her canonical regulations.

The Vocation to the Diaconate and the Minor Orders

A contrary problem is posed by the fact that at present, in the Western Church at least, the orders below the priesthood are no longer conferred except as stepping-stones to this order. The consequence is that either all or some of the functions originally belonging to deacons or inferior orders have now fallen to priests or else are carried out by laymen, who may not always have been adequately prepared for them and do not have the benefit of a sacramental grace directly adapted to the responsibilities they assume.

We have no intention of examining this question as a whole, but simply from the angle at which it touches the spiritual life of those concerned. We shall restrict ourselves, therefore, to recalling, to begin with, that it was formally intended by the Council of Trent that in each diocese and, if possible, in each parish, the complete hierarchy of minor orders and sacred orders should be reestablished, from the simple clericate to the priesthood. The Council passed decrees to this effect.

Unhappily, they have never been applied in practice. We see the result today. Numbers of priests find themselves overwhelmed by affairs of administration or practical charity which had far better be (and were in all Christian antiquity) the business of deacons. The same can be said, in many places, of tasks of teaching, which the priest should doubtless guide in the sense of providing integral religious formation, but of which a large part could be left to deacons or even to lectors, or laypeople. In the same way, the functions carried out by priest-sacristans or choir-masters in large churches would more normally be given back to sub-deacons.

And, conversely, laymen are entrusted with tasks properly those of porters or acolytes. And the good laypeople who teach catechism or participate actively in works of charity are carrying out the duties of lectors, exorcists or even of deacons.

Here we certainly have, on the one hand, a dissipation of effort which burdens and paralyzes the priestly minister, and, on the other hand, an improvised and basically deficient organization of ministries really requiring men who have been especially prepared and consecrated for them.

This situation leads to the suggestion of two possible reforms. Either the present canonical legislation could be left unchanged: looking forward to conferring the priesthood on all clerics sooner or later, only those destined to the superior order are admitted to the clericate. The present obligations of deacons and sub-deacons also would be retained: the recitation of the whole Divine Office, and celibacy. But, in practice, candidates would be admitted to the priesthood only after more or less extensive periods of actually exercising the functions of the lesser orders in parishes.

Or else something of the Oriental practice, at least so far as the diaconate is concerned, might be brought over into the West. There might again be admitted, as a practical possibility, the idea of a vocation to the lesser orders including the diaconate, a vocation which would not necessarily include orientation (in any case, immediate orientation) to the priesthood. Then priests would once again have the regular assistance (in secondary liturgical functions, in subordinate religious teaching, in administrative duties in the Church and responsibility for works of charity) at least of deacons, who would in principle remain permanently in this office. They could, perhaps, be dispensed from the obligation of celibacy, and, if their services in a given parish did not amount to a full-time job, they might be allowed to exercise some secondary work, such as teaching, which would be in accord with their sacred profession.

It would seem as though, simply from the spiritual point of view, suggestions of this kind might contain a twofold advantage. In the first place, they would do justice to a situation which, it seems, cannot be ignored; for there appear to exist, among laymen as well as religious who are not priests, positive vocations to the service of the Church which nevertheless are not vocations to the priesthood itself. As things are, these vocations find no status to correspond to them. And, perhaps, this simple fact may help to explain the permanent crisis in Catholic Action, divided as it seems to be between tasks that are directly apostolic and, as such, clerical, and those that mean simple Christian witnessing in the midst of ordinary occupations.

In the second place, the setting apart of priests from the laity as a whole as a result of the sacredness of the priest's occupations (which in theory are exclusively so)—a setting apart still further accentuated by celibacy—could be maintained for the great advantages afforded the Church by the presence in her midst of men who are exercising pastoral responsibilities in a total consecration to the spiritual. This setting apart would be the more effective by reason of the fact that priests would no longer have to be concerned with a multitude of tasks that have nothing priestly about them, but which at present priests have to carry out nonetheless. And conversely, the permanent restitution of the original stages between their life and that of the ordinary layman, by surrounding them with these intermediary co-workers, would certainly compensate for the risks which a priestly life too cut off from that of the people might otherwise run. The role of intermediary between the priest and the people, which is that of the deacon in the Eastern liturgies, would thus be extended to the advantage of the whole life of the Church.

The Problem of Priests Exercising
Non-Priestly Functions

In the suggestions just outlined there might also be found at least one element in the solution of a problem which the creation of priest-workers tried (vainly in fact) to solve and which their suppression has left in mid-air. This problem consists in the fact that the missionary work of the Church, both in missionary countries properly so called and perhaps still more in de-christianized countries in which prejudices have accumulated against the Church, seems to call for apostles who have at their disposal far more spiritual resources and responsibilities than ordinary laymen would normally possess, but who nevertheless were not so entirely and exclusively devoted to sacred functions as tradition has shown it desirable for priests to be.

The experience of the priest-workers would seem to have established two things. The first is that if the priest-worker wishes seriously to be a worker, he cannot seriously be a priest: in other words, he cannot devote himself sufficiently freely to his spiritual duties and responsibilities to provide the laity with the precise doctrinal, sacramental, pastoral aid that they have a right to expect from him. The second is that the best of the laity, in certain modern environments, can render only an inadequate witness—either because they are not sufficiently organized to be effective or because they do not sufficiently engage the Church as such in a fraternization with those who live in these environments—without which they remain strangers to her, as she has in fact become strange to them. The existence of Christian workers who would belong to the clergy, perhaps up to the diaconate inclusively but not including the priesthood, without thereby ceasing to be workers, and surrounding priests who were living as priests in these environments, might perhaps answer a need by no means imaginary, as the existence of the priest-workers could not answer it.

For, in the priest-worker, there exists the same at least latent contradiction as in the priest-manager, the priest-doctor, the priest-businessman, the priest-politician, etc. . . . which has led the Church from early times, to reject this dividedness and, finally, by the imposition of celibacy, to emphasize the separation necessary between the priesthood and profane tasks, even when these are consecrated by the profession of Christianity. For the tasks of the human city, and the marrying which ordinarily goes along with them, take up all the energies of the man who gives himself to them—all the more so when work and marriage are conceived and carried out in a Christian way. And it is the same with tasks that are directly sacred and with the pastoral responsibility connected with them.

Meanwhile, it goes without saying that what has appeared with such force in the case of the priest-workers must also appear in the case of priest-administrators, of priest-organizers of works which have nothing priestly about them, even when the administration in question or the works to be done touch directly on the life of the Church. Every priest who does not devote the essential part of his time and his efforts to priestly functions and preoccupations as we have defined them is assuredly in a situation which is as equivocal, as dangerous for him spiritually as it is for the priesthood in general.

This does not preclude the possibility that there may be exceptional cases, of which authority is finally the only judge; but it is in the nature of these cases to be rare and, normally, provisional.

What has just been said does not apply so directly, however, to priests who assume the task of educators, even though there is sometimes a tendency to think so by way of a harmful generalization. If the education is truly integrated and if it is an authentically Christian education, the task of educator becomes one of the most important forms that can be assumed by spiritual fatherhood. And for that reason, it seems to be particularly appropriate to the priesthood.

This is true even when the priest devotes a more or less important part of his time to teaching subjects that may be profane in themselves, when this teaching lends itself to giving a Christian formation to the whole of life. But this teaching must also be conceived and carried out with this precise end in view, and it must furnish the priest who undertakes it, not only with leisure, but also with positive opportunities to exercise his sacred functions and his pastoral responsibilities. A priest who never directly proclaims the Gospel, who never administers the sacraments, who has no real charge of souls, is only a priest still-born, his priesthood a stunted priesthood. When the task of a teaching priest has come to such a point, even if it forms part of a whole Christian education of indisputable value, he is not in his proper place. The place he occupies should be returned either to a layman or to a religious who is not a priest.

The Various Forms of the Active "Religious" Life

These last considerations lead us to the problem of the vocations to a "religious" life—a life defined by the three great vows already mentioned in connection with the monastic life, yet one in which these three vows are not applied in such a life itself but in a life of consecration to God in an activity more or less directly apostolic.

It should be emphasized that the progressive but more and more complete dissociation that has come about between the "religious" life defined by these vows and the monastic life is a

phenomenon exclusively proper to the West, as is the multipli-
cation of "religious orders" or "congregations" which has been
its consequence.

This is not to say that, in the East also, the religious (here
one and the same thing as the monks) cannot be and are not in
fact employed in all the tasks which we have come to describe as
"apostolic." Together with the priesthood, monks soon received
all the other orders. The episcopate of the Eastern Churches
from early times came to be recruited entirely from monasteries—something which has never been other than exceptional
in the West. From the end of the fourth century, on the other
hand, in Cappadocia with St. Basil and in many other places,
the monasteries took on all kinds of educational, social, hos-
pital work. Finally, the monks of the East, whether priests or
not, have been found as were also the monks of the West in the
front rank of the missionary expansion of their countries (this
happened even in the middle of the nineteenth century in the
evangelization of Siberia by the Russian Church).

But, in all these cases, the question was one of tasks being
undertaken from time to time by monks judged by their superiors to be fitted for them—by virtue of the maturity they had
attained in the monastic life as well as their own inclinations
or particular preparation. In the East, in any case, we do not
find any organization of religious established precisely in view
of some work of this kind and consecrating its members to this
work by the very fact of their profession.

The contrary is what has come about in the West, first of
all as a result of a systematic effort, which appeared at the end
of the fourth century, to lead the clergy as a whole to practise at least the three great monastic renouncements. From this
effort issued what were later to be called the regular clergy—at
first simply a diocesan clergy living in communities practising
poverty, continence, and obedience to the superior of the local

Church. This is what was soon to be called the canonical life. It had its ups and downs, in the sense that the majority of the chapters of "canons" (despite the "canons," the rules, supposed to regulate their lives) returned more and more to a life in which chastity alone was imposed (at least in theory), but no longer poverty in any way, nor even obedience understood in the strict sense.

In reaction, especially from the twelfth century on, a rebirth of the regular canonical life was effected (with St. Victor or Prémontré, among many other attempts). With the "mendicant" religious, this life was detached from cathedral or parochial churches: the Dominicans and the Friars Minor thus forming the first "orders" on the fringes of the diocesan clergy, undertaking missionary work or, as we would say today, a work of re-christianization.

The sixteenth century in turn saw a new and more radical mutation in the religious life with the appearance of the Jesuit as a religious priest pledged to apostolic tasks, but, apart from the vows, no longer keeping anything of the ancient forms of the monastic life, even those still retained by the mendicant orders such as the choral celebration of the Office.

Meanwhile, but as the result of an opposite line of development (pious laymen attached to the monastic life at Citeaux, embracing its vows but not its observances as a whole; then the lay brothers of the mendicant orders; and, finally, the coadjutors of the Jesuits themselves) appears the active religious, more or less directly apostolic in his effort but destined neither for the priesthood nor the clericate: whether he cares for the sick, like the Brother of St. John of God, or teaches children, like the Brother of the Christian Schools.

Whatever the infinite variations may be distinguishing these more and more numerous "orders" or "congregations"—for women as well as, and even more than, for men—they all have this in common: the three vows called those "of religion" are taken, not in view of the monastic life, but in view of some activity, directly or indirectly apostolic, which is proper to the order or the congregation as a whole and which serves to specify it.

It remains true, however, that just as in monasticism the vows themselves are always ordered immediately toward the Christian perfection of those who take them. Nevertheless, apart from this, perfection is no longer sought in a life simply freed from the world and lived apart from it—which is the monastic life—but rather in a life collectively devoted to carrying out a particular work of the Church, whether this work be one properly belonging to the clergy or not. In other words, devotedness to some "service" of neighbor (like the "liturgy" which is, in the etymological sense of the word, the "public service" of the sacred ministers) here seems to be substituted, as the way of consecration to God, for the traditional life of the monastic observances.

At least this is what we might be led to think from a somewhat over-simplified outline of this development. But, actually, a somewhat deeper examination of the modern forms of the "religious life" indicates that the reality is much more complex. Along with the tendency, common to all "orders" and "congregations" since the establishment of the canons regular, of the mendicant orders and then of the Jesuits, to seek sanctification in "service" and thus to depart from the ancient monastic ideal, we must recognize an exactly contrary tendency: a striving, in reaction against an increasing institutionalizing of the monastic life, to regain the original evangelical inspiration of that life itself. Thus the "mendicants" returned to a more real poverty, as well as to a simpler and more flexible social organization, than what was practiced at the time in the great monasteries of Citeaux and Cluny. And, to go a little more deeply into the matter, it would be very interesting to determine the place that was given, in the most traditional Jesuit formation, to the

Fathers of the desert and to Cassian their heir, in periods when hardly any Western monk, either in the line of Citeaux or that of Cluny, ever read them any more.

Thus, together with the concern to serve, we must recognize in the medieval orders a kind of condensed version of traditional monastic practices, which in many respects renewed them in their reality as well as in their primitive significance. Moreover, with the Jesuits and other modern orders, the essential mortification of the will, proclaimed by all ancient monastic literature as more fundamental than any other ascetic practice, is placed at the very center of the ascetic effort defined by the vows. Thus it is possible to maintain that these different orders represent equally attempts to acclimatize the spirituality of the desert to the world and to sanctify oneself in the service of men.

The Spiritual Significance of the Active or Apostolic "Religious Life"

The central spiritual problem of the vocation to a "religious life" thus understood, therefore, is finally that of the relationship between these two aspects: that of personal sanctification by a quasi-monastic existence, and that of personal sanctification in dedication to works of the apostolate or of Christian charity.

At first sight, such a life must seem to be only a mixed life, half monastic and half lay or clerical. But already, in the person of St. Thomas himself, the mendicant religious of the thirteenth century had refused this ideal, judging it to be inferior to the monastic ideal which they desired to renew, nay even to surpass.

St. Thomas, indeed, having identified the monastic life with the contemplative life, proclaims its absolute superiority over any kind of active life, even one motivated by charity. He deduces its equal superiority over a merely "mixed" kind of life, in which contemplation would be present but in alternation with action. Nonetheless, he declares the apostolic life as he defines it to be superior to all these forms: being a contemplative life in which from contemplation itself flows an activity which is not simply any land of activity, but one which consists in communicating to others what one has contemplated. Thus, "to contemplate and to hand on to others what has been contemplated" has become the ideal of the Order of Preachers, taken up or shared with some variations by the Franciscans, the Carmelites, etc. (*Summa Theologica,* Ila Ilae, q. 188, a. 6).

It is interesting to notice that this Thomistic presentation is a faithful echo of the most primitive monastic tradition, according to which the most radical anchoritism should normally fructify in a boundless spiritual fatherhood. The whole difference is that, in general, the modern orders which took up or accepted the Thomistic ideal considered it possible to economize on the journey through the desert and on a greater or lesser part of the traditional monastic observances. With the three vows and the minimum organization of life necessary to allow them to fructify in the life of prayer and asceticism, this contemplation, which in some way is extended and outpoured in the apostolate, can be attained.

We cannot profitably discuss this possibility until we have gone more deeply into this idea of contemplation as the supreme end of the monastic life and as the source of the apostolate in the ideal religious life. But, for the moment, it will be useful to recall certain points that seem to stand out.

The first is that the Thomistic presentation of the ideal religious life has not been accepted without increasing reservation, particularly in the more recent orders. The primacy of contemplation, which it admits as an essential postulate, is vigorously challenged in favor of the primacy of charity alone. To this it might be answered that, for St. Thomas himself, there is no

Christian contemplation which is not accompanied by a radiation of charity, even if it is true that the beatitude of the saints consists more in an act of the intelligence than of the will (a position which the Franciscan school had already opposed). But, above all, if contemplation is taken in the sense of ancient monastic tradition, there is no doubt that charity is included in it, the "knowledge of God" which culminates in contemplation being that of the Bible: knowledge which is love and union.

The second point is that modern thinkers likewise contest the scheme of progressing from action to contemplation to apostolate, maintaining that, in virtue of its requirements, the apostolate itself is as sanctifying as contemplation (in whatever sense it be understood) and even independently of contemplation.

We have already met this point in passing. For the moment, it is enough to say that here again we touch on one of those problems in which the alternatives are factitious, in which the very hypothesis of a possible choice is removed by a more attentive examination of the normal development of the spiritual life, and, above all, of its inherent rhythms. Let us remark, however, that there are doubtless many souls who would find a more or less radical type of monastic life psychologically inassimilable, but are nonetheless obviously called to practice the great monastic renouncements in the permanent way in which the vows engage them. For such souls, a life of dedication more or less directly apostolic, or even quite indirectly so in the exercise of fraternal charity alone, is indisputably very sanctifying. But, once again, such a life cannot be sanctifying if it neglects the interiorising asceticism developed by monasticism, but only if it more or less successfully integrates this asceticism, in an indefinite number of forms varied according to individual temperaments, with a life of activity pursued in the world without being of the world.

It is in this sense that it is legitimate to speak of many spiritualities corresponding to the diversity of human vocations. Yet we must always insist on the fact that these spiritualities all overlap, not only in their recourse to the common objective elements which are the soul of all authentically Christian spirituality, but also in their recourse to the fundamental ascetical practices which monastic experience itemized for the first time. These may certainly vary in the modalities of their concrete application, but in their substance they correspond to the unchanging substratum of the human soul in the actual condition, in which, fallen by sin, it is called by Christ to raise itself up in carrying the cross after him and by his grace.

Contemporary Experiments in the Religious Life and the Secular Institutes

The tendency to immerse the "religious" life more and more completely in life as such has continued in our own times. It has led to the formation of religious congregations still living in community (even, in many cases, no religious habit is worn)—with vows (sometimes simple private vows and thus more capable of dispensation, sometimes even of merely temporary vows)—but with no cloister at all and no separation from the world and, finally to the appearance of secular institutes whose members, even if they take vows, live separately in the world and practise a profession, thus seeming, so far as externals go, to be in the same condition as laymen.

What are we to think of these new efforts and new attempts, the development of which was also prepared, after the Middle Ages, by third orders and pious associations or fraternities of the laity which are still in existence?

New beginnings are certainly to be found here which may prove most fruitful for the apostolate carried out among those who have not only lost all contact with the Church but who are kept far from her by accumulated prejudices against her traditional institutions. These efforts may, at the same time, prove to be the source of a renewal of these same institutions, bringing them back to the spirit of their origins, even when a break has been made with their development over the centuries (somewhat as was the case with the appearance of the mendicant orders).

From the spiritual point of view which is ours in this book, these various institutes may serve to satisfy many Christians who seek to consecrate themselves to God in a particularly fervent life, and who do not find in the traditional orders forms to which they could adapt themselves. Nevertheless, the same remarks that we made in general concerning the life of the laity in the world and explained more fully as to various important aspects in connection with the life of secular priests, apply here *a fortiori.* To interpret the creation of these forms of "religious" life as being a means finally made available whereby to realize a spirituality of adherence to the world as simply opposed to flight from the world, or a spirituality of creation as opposed to the spirituality of the cross, would be to enter (and to risk bringing others to enter) on a dead-end road.

More generally, there is no sanctification by means of action alone, but only by action vivified by prayer; and action cannot be thus vivified unless it is marked with the sign of the cross of Christ. What we have already said on this subject excuses us from returning to it again.

One last admonition may perhaps be necessary concerning these new attempts in the "religious" life. There can sometimes be perceived in them the temptation to will the impossible, whether by deluding oneself as to the simultaneous attainability of several objectives which it would not seem possible to achieve in this way, or by some misunderstanding of the normal rhythms of spiritual development. To imagine, for example, that an integrally contemplative life can be attained without any separation from the world would seem, except in the case of exceptional personalities, to be a chimera. And still more, to launch novices in the "religious" life, whatever may be the forms that their life is to take later on, into a witnessing, and, still more, into an apostolate, which plunges them into a dechristianized world, again under the pretext of sanctifying them by action, would seem to be falling once more into the errors mentioned above.

Catholic Action and Spirituality

Many of the things we have said, both in connection with priestly spirituality and with that of active religious, can, with some transpositions, be applied to the spirituality of those who dedicate themselves to some form of Catholic Action. Everything that touches the reciprocal relationship between personal sanctification and apostolic action applies to them also and only needs to be placed in the general context of all lay spirituality, as we described it at the beginning of our study of the various vocations.

Yet there remains a problem peculiar to laymen responsible for movements of this kind, a problem which we touched on in passing, but which, at the end of our study, we must now deal with more directly. This is the question of the Christian's enlisting in a certain political, social, or cultural line of action which does not depend necessarily, or evidently, on the faith alone, but also on elements of concrete evaluation determinable only by reason applied to experience, in which all kinds of personal or collective factors should allow for the free play of various opinions.

Here there must be a very clear distinction between the choices which the individual Christian can and should make, and those which a Catholic Action movement, as such, should or should not make. The latter, by force of circumstances, concern and may even involve the Church as a whole. It is therefore hard to see how those responsible for a movement which is lay but also of the Church can, under the pretext that they are laymen, pretend to commit themselves and to commit others independently of the hierarchy. Here we are inevitably led to ask ourselves whether such guiding spirits could and should still consider themselves simply as laymen or whether they should not recognize that in fact, if not by right, their very responsibilities attach them to the clergy. This brings up again, under a new light, the problem of the cleric-lay contrast and invites us to emphasize for one last time how false it is, on the one hand, to identify this contrast simply with that between sacred and profane, or, on the other hand, to limit the clergy for practical purposes to the priesthood alone, to try to apply to every cleric what may be true only of the priest.

Chapter 10

THE DEVELOPMENT OF THE
SPIRITUAL LIFE: PURIFICATION

U p to this point, we have examined, first, all the elements
which together constitute a spiritual life and, second, the
different vocations which may modify not the composition but
the mutual adjustment of these elements. We still need to examine what might be called the dynamism of this life, after having
seen the statics of its components: how, given these elements, it
comes to integrate them little by little, precisely by living—or
how, which comes to the same thing, this life itself is developed.

That the spiritual life, like all life, is a development is
asserted by the whole Bible and, most expressly, by the New Testament. St. Paul teaches this in particularly remarkable terms,
for they imply not only the fact of a development but also the
necessity we are under of applying ourselves to it deliberately:
"Forgetting what is behind me, tending toward what is ahead,
I run toward the goal, toward the prize of the vocation from on
high in Christ Jesus" (Phil 3:13).

This development of the Christian is engrafted into the
growth of the whole Church, the goal which St. Paul again

describes: ". . . that we may all meet in the unity of faith and of knowledge of the Son of God, [so as to form] a perfect man, to the measure of the mature age of Christ" (Eph 4:13).

Furthermore, he speaks of new Christians as being children who should, after having been fed with milk, come to taste a more substantial food (1 Cor 3:1; cf. Eph 4:14).

Progress and Alternations

This growth can, therefore, certainly be described as progress. In fact, the Fathers of the Church, and St. Gregory of Nyssa in particular, emphasize the unceasing and perpetual progress in which every Christian life must consist. St. Augustine does not hesitate to say that anyone who does not make progress in it must be regressing, nay must even be in danger of falling away entirely.

Beginning with the end of the fourth century, there has been much concern to define the principal stages of this progress. After various tentative sketches, a first definite division into three stages was made by Evagrius Ponticus and then taken over by the majority of writers. They did not usually adopt these three stages under precisely the form they took with Evagrius but rather under the form they assumed a little later with Pseudo-Dionysius. Borrowing a vocabulary already familiar to Neo-Platonism, they speak of the three successive ways of purification, illumination, and union with God: the purgative, illuminative, unitive ways.

Some hints at least of this scheme are found even in Origen who, in dealing with the reading of the various sapiential books, is concerned to connect them with the three successive stages of the spiritual life: infancy, youth, and maturity (to which correspond respectively Proverbs, Ecclesiastes, and the Canticle).

Yet Origen does not devote himself so much to this regular division as to what we might call the rhythms of the spiritual life. Tracing these out, following the example of Philo and the Jewish Haggadah, in accordance with the history of the people of Israel, he sees the spiritual life as a succession of obscure and luminous phases, alternating in such a way that progress does not take place along a straight line, so to speak, but rather a spiral, seeming to go back again and again over the same points and yet continuing upward by means of these very returns. Gregory of Nyssa deepens this view by showing that the darkness and the light are only relative: what is light when we first reach it becomes dark when we linger in it, and thus we are always urged to go on toward further light. Evagrius to a certain degree and, more explicitly, Pseudo-Dionysius reverse these images: according to them, it is the darkness in which faith loses itself beyond the reach of ordinary human understanding which becomes light when grace causes us to attain it. . . .

Nearer our own times, St. John of the Cross, in his succession of active and passive nights of the senses and of the soul, combines in a particularly happy way the scheme of the three phases of the spiritual life with the perpetual rhythm of alternating shadow and brightness.

The Three Ways

Before undertaking any explanation of these traditional ideas on spiritual progress, it is most important to emphasize the fact that the distinction between the three ways should not be overdone. On the one hand, all the authorities agree in saying that there is no peak in the spiritual life here on earth so high that it cannot be transcended. Conversely, God can, without doubt, in certain more or less exceptional cases, raise a soul from sin to a high degree of sanctity without any very apparent period of transition. But, even more important, Evagrius himself, who was the first to present with precision the distinction between the three stages of the spiritual life, was also the first to set out clearly what is merely relative about them. Although in theory purification precedes illumination, he emphasizes the fact that purification is only completed in and by illumination. As he says in a formula to which we shall return, *apatheia* is only perfected by *gnosis.*

In truth, the distinction in question here is rather one of predominant aspects in the spiritual life during one or another of its phases than of rigorously successive forms.

Taking into account these various reservations, let us now see how the traditional scheme of the three ways, or, if you prefer, of the three ages of the spiritual life, is presented.

The first phase, as its name (the purgative way) adequately indicates, is dominated by the struggle against habitual sins, against the vices encumbering the life of fallen humanity. This conflict against the forces of sin is, from the outset, developed in an effort, sustained by faith, to extricate ourselves from the pressure that the spirit of evil exercises on our weak will by the intermediary of the world and the flesh.

To the extent, however, to which victory can be glimpsed, to which freedom manifests itself, the virtues are developed. We might say that we go from the purgative to the illuminative way from the moment when virtues begin to outweigh vices, or, in other words, when the grace of Christ bears some positive fruits within us. This new phase is described as "illumination" because the relative dominance over the sensible impressions, which hitherto have carried us away, allows us to develop an understanding of the truths of faith which takes on substance to the degree to which we become in accord with them. Formerly foreign to our experience and thus obscure, they are now filled with light and enlighten our whole existence.

From this moment on, the soul tends to union with God in a superior form of contemplation in which the charity poured out in our hearts by the Holy Spirit finds its development. Then, according to the authorities, the "gifts" of the Spirit, moving the soul directly and, as it were, perceptibly, outweigh the still laborious exercise of the virtues. It is truly life in the Holy Spirit that now begins—"charismatic" life in which we are at once wholly in the hand of God and arrive at a higher freedom and spontaneity.

Purification

The preceding scheme, as we can never repeat too often, should not deceive us and make us believe that the virtues can only develop in us after the vices have been destroyed. Quite the reverse, it is a first development of the virtues which alone can gain the upper hand of our vices, just as, later on, these will be completely uprooted by the flowering of the virtues and, finally, by the highest gifts of the Spirit.

In particular, as Evagrius emphasizes, it is on the basis of faith that the Christian is to carry out the whole spiritual warfare against sin and what incites us to sin. This combat, indeed, cannot be victorious unless it is from the beginning the work of divine grace in us. The spirit of evil is not driven out except by the influence of the Spirit of God.

Sin, let us repeat, is always in its source a proud revolt: the act of a creature wishing to take itself as its law and its final end, as if it were the Creator himself. In man, this revolt becomes concrete above all in the desire for some form of enjoyment, for some sensual pleasure sought egotistically, in defiance of what justifies pleasure in our nature as God has willed it. Thus, there is created in fallen humanity an inclination to disobedience which makes the individual a plaything in the hands of the spirit of evil, making use at once of the desires in our own flesh disordered by original sin and of the innumerable stimuli provided by a seemingly perverted world which come to reinforce these desires.

Against all this, the only liberating power which can be truly and radically effective is divine grace. This, in the strongest sense that the word can have in Christian language, is the fruit of the Holy Spirit present in us, driving the wicked spirit out of our heart and recreating in it, not only the aspirations toward a life in conformity with the Law of God which are to be found more or less buried there but, as St. Paul says, "the willing and the doing."

This activity of grace in us should in no way, however, be understood as a pure and simple substitution of God for ourselves in such a way that he would work in us as if in our stead. Quite the contrary, the same St. Paul who tells us that "God creates in us both the willing and the doing" exhorts us, precisely for this reason, to "work at [our] salvation with fear and trembling" (Phil 2:12–13). In other words, this "willing" and this "doing" that God creates in us are nonetheless our own. To repeat once more, God does not substitute himself, by his grace, for our own nature: he regenerates it. This active presence of God in us remains profoundly mysterious, and it is this presence that is the primary object of faith. We are called to act, that is, trusting in the powers of another and not at all in our own, but yet to act ourselves, we who see nothing in us but weakness. Whence the laborious character of the salutary warfare against sin, a character which is in no way abolished by grace. Quite the contrary, it is thus that we are saved by faith and not by any confidence that we might put in anything that we see in ourselves and that we might consider our own.

The substitution in us, in our heart, of the Spirit of God for the spirit of evil comes about at first without any outward indication. Even before faith and Baptism, the two spirits are at war: a war of which we are not only the prize but the terrain. The change brought about by Baptism is that while previously the spirit of evil was established as master within us, but a master whose empire was contested by the Spirit of God, now the situation is reversed. It is the divine Spirit who is established in the depth of the soul, while the spirit of evil, now driven out, does not cease to make use of all the allies he still retains in our flesh and in the world around us to reverse the situation to his advantage.

Such is the origin of the spiritual combat within the Christian himself. Its objective is progressively to overcome this dividedness, this *dipsychia* as the ancient writers call it, to attain a complete restoration of "simplicity of heart." This will be regained when the divine Spirit within us has completely subjugated the evil spirit. It can be said, then, that the presence of the Spirit in the soul, as its master recognized by faith, is the principle of the spiritual combat, while his effective dominion in our whole being is its goal.

Under these conditions, it is possible to see the exact bearing of the term "purification" applied to the first phase in the spiritual life. The Fathers made abundant use of Neo-Platonic formulae to describe the effort required to extricate the divine image within us from everything that has befouled it. But it would be completely wrong to understand them as if the question were simply one of bringing to light an inalienable likeness, remaining in us and merely hidden under the effect of sin—a likeness which we would merely have to rediscover by our own efforts, simply aided by grace. In taking up this theme of the image of God, the Fathers always explain it as being like an image in a mirror: for such an image to shine out anew, it is not enough to have the mirror cleansed of all encrustations; the living presence of the model must also be restored. As Evagrius again says, it is not the spirituality of our nature which, by itself, makes us images of God: that nature must also become (or become again) the temple of the Holy Trinity.

In other words, the grace that restores us, that purifies us does so only through raising us to a participation in the divine life, a participation which cannot be conceived apart from the living presence, at once personal and active, of God within us, a presence which, by its sole and proper power, makes us live in union with him. As Latin scholasticism says, it is on the basis of habitual or sanctifying grace, flowing from the vivifying presence of God in our soul, that his actual graces, in all our regenerated actions, cause us to act in such a way that what we do, while being fully our own activity, will also be wholly God's and so sanctified.

To such a vision of the work of grace in us should correspond, on our part, an activity in the spiritual combat and in prayer which proceeds wholly from faith. In order that the divine action, the divine life may thus pass into us, we must open ourselves out to it, and we cannot do so except by continually reactivating our faith in the Word that assures us of it, by the prayer that opens us out to it. Once again, we must recognize in the very prayer which carries us toward God and which strips us of all confidence in ourselves to give us up to an action proceeding wholly from his grace, both the first divine grace and the source of all others.

The Vices

Although sin has but one source, it has many branches in its manifestations or applications. The struggle against it must then begin by taking account, in the light of the divine Word, of the different forms in which it clothes itself. For it is under these multiple appearances that it must be attacked so that the old self in us will die and in its place may be developed the new self, who is nothing other than Christ in us.

St. Paul and the primitive catecheses multiply descriptions of these forms of sin, but to the slowly systematized asceticism of monasticism is due their more or less strict classification. Here again, the role of Evagrius is decisive. He clarifies how sin becomes molded within us, so to say, according to what he calls the "eight evil thoughts," meaning by this ways of looking at life for practical purposes which fashion it contrary to the design of God. In accordance with the account of the first sin in Genesis, he first distinguishes gluttony: the attraction of the forbidden fruit, the disordered desire for sensible pleasure in its elementary forms. From this in turn is born lust, which gives up to sensuality not only a superficial zone of our sensibility but what is, as it were, its core. To satisfy gluttony and lust, the love of money next enters in. But this, by its very inanity, installs sadness, that is, incurable dissatisfaction within us. Sadness in turn, trying vainly to obtain at any cost what is lacking to it and what it can neither gain nor even define, engenders impotent explosions of anger. These are, as it were, the converse of *acedia*, the spiritual debility which sin induces little by little: with the sensuality which cannot satisfy itself is paired a growing insensibility to spiritual realities. Then vainglory makes us seek all around us, by a display devoid of substance, for the satisfaction which we feel confusedly we can no longer find in ourselves. And underneath all this, what is revealed in the final analysis, when all the more or less carnal coverings in which it was disguised are stripped away, is the root sin of the rebel spirit: pride.

In place of this progressive revelation of the malice of sin, disclosing all its depths as it unfolds, the medieval spiritual writers adopted a more theoretical classification which still covers the greater part of the preceding one. This is the classification according to the capital sins, the sources of all the others, as connected with the threefold lust described by St. John in his First Epistle: the lust of the flesh, the lust of the eyes, the pride of life (2:16). To the "pride of life" is linked pride in the strict sense (the tendency to make ourselves the center of everything), the limitless envy which results from it, and the anger which comes from envy frustrated. From the "lust of the flesh" proceed gluttony and lust as well as the sloth that ensnares us in pleasure. In the "lust of the eyes," finally, is seen the motive force of all avarice, attached to apparent riches at the expense of what is truly good.

These different classifications are, obviously, neither exhaustive nor absolute. They are only attempts to take cognizance of, and cover, the concrete reality of sin in the whole detail of our life and so to gain the realistic consciousness of ourselves which is the first condition of all progress (as antiquity had already perceived in the Delphic precept "know thyself"). In this regard, we cannot overemphasize the importance, both at the beginning of the spiritual combat and throughout its whole course, of uncompromising truthfulness with ourselves. The devil is the father of sin in being the father of lies. We cannot escape from him unless we have, from the beginning, determined to avoid all lying and, above all, the fundamental lie which consists in deceiving ourselves, in avoiding the sight of what we really are so as not to have to change ourselves.

Yet inasmuch as sin has troubled our flesh, itself ensnared in the world perverted by sin, such lucidity is not possible without faith. Without faith, furthermore, even if it became possible for us, it could only lead to despair. But faith, restoring by adhesion to the divine Word the very principle of our perception of true reality as God sees it and wills it, makes such self-knowledge possible and salutary. It gives us back, together with the perception of true values, the sense of our faultiness. And, in causing us to measure our abasement, it not only explains it but discloses the means to escape from it which God has put within our reach.

It is in this sense only that we can accept the Socratic teaching according to which sin is an error from which we can escape only by recovering a true view of things, one not dominated by the sensible appearances in which we are actually immersed. For this is true only if knowledge bears not only on the world and humanity as they are at present but also as God wishes them to be and on the means he has put within our reach of going from one condition to the other. And, we must also add, the initial error, like the regained true knowledge, is not simply theoretical but also practical; perversion of the will is here inseparable from false judgment. In this sense, the error of sin is a voluntary error, just as the knowledge that saves presupposes at least an embryonic love of God revived in us by grace.

The Struggle Against the *Pathe*

It is Evagrius again who has given us the first and most interesting systematic presentation of the struggle against the sensible impressions, of the flesh and the world together, by which the devil holds us in slavery to sin. For him, the whole spiritual combat is centered on these *pathe,* which more modern authors translate as "passions" but which are not to be understood in the modern sense of this word. What is meant here is not a psychological complex focusing our sensibility and desire on a particular object but, once again, the impressions produced on our will by a sensibility which the exclusive quest of egotistic pleasure has, as it were, crazed.

Faith, to repeat again, is the principle of this warfare since it restores to us the certitude, still obscure but nonetheless potent, of the superior reality of the divine Spirit and of the life to which he calls us. It is thus that faith, as Evagrius explains, engenders that holy fear which sin has, as it were, put to sleep and which makes us respect the prohibitions of the divine Word, hitherto obscured for us by the appeal of the senses.

From fear in turn proceeds *enkrateia*, which, as we have already said, is continence but a continence which restrains not only the sexual appetite but also all the other attractions of the senses. It is here that sensible mortification comes in, refusing to our sensibility the satisfactions it demands. Fasting and ascetical abstention, by repulsing pleasure, hold desire checked and curbed. A further step is, through patience, not only to resist in the light of faith the hitherto victorious attraction of pleasure but to endure whatever is painful about the present life, especially the ascetical life which we may have embraced in one or another form.

Continence and patience do not develop without the rebirth of hope as well: along with the ability to rule the desires aroused only by the taste for pleasure and to accept the hardships which oppose these desires, is developed the taste, hitherto stifled, for spiritual good things—for those promises God makes to faith which are the counterpart of his demands.

The climax of all this development, which corresponds to the progressive extinction of the vices, is what Evagrius (following Clement of Alexandria but with a great deal more precision in his thoughts and his formulations) calls *apatheia*. As we have said already, *apatheia* is not insensibility and still less impeccability. It is simply domination over sensible impressions as this has become habitual in the believing soul which has thus "mortified its members which are on the earth," according to the phrase of St. Paul, to regenerate its taste for the things of God. It is no longer its unbounded desires that rule it henceforth, in subjection to the flesh and the world, but the very Spirit of God. The attainment of *apatheia* has, then, as its immediate counterpart the diffusion in our heart of the love of God, of that heavenly *agape* poured out by the coming of the Holy Spirit.

In describing the state resulting from the purgation of the soul by mortification of the *pathe*, the Fathers draw largely on the teaching of the Stoics. These had already made the name (*apatheia*) the property of their prudent ideal of self-mastery, realized in the voluntary subjection of reason to the master of the universe, to the contempt of sensible impressions. Yet the Christian *apatheia* differs from the Stoic first of all in that it is not acceptance merely of the impersonal law that rules the universe but of the will of a free and all-loving God known by faith. And this God leads us to *apatheia*, not by the constraint of his almightiness to which *we* could only resign ourselves passively but by the condescension of his grace. To this we adhere, not only freely but through an act of faith vivified by love which is, as it were, the very restoration of our liberty hitherto captive under the yoke of sin, of the flesh, the world, the devil. We might even say, along the line of St. Paul, that here love is victorious over the Law of God himself in the sense that *apatheia* does not move us to submit ourselves to a law imposed from without as a constraint upon our will but to adhere with the freest possible filial love to the generosity, to the creative spontaneity of the Father's love.

It is in this sense that St. Gregory of Nyssa, for example, and, a little later on, St. John Chrysostom take up and transpose the Stoic comparison of the wise man to a king. For by *apatheia*

we are introduced into that kingdom of God in which we are
not merely subjects but heirs of the Father, coheirs with Christ,
because our soul, instead of being enslaved to the flesh and by
the flesh to the world, being now subject to the Kingship of
Christ, reigns once more over its own body, and at the same
time, by its faith, triumphs over the world.

Purification and the Practice of the Counsels, Particularly Obedience

As we have said, purification presupposes mortification. In other
words, there is need for that fasting, in the most general sense of
the term, which, as has already been explained, must be given
its place in every authentic Christian life. However, as has also
been said already, since purification should simply make room
in our heart for the love of God, fasting normally goes along
with almsgiving, or, more generally, with a self-giving to the will
of God which takes the form of serving others.

Fasting and almsgiving, detaching us from the flesh to give
us up in charity to the Spirit, are perfected, in the "religious" and
particularly in the monastic life, by that *xeniteia*, that effective
adoption of the state of "pilgrims" and "travelers" which uproots
us from the world. Poverty and celibacy form its basis, but
obedience is its core: here is attained that necessary and radical
disappropriation of self without which we cannot be wholly
God's. Obedience plays a particularly important part at the
beginning of the spiritual life, and here it takes a special form,
which has been well defined by William of St. Thierry, certainly
the greatest theoretician of asceticism in the Cistercian school.

At this point, the man or woman who is still fully occupied
with the initial striving for purification has only a bare faith in
spiritual realities; this is faith pure and simple as Origen calls it.

This faith adheres purely and simply to the divine Word because it has recognized it as such, but the content of the Word is as yet almost entirely obscure to it because the realities it speaks of are still deeply foreign to the experience of the believer. In this state, at this stage, it is strictly true to say, as does St. Paul, that faith comes "from what one has heard," as it were, by hearsay.

The result is that the novice in the spiritual life cannot make sure progress without a master who, knowing his or her particular case, will watch over this faith which is still so little rooted in the believer and draw out the vital consequences of it for him or her. This master, as a spiritual father, should be a tried believer, one whose faith has passed over into his own life and who, therefore, has at least begun to experience the objects of faith. To the degree to which his obedience has submitted to the requirements of faith and has made a first test of its promises, it has created in him a connaturality with these objects, a connaturality which the sinful man or woman, does not, or does not yet, possess.

Thus, as beginners receive their faith from without, the obedience through which faith is to inform their whole life must be presented to them from without—that is, at this stage, above all by a master who himself knows from experience the bond between faith and life. It is in this way, and in this way only, that novices can in turn effectively make their own faith enter into their own life. The obedience to another, which is basically obedience to a tried master, is thus a necessity or a quasi necessity for a beginner; it is what William calls *obedientia necessitatis*.

Accompanying this spiritual direction and giving obedience to someone else its own special necessity at the beginning of the spiritual life, is the practice of the examination of conscience. By this is meant a self-examination which takes up one by one the vices, or the virtues opposed to them, to try to determine concretely our position in relation to each according to the particulars of our most recent behavior. This, again, is an inheritance from the Stoics adopted by the ancient monks. Above all, when carried out under the guidance of a wise spiritual father, this practice can be extremely fruitful in the gaining of true knowledge of self and so in progressing with assurance.

Yet it must be guarded from excess in two ways. The considering of ourselves, even at the beginning of the spiritual life, must never come to take precedence over the contemplation of Christ and his mystery. The particular examen must never come to take over the whole of prayer. On the contrary, the particular examen is simply a means by which prayer is to have its practical effects in our lives. In the second place, the particular examen should not go into such minutiae as to destroy the spontaneity of our interior life. It is good to be clear-sighted about ourselves, but it is never good to adopt permanently a reflex consciousness of all our actions that has us live as if we were continually looking at ourselves in a mirror. It is to prevent such misuses and excesses that the help of a guide is so necessary.

The Beginning and the End of This Purification

In conclusion, something should be said about the beginning and the termination, in so far as any exists, of the stage of purification. We enter into this first phase of the spiritual life originally by way of penitence, or, more precisely, by what the New Testament calls *metanoia,* which is precisely a "change of spirit," a conversion. It is very difficult to give any analysis, much less a description, of this process. Divine grace, as we have already seen in connection with the different vocations, has many ways of leading the souls given up to it and, it would seem, an even greater variety of means for turning toward it those who have previously ignored or misunderstood it. In fact, whether they are slow or sudden, conversions constitute a type of human experience in which a great variety of forms may clothe what remains substantially the same: the substitution of a living faith for a dead faith or for no faith at all.

It should be emphasized, however, that the most speedy conversions, even those so sudden as to seem almost instantaneous, are so, ordinarily, in appearance only. The experience of St. Paul on the road to Damascus must have been prepared, without his having been aware of it, by the sight of St. Stephen's martyrdom and, long before that perhaps, by whatever provoked him to such violent opposition to the Christians. More important still is to observe the fact that the most violent transformations, those which seem the most complete, may still be only the beginning of a progressive assimilation by the whole personality of what it has seized in a flash. Even though a single act of living faith, that is one in which the love of God is reborn in contrition for sin, in the firm hope in grace, is enough for the justification of the sinner, still his or her integral sanctification can never be other than the work of a whole life: preeminently the work of God, but a work in which it is we ourselves who are re-created in true liberty; and this implies that we cannot become so without our cooperation, even though this cooperation remains, and in a sense remains entirely, the supreme fruit of grace.

A special question that arises here is that of the first personal developments of the spiritual life in a Christian who was baptized before the awakening of his or her conscience and who has thus initially entered the faith before this first awakening. In such a case, can we speak of "conversion"? We most certainly *can* do so, even if childhood or adolescence do not involve grave faults later requiring a radical reform. For there is a decisive moment in every life in which the personality freely and consciously ratifies what was communicated to it before it enjoyed its proper autonomy or breaks away from it. Yet here, even more than in adult conversions, the diversity of ways taken by grace defies all methodical description. Here above all, in many cases, the fixing of the precise moment in which the decision was taken escapes even the person concerned. Adolescence, obviously, is for the majority the period in which such decisions are taken. But in this respect there are personalities whose spiritual precociousness is astonishing, and others whose indecisiveness is prolonged beyond belief.

What must surely be emphasized in connection with the beginnings of the spiritual life in children and adolescents brought up in a Christian way is, first, the necessity for a training in which religious formation goes along with formation for existence in general. This should be understood as applying to the communication of the truths of the faith (what is called "religious instruction") as well as to the application of faith to life. But later on, when the personality awakens, it is surely important to avoid, here more than anywhere else, any kind of constraint, purely moral constraint furthermore, proving worse than any other kind. The person called on to make personal decisions that will involve his or her whole life should be given every kind of enlightenment by his or her educators and every possible encouragement, but these educators should resist the temptation to believe that they can ever make these decisions for him or her.

What is true of personal conversion is even more true of choice of vocation, whether there is question of a priestly or religious vocation or of that vocation to human tasks and human responsibilities (marriage, a family) taking on a Christian meaning, the importance of which we have already pointed out. Here we can enlighten young people as to the nature of the choices open to them; we can, when one or another choice begins to be clarified, give it prudent encouragement, but we can never anticipate it, still less force it, without risking very serious errors.

The end of the stage of purification in any life, as we have already said, is even less precisely determinable than the exact moment of conversion. Just as the heights of union with God certainly begin to attract us and become the object of some indefinable presentiment from the time of conversion and even before this has been fully accomplished, so purification goes on to the end.

We can, nevertheless, name certain signs which indicate that the most decisive part of this work has, perhaps, been accomplished. Still, as we have said, this in no way makes impossible lapses pure and simple, still less new and more serious failings such as those of spiritual pride, which prove ever more threatening the higher we mount toward God. Having taken account of these limitations which must always be kept in mind, here are some of the best-known signs of an effective purification of the soul. Evagrius, again, first grouped them together in his description of *apatheia* tending toward its proper perfection. The first sign he indicates is the possibility of praying without distractions. The purified soul is no longer the slave of sensible impressions; on the contrary, it is faith that is victorious over everything else. Prayer, in which the soul can give itself up to faith, then takes possession of it with no further resistance.

More generally, the purified soul is no longer subject to the impressions made on it by the things of this world, nor to the impressions that emanate from the world but continue to echo within us even without their actually being present to us. Such a soul has mastered, in other words, not only the immediate attraction of things or beings and the attraction of the sensations they produce on it but also the far more subtle attraction of memory and the imagination. The thought of the things or the beings of this world henceforth disturbs it no more than does the fact of their presence.

More profoundly still, as Cassian emphasizes even more than Evagrius himself, if purification is fully authentic, it must go beyond the limited field of our consciousness and extend even to our unconscious. Modern depth psychology has fully verified the assertion of the ancient writers that a purification which bears only on the conscious as such may be very questionable. It may only be the artificial termination of a process of repression which, far from healing the personality, runs the risk of increasing in its depths the tension of forces that may sunder it.

Here appears, again in accord with ancient monastic tradition, the importance accorded to a knowledge of self that goes beyond appearances and of entrance into the desert of complete solitude. For it is only thus that all the superficial coverings of our "I" will be shattered and that the demons we all bear within us will finally show themselves so that we can really confront them. And it is here, to put it briefly, that it would indeed seem as if only the monastic life, in its most rigorous form, is revealed as capable of leading a soul so far, where even the most generous types of "religious" life which do not include this entrance into the desert cannot lead by their very nature. It is understood, of course, that many monks, even very earnest monks, may in this respect remain on this side of the possibilities offered by their vocation. Conversely, many other religious and, as ancient monastic literature untiringly repeats, many laypeople living in the world may prove to be monks according to the Spirit. In any case, it is the trial of solitude in the presence of God that alone can make us meet and overcome in the last strongholds within us that "old self" which the "new self" in Christ is to supplant. And this is why the Gospel exhortation to enter into a place apart is addressed to all.

This explains why Evagrius, or Cassian after him, who believes along with modern psychologists that the purification of the soul is not completed until a calm passing over from our waking life to our unconscious life manifests itself even in our dreams, finally places the height of purification in a capacity to make a perfectly objective judgment with regard to self. Perfect purity of soul, in other words, is the exact contrary of a false innocence. It does not exist, in fact, until the moment when we can, without faltering, view ourselves wholly as we are; see ourselves as God sees us; and judge ourselves as he judges us.

It is when we are conscious of this that the statement of Evagrius becomes obvious: if purification, in a sense, comes before any effort toward illumination and union, it nevertheless cannot be completed except at the heights of illumination (and perhaps, we would add, of union). "*Praktike* [this is one of his most common terms for the first stage of the spiritual life]," he says, "is a spiritual method for purifying the sensible part of the soul. But the energies of the commandments do not suffice perfectly to heal the powers of the soul if contemplations do not then come to take hold of the *nous* [the spiritual intelligence]."

St. John of the Cross, for his part, shows better than anyone before him how the process of purification must take place not once but several times in the course of a spiritual life. Apparently dominated at first by our voluntary efforts, it becomes progressively a work of God that is essentially mysterious, the course of which escapes us. First applied to the senses, it must be continued in the most interior, the most spiritual aspects of the soul, and it will not be completed until the soul is wholly immersed in God and, at the resurrection, its very body. These are the nights, first active and then passive, of the senses and of the spirit, of which we shall speak again when, having finished our general description of progress in the spiritual life, we shall

come back to the rhythms and the alternations essential to all
spirituality.

Chapter 11

THE DEVELOPMENT AND THE
RHYTHMS OF THE SPIRITUAL LIFE:
ILLUMINATION AND UNION

The counterpart of the purification through which every soul must pass in entering on the spiritual life is what has been called "illumination." It cannot be said flatly that illumination comes after purification, as though they were two operations having nothing to do with one another. The fact is, as Evagrius already brought out, that since the principle of all Christian purification is faith, there can be no true purification otherwise than on the basis of a first and fundamental illumination. Conversely, as Evagrius again reminds us, purification cannot be completed except by "gnosis," taking the word in the sense in which the most orthodox Fathers take it; that is, the understanding of God, the development of which characterizes the illuminative way.

It could be said, however, that the positive aspect of illumination predominates in the spiritual life to the extent to which, purification having done its work, the soul is no longer preoccupied and, as it were, encumbered by a wholly sensual view of things. Then faith is no longer what Origen calls "faith pure and simple": acceptance of divine truths solely on the authority of the divine Word while they remain almost totally obscure to us. It now becomes what he calls a "scientific faith," meaning by this not in the least a well-informed, a reasoning, or a scholarly faith but one that begins to have some experience or some foretaste of those truths, the faith of someone whose life has been put in accord with these truths and who has thus become fit to assimilate them.

The Illuminative Way and the Development of the Virtues

This amounts to saying that the illumination we are concerned with here is not the affair of the intelligence alone; our whole being is engaged in it. As St. Paul says, the question is not only of seeing the face of Christ but also of reflecting it (cf. 2 Cor 3:18). This is why the development of the most positive virtues is connected with the illuminative way, as the extinction of vices is with the purgative.

Still following the formulations of Evagrius, let us recall that the purgative way tends to *apatheia*, that is, to the mastery, gained as our faith in Christ and our hope in him take possession of our whole being, over the *pathe*, those seemingly irresistible impressions of the flesh and the world that dominated our sinful being. It is thus that *apatheia*, far from making us "insensible" in the ordinary meaning of the word, gives us up without let or hindrance to charity, to *agape:* the very love with which God loves, poured out in our hearts by the Spirit he has given us. To the illuminative way corresponds, then, a flowering within us of charity illuminating our whole being, in such a way that faith in God who is himself charity finally enlightens an intelligence attuned to know him.

For it is charity that makes us like to God, that makes us apt to understand what He has revealed to us, with a knowledge no longer wholly enveloped in darkness, as was our faith in its beginnings in our soul, but a knowledge that presupposes a true sympathy with its object, founded on a true connaturality with it.

This development of charity within us branches out, in a way, into the development of a whole series of virtues. Their appearance, or their reappearance, in us corresponds to the restoration of our human nature in its integrity as originally willed by the Creator. For this restoration within us of a nature made to the image of God must accompany its being raised to a participation in the very life of its eternal model.

It is in this sense that the medieval authors, St. Thomas in particular, developed their theory of the supernatural virtues infused together with charity. These virtues correspond to the natural virtues already described by the greatest moralists of antiquity as the integral parts of the harmonious life of a nature faithful to its ideal. The supernatural virtues correspond to these natural virtues, but they differ from them, not only as to their origin but also as to what gives them a meaning and a perfection previously unknown.

The ancients, particularly Aristotle, distinguished four chief virtues called "cardinal" (from *cardo* signifying "hinge") because it is on them that the whole moral life turns. These virtues are fortitude (or courage), prudence, justice, and temperance.

Fortitude, meaning moral courage, is as it were the vigor of the whole life of the soul. Without it, this would not be life at all, not a real life in any case. It needs this primary energy to make it come out of its inertia and be able then to overcome the obstacles which virtue will inevitably meet with on its path.

The primordial importance of this virtue of fortitude signifies that there is no virtue which is merely negative. Virtue cannot simply result from the absence of sin; it is sin that is only the negation of virtue.

And this fortitude must be rightly applied. Whence the importance of prudence, which is the habitual disposition to form a sanely balanced practical judgment. A critical clear-sightedness in the evaluation of human actions beginning with our own (which presupposes that we have given up not only deceiving others but also fashioning illusions for ourselves while also avoiding exaggerated pessimism) should develop into a wisdom that impregnates all our decisions before it forms our actions.

It is thus that justice, which consists in giving each his or her due and, more generally, putting our whole life in accord with the exact perception of true values, can dominate our existence and characterize our whole personality.

And, for this to come about, it is also necessary that temperance be firmly established in us, that is, not only moderation imposed on all our instinctive impulses without which all the other virtues would remain powerless but also moderation acquired in the practice of the virtues themselves, keeping them from all excess, from all malformation due either to some exaggeration or to a faintheartedness no less opposed to the true greatness of the soul.

All these virtues, with the ancillary virtues that extend and diversify their application to the different spheres of human existence, are gained in the natural order of things by the exercise and repetition that make them little by little into *habitus*, habitual dispositions of the soul. But with the Christian, their principle is supernaturally infused by the Holy Spirit, together with the charity of which they are the necessary accompaniment and, as it were, the substructure. For they are nothing other than the rectitude of the soul necessarily implied in any union of the soul with the life proper to its divine model.

This infused character of the virtues does not mean that their exercise requires no effort but that this effort is to rest not on trust in ourselves, in the innate capacities of our soul, but, on the contrary, on faith in grace that heals our nature by the same movement with which it raises it to God. And when they are motivated by charity—the confident love which, in us, is total self-abandonment to the divine love that is the supremely generous gift—then fortitude and prudence, justice and temperance gain a depth, a fullness of meaning and reality that the ancients never even suspected. Instead of simply setting us in our place in a static universe, they draw us into the creative and saving impetus of Christ's love. Above all, in this very love, they open us out to the contemplation—assimilating us to what we contemplate—of that love which is the very life of God, in what is most personal about it, most transcendent to natural humanity even at its most upright.

The Knowledge of God

It has become more or less fashionable in the last fifty years, first of all among Protestants and later by an infiltration of contemporary Protestant ideas among many Catholics, to consider everything contemplative in Christian tradition, any knowledge of God that tends to take a central place, as being a Greek contamination. We are to take up this question more deeply when we speak about mysticism, but at this point we need to emphasize the fact that this is a mere prejudice, born of a study of words taken apart from their meaning in the texts, the meaning that arises from the context in which these words are found.

It is quite true that Greek thought, in amply developing its reflections on knowledge itself, had worked out a rich vocabulary which the Christians of Greek culture naturally made use of in expressing their faith. But, on the one hand, Christianity had had no need to wait for any meeting with Hellenism in order to give a central place to knowledge, especially to the knowledge of God. And, on the other hand, this "knowledge of God" was so specifically Christian (and primarily biblical and Jewish) that once this meeting had taken place, far from allowing itself to flow into unchanged Greek molds, as would appear to be the case to a quick and superficial view, Christianity rather refashioned to its own way of thinking the Greek notions it had borrowed.

The "knowledge of God" of the prophets is the knowledge that only the Word of God can produce in the person who hears it with faith. This means, as we have already explained, that it is an eminently personal knowledge, wherein the person of the believer is awakened in the adoring recognition of the divine, creative personality who is arousing it by summoning it. Under this aspect, as we have emphasized, it is a knowledge which is at once union and conformation.

It is very typical of the Hebrew vision of things that the word "to know" should be used freely to designate the sexual relationship between man and woman. And, far from there being in this any depreciation of knowledge, it is most remarkable that, conversely, the knowledge of God by the People to whom he revealed himself in his Word is compared to the union of man and wife in marriage. This is what we find particularly in prophets like Hosea and Ezekiel.

But the aspect of conformation is no less essential to the knowledge of God than is the aspect of union. Because the People of God is the People that knows him, its members must become like him. Thus it is that the revelation of the divine name to Moses, representing the people, was followed, on the same mountain, by the revelation of the divine Law. For the whole meaning of the Law, for Israel, is to mark the people with the divine seal: "Be ye holy as I am holy," Leviticus endlessly repeats. Jesus carried the same idea to its extreme when, at the end of the Sermon on the Mount—the whole object of which is to teach us to love with that generous love which is proper to God—he said: "Be ye perfect as your heavenly Father is perfect."

Here is the place to dispose of one of the grossest confusions underlying the fantastic notion that the importance given to the knowledge of God by early Christianity originated in Hellenism. In many comparative studies, we are told again and again that the idea of a transforming contemplation, bringing the contemplative to resemble that which he contemplates, is a notion of a typically Greek and, more precisely, Platonic origin. And so, whenever we encounter an idea of this kind in ancient Christian (or even Jewish) texts, we are told to see it as borrowed. But to do so is not to see that this means confusing two schemes of spirituality in which undeniable analogies still conceal a radical opposition.

For Platonism never speaks of a contemplation that brings one to resemble what one contemplates; this notion only appeared very late in Hellenism, more precisely in the writings called Hermetic under influences which were at least Jewish and perhaps even Christian. Plato did develop the idea that like could only be known by like, so that to know God, we must strive to make ourselves like him. In his thought, in other words, knowledge and likeness are closely connected, but here knowledge results from likeness and not the other way around. This amounts to saying that it is not the idea of knowledge as making us resemble what we know which has Hellenism as its source but rather the contrary: a likeness that calls forth or favors knowledge. In contrast, it is Judaism which is the source

of the idea of knowledge as causing resemblance. Indeed, this is
a direct consequence of the fact of revelation, of the God who
makes himself known by his Word and who, by one and the
same act, thus reimposes his image on his disfigured creatures
who had lost their original likeness to him by closing themselves
to his initial Word.

In this sense, the knowledge which causes likeness on our
part is only a consequence of the antecedent knowledge God has
of us—a knowledge which on his part is not a simple statement
or a cold judgment but a choice, an election, and a predilection.
This is what brings him not only to make himself known but
to communicate himself, to give himself to us in the revelation
of his Word. What we should tend toward in consequence, as
St. Paul says, is to "know even as I am known" (1 Cor 13:12).
This not only means that our knowledge of God always flows
from the primary knowledge that he has of us but also that as
his is communication and self-giving, so ours in turn should be
a loving opening out and self-abandonment.

This conformation to the God who has made us to his
image, resulting from the living "knowledge" we have gained
of him, explains how obedience is connected with faith. It is,
more precisely, the obedience *of* faith, as the apostle says (Rom
1:15), an obedience, that is, which normally follows on faith;
which is produced in us, created in us by that Word to which
faith adheres and gives itself; and which itself "creates in us
the willing and the doing" in such a way that we "work at our
salvation with fear and trembling" (Phil 2:13).

In return, it is true that, in conforming us to the Word
received in faith, this obedience makes us the more capable of
realizing our faith in the consciousness that we gain of it. To
repeat: as what the Word speaks of becomes interior to us, as the
love of God is poured out in our own hearts, we become capable

of knowing and recognizing what this love of God, which is the great object of faith, is in itself.

This is what justifies the Fathers in the use they make of Platonic formulations, insisting in their turn on the necessity we are under of working to restore within us the image of God disfigured by sin so as once more to be in a position to know him. Placed in their new context, these formulae now are to be understood in the sense of the interior dialectic of faith's development within us. It is faith, let us repeat, which is the starting point for the only effective purification: that is—as is explained by the Fathers, such as Gregory of Nyssa, who used the Neo-Platonic vocabulary of purification—the reestablishment of conformity between our will and the will of God. But, in the soul thus purified by obedience, the knowledge of faith, without changing its nature, begins to be illuminated for us. As we become like him in whom we believe, we assimilate what we believe of him.

The Development of "Gnosis"

This process is what Christian antiquity as a whole called the passage from simple faith to "gnosis." Here again, in spite of the many prejudices which encumber the manuals and which, in this case, originated in what of the scholarship of the nineteenth century has been most completely outmoded by modern discoveries, this vocabulary should in no way alarm us. It is completely untrue that the Greek word *gnosis,* meaning knowledge, was borrowed by the Fathers (Clement of Alexandria and Origen) from the vocabulary of the heretics whom the scholars of the nineteenth century commonly called "gnostics" as if the term applied to them alone. The fact of the matter is that the Fathers called these heretics "Pseudo-Gnostics," reserving true "gnosis" to the one Catholic Church. And it is equally wrong to fall back into the perennial error of overzealous comparativists and to think that the first use of this word "gnosis" originated in Greek philosophy.

The fact is that the term "gnosis" (which, in classical Greek, signifies knowledge in the widest sense of the word) never had any more limited meaning in Greek philosophy. The knowledge which is properly philosophic is always described by the word *episteme* and never by the word *gnosis*. It was in the Greek translation of the Bible, in the Septuagint, that the word *gnosis* came to take on a particular meaning: that knowledge of God so characteristic of the prophets, which we have just described. It was later on with Philo of Alexandria, but always in dependence on the biblical texts which he quoted in Greek, that *gnosis* was regularly used to describe a knowledge specifically religious and, as such, salutary.

And it was either in immediate dependence on him, or in a more general dependence on the Judaism using Greek modes of expression, that in Alexandria itself Hermetism came in turn to use "*gnosis*" with the same shade of meaning. And, finally, it was in the same dependence with regard to Judaism and the Bible that the heretics later called "Gnostics" came to use it themselves. The Christian writers, such as Clement of Alexandria, who fought against them by a recourse to Greek philosophy in no way borrowed from them this vocabulary of gnosis. And neither did they owe it to philosophy. It is equally present in those who, like Irenaeus, fought against "pseudo-gnosis" while ignoring philosophy. And it had already been used by the first Christian writers, like St. Paul, simply because they were Jews living from the Bible.

In Palestinian as well as in Greek Judaism, indeed, by reason of the heritage of the prophets received through the "sages" of Judaism, the single word for knowledge (*dahat* in Hebrew, *gnosis* in Greek) came to cover a very rich, very complex, and yet very unified religious reality. And it was this reality that was taken up by primitive Christianity so that in Christianity it might attain its full development.

The "gnosis" of the Judaism contemporary with Christian origins is always, basically, the "knowledge of God" of the prophets. But it is also the "knowledge" which the sages had probed and deepened by their reflections: the knowledge of the ways of God in accord with which humanity should regulate its own ways. It is, consequently, the practical discernment which should guide the whole life of the thoughtful Israelite for whom "the fear of God is the source of Wisdom" (Prv 1:17). Yet, as it was finally revealed (cf. Dn 2) that God alone is truly wise, that he alone can communicate wisdom to whom he wishes, this practical knowledge, like the "knowledge of God" from which it proceeds, finally came to consist in the "knowledge of the scriptures." In the tradition of the rabbis, teachers of the Law, this was the proper object of *Halakah*, the casuistry on the basis of the traditional scriptural commentary which went to the Bible to seek solutions for the all concrete problems arising in the life of the devout Jew.

But the rabbinical *halakah* was not separated from the *haggadah*, that is, the commentary which Philo was the first to call "mystical," which searched the scriptures so as to apply the history of the past, the great deeds God had wrought for the forefathers of the people, to present history and to the history of each individual. With *haggadah* is connected the whole literature called "apocalyptic," which examines the scriptures to gather from them a "revelation" of the supreme designs of God, of the ways by which he will finally, in spite of everything now opposing his will in this world, assert his kingdom and thus bring deliverance to his own.

At this point, the apocalyptic *haggadah* becomes an anticipated vision of the designs of God in their ultimate, or, as is said
today, "eschatological," realizations. And it is thus that knowledge, "gnosis" in the Jewish texts of Qumran, becomes particularly the "gnosis of the mysteries"—that is, of the final secrets
of history, of the messianic kingdom ready to be inaugurated.

But, for believers, for the faithful who have sacrificed everything for this expectation of the kingdom, the faith animating
their soul in some way anticipates the kingdom. Inspired by
the prophetic Spirit, they not only see, but also to some degree
realize in advance, what God has in reserve for those he has
chosen. . . .

Thus "gnosis," "knowledge of God" in the biblical sense,
becomes a discernment of the way of salvation which the
believer is to follow, an anticipated discernment of the ways by
which God himself is coming to meet his own, and also finally
a quasi-ecstatic contemplation of the radiant future advancing
toward us together with him, even in the midst of the worst
trials which still await the elect.

In the words of Christ as the synoptic gospels report them
to us, the "gnosis" of these mysteries of the kingdom is given,
under the veil of parables, to those who believe in this kingdom
as inaugurated in the very person of the King, Jesus. The famous
logion of St. Matthew and St. Luke already concentrates this
"gnosis" on the person of the Son, known by us (through revelation) with a "knowledge" which is participation in that which
the Father himself has of the Son and which, reciprocally, opens
to us the knowledge of the Father himself: "No one knows the
Son but the Father, and no one knows the Father but the Son
and those to whom he wills to reveal him" (Mt 11:27; cf. Lk
10:22).

With St. Paul, "gnosis" retains all its Jewish connotations.
But emphasis is given to the fact that it is a gift of the Spirit,

preeminently an eschatological gift, and that it is achieved in the "gnosis of the mystery," of the unique mystery which is Christ and particularly his Cross, but also "Christ in us, the hope of glory" (Col 1:27)—that is, Christ definitively illuminating the scriptures by fulfilling them.

As early as the Second Epistle to the Corinthians, for St. Paul, "knowledge of the scriptures"—which evidently is one with the "gnosis" of 1 Corinthians 12 by which we come to know God as we have been known by him "in Christ"—is defined as "reflecting with unveiled face the glory of the Lord, being transformed to his own image from glory to glory as by the Lord who is Spirit" (3:18).

The Epistles of the captivity deepen this idea without adding anything to it, showing how the "gnosis of the mystery" (Col 2; Eph 1:9) has us discover in Christ himself all the treasures of the wisdom of God which are the treasures of his love, inexpressible otherwise than by the Cross.

St. John, finally, (who never uses the noun *gnosis* but rather, very frequently, the infinitive *gnonai*) has "to know" Christ as that in which living faith will find its realization: a fellowship which is the reciprocal knowledge by which Christ and his Father live within each other, are one with each other, a fellowship which transports us all within their unity, their community of life in love (chapter 17, particularly the beginning and the end).

The early Church, then, like Judaism before her, gave thanks in her Eucharist for the inseparable gift of the life and the "knowledge" given us in Christ and particularly in his Cross.

Before the appearance of the properly intellectual and relatively Hellenizing tradition first of the apologist Fathers and then of the Alexandrians, the Church, with Irenaeus in particular, made "gnosis" a living perception of the "hypothesis of the faith"; that is, of the traditional vision of faith which in Christ illuminates the whole meaning of the scriptures. It is offered to every Christian eager for the perfection of the Spirit, which is not reserved to an intellectually aristocratic elite but given to all practicing believers together with their faith. In this perspective, the supreme "gnostic" is the martyr.

Clement of Alexandria, as has been too little brought out, takes up all the "gnostic" themes of Irenaeus. For him also, it is the martyr who has attained the height of "gnosis," and "gnosis" is nothing other than discovery of the "symphony of the scriptures" in Christ. This "gnosis" is not accessible except to those to whom its true meaning has been opened out by that mysterious tradition he praises, which is but one with the acceptance of the "ecclesiastical canon," that is, the Church's rule of faith.

Certainly, he insists for his part on everything a wide culture could provide to aid in developing this "gnosis," particularly in facilitating criticism of fallacious, purely verbal, interpretations of scripture. But this appearance of intellectualism assured by the orthodox Alexandrian "gnosis" is dissipated by Origen who, better than anyone else, reaffirms and develops throughout his meditation on scripture the theme that there is no Christian "gnosis" which is anything other than a "gnosis of the mystery": that is, "gnosis of Christ," especially of his Cross, and of his Cross seen in all the perspectives of the Resurrection and the Mystical Body.

And, finally, it was in monastic literature, and once more with Evagrius, that "gnosis" attained its full spiritual development. For Evagrius—who was the disciple, but the very individual disciple, of Clement, of Origen, and of the old Egyptian monks wholly evangelical in spirit, such as Macarius of Scete—"gnosis" begins on the basis of *apatheia* when this has become, if not perfect, at least sufficiently real for the development of *agape*, charity. Together with the development of *agape* in the soul "gnosis" itself develops. Nourished with the words of the Lord, the *logoi*, it restores true "reason" in us, which is simply the adherence of the human spirit to the archetypal "reason," the personal *Logos* of God, Christ. As it thus develops, it goes through five phases, which Evagrius enumerates in various places, and defines as the "gnosis" of corporeal realities, of incorporeal beings, of divine providence, of the divine judgments, and—wholly transcendent to the preceding—the "gnosis of the Holy Trinity."

The gnosis of corporeal realities is a vision of this world proceeding from that which God himself has of it and which his Word communicates to faith and substitutes for the narrowly sensual vision of fallen humanity enslaved to the *pathe*, as we have already described them in the preceding chapter. We now see the world, this very physical world in which we are immersed by our body, no longer as a mere excitant of our appetites, as the satisfaction offered to our taste for egoistic pleasure, but as a primary revelation of God, as the product of his Word in which the Word is, as it were, materialized, and as the ready instrument of the glorification we are to give to its Creator.

This elementary gnosis, nourished in us by the teaching of scripture and especially of the Psalter, leads us toward a superior stage: that in which we recognize that the profound reality of the created universe is spiritual. Not only is the body expressive of the spirit in man, but also the reality of the whole sensible universe is merely a mysterious manifestation of an intelligible, spiritual universe in which personal being is the true being and in which is shown forth both the original grandeur of that being, as the image of the greatness of its Creator, and its Fall. This is the angelic world, a world wholly spiritual in principle, whose disobedience has darkened the "sensible" world itself and made it what it is: a lure attracting people to sin when it should incite them to praise.

From this second stage of "gnosis" which causes us to discover the world as simply the locus of a spiritual drama, we go on to the "gnosis of providence." This causes us to discover how God has disposed everything according to his sovereign wisdom and boundless love, in such a way that "all things work together for the good of those who love him," as St. Paul says (Rom 8:28). In other words, the world we are in, tragically marked by the Fall, is at this stage revealed as affording, in the very consequences of the Fall, the opportunity for its resurrection: suffering and death, the consequences of sin, afford the opportunity for sacrifice, for the purifying asceticism which repairs what sin has damaged by overcoming death and restoring to us life in fullness, the life of the resurrection.

Whence comes the "gnosis of the judgments of God" which causes us to understand how human history, which to the simply sensual "view" is only the history of sin and its consequences, is discovered in the "faith" given by the Spirit to be the history of judgments, of condemnation of the power of sin, as well as the history of justification, of the liberation of believers, following upon the Cross of Christ crucified.

Arrived thus far, we are ready to be raised to the supreme gnosis: the "gnosis of the Holy Trinity," raising us above what Evagrius calls the "gnosis of beings" and the "gnosis of the eons," that is, of the successive dispensations of the judgments of God carried out in the sacred history of the Incarnation. The "gnosis of the Trinity" at the heights of "pure prayer" raises us out of this world, transports us even to the "dwelling place of God." It belongs no longer to what Pseudo-Dionysius himself describes as the illuminative way but rather to the unitive way, causing us to enter into the divine darkness, to journey out of this world, out of our very selves, in order to be transported even into that inaccessible light where God dwells, which is only revealed in the extinction of all inferior lights.

The "Knowledge" Proper
to the Illuminative Way

From what has just been said can easily be gathered the characteristics of the "knowledge," the flowering of which within us constitutes the illuminative way. This "knowledge" is the immediate fruit of meditation on the divine Word, taking an increasingly contemplative orientation, in the sense we have defined in speaking of prayer. It presupposes, as we have emphasized, that we hear the divine Word in the school of the Church; that is, that we enter into the mystery of faith which constitutes the living unity of this Word in accepting, at once passively and actively, the tradition which gives it to us, chiefly through participation in the liturgy. For it is here that the Word retains its perpetual actuality; it is here, in the sacraments and chiefly the Eucharist, that the reality which is the object of the Word is communicated to us; it is here that everything expresses that living response by which the People of God make their own the Word addressed to them by giving themselves up to it, in the power of the Spirit.

Yet the very reality of this giving up of our being to the Word that is Spirit and Life presupposes that we give ourselves up, by asceticism, to obedience to faith, which is also and necessarily obedience to the cross. It is in this way that sin and its consequences (negation, refusal to believe becoming incapacity to believe) are overcome by charity which grows in us together with all the positive virtues of a soul restored to the image and likeness of God.

It is in and by our restoration to the image of God, itself the fruit of a living faith working through charity, that the Fathers, especially Gregory of Nyssa and Evagrius Ponticus, see the soul going on from "simple faith" to "gnosis," that is, to an apprehension that is real and not simply notional of the truths of faith. At this stage, these truths are unified for us in an increasingly simple and profound view of the supreme and unique mystery of the Word of the Gospel: "Christ in us, the hope of glory," according to the phrase of St. Paul.

It is in this "gnosis" (which he calls *scientia*) that William of St. Thierry, again following St. Gregory of Nyssa, sees the soul as recovering, by already entering into the divine kingdom, its proper rule over its own body.

It is here that, having become like to God by the living faith which has caused us to assimilate in love the mystery of Christ, we begin to know God as we have been known by him: with a knowledge which is relationship, union, conscious connaturality.

At this stage, as William of St. Thierry tells us, the obedience in which faith began to work by charity, according to the word of St. Paul, is transformed. Let us recall that it began by being an "obedience of necessity" to a "spiritual father," who already possessed the experience of spiritual realities which hitherto we ourselves had lacked. Now it becomes "obedience of charity," moved by love, a love which obeys the more perfectly now that at last it understands the meaning of what is imposed on it. This obedience to the orders of superiors, even while it is much more perfect because interiorized, in some way goes beyond and overflows them. In imitation of the obedience of Christ to his Father which placed him, out of love, at the service of his brothers, it gives us up to serving the wishes and the needs of all our brothers in Christ whether they express these needs or not.

The knowledge that we have acquired of the heart of God makes us indeed all the more able to penetrate into the hearts of others, and gives us up to the most devoted love of them in giving us up to the infinitely generous love of the Father who has already begun to make us his sons and daughters, not simply in words but in fact.

It might be said that this "knowledge" is, as it were, a new conscience which progressively awakens in the course of the illuminative way. It is so intimately allied to the restoration of the divine image in us because it is the filial conscience which has us enter into the designs of God as into designs which are no longer foreign to us. In turn, in giving us up to these designs, it perfects in us this likeness, this participated adoption as sons and daughters. Thus is set up, as it were, an interchange between the knowledge that conforms us to him whom we know and that more perfect conformity which causes us to know him more intimately.

In the course of this progress, it is normal that prayer should tend to be simplified. The part that may have been given in the beginning to reasoning and to consciously aroused affections is increasingly reduced. When the soul fixes its thought on a word of scripture, on a particular mystery, or on the mystery of Christ in the fullness and unity that attract it more and more, it is simply absorbed therein. It has no further need of thoughts or sentiments nor even of particular decisions; not that it becomes slothful but that the perception of the things of God and the adhesion of the whole soul have acquired such a depth that its activity goes beyond the reach of the superficial consciousness in which all this has taken place previously. At this point, God's control of the soul, its belonging to Christ, and the motion of the Spirit have become almost directly perceptible to it. We are at the moving shore which, to use a happy phrase of St. Teresa, takes us from the prayer of recollection and simplicity to the prayer of quiet, in which the activity of God in us seems to absorb our own. We arrive, that is, at contemplation in the deepest sense that the term has taken in Christian language.

Thereby the transition is prepared from the simply illuminative to the unitive way.

The Transition to the Unitive Way

The unitive way characterizes the highest summits of the spiritual life accessible here below. It is the perfect way, that in which contemplation normally unfolds. Here the presence, the activity of the Spirit within us, becomes, as it were, the object of direct experience, though this is obviously an experience entirely *sui generis* of which we are in no way the masters since it means, on the contrary, that it is God who is now sole master in us.

If the purgative way was characterized by the extinction of the vices and the illuminative way by the development of the virtues (chiefly charity), then the unitive way can be defined by the predominance of the gifts of the Spirit. The same scholastic writers who worked out the theory of the infused virtues distinguished the gifts of the Spirit (traditionally listed in accordance with the beginning of the eleventh chapter of Isaiah) as being wholly new and supernatural instincts of the soul. When the activity of these gifts predominates, they cause the soul to act with a holy spontaneity which is that of the Spirit within it.

They are described, following the sevenfold formula of Isaiah, as the gifts of wisdom, understanding, knowledge, counsel, piety, fortitude, and fear of the Lord. But there is great agreement on the fact that these are only various and complementary aspects of a new life of the soul which is properly the life of God in it, lived as such. This is what Pseudo-Dionysius, coming at the end of the whole spiritual tradition of the Greek Fathers, describes as a union with God, on the basis of faith, become a true divinization. We should understand this as meaning that our adoption in the Son becomes so real that it is no longer, as it were, simply a reflection of the life of the Father that the Spirit projects on us but this life itself that wholly possesses us.

Such an experience is so marvelous that we should not be surprised to find in tradition apparently contradictory formulations attempting to describe it. While Evagrius insists on the uprooting from its natural element (the *ekdemia*) that the soul must undergo, snatched away from its merely human ways of thinking and living, he says that it is at the same time and inseparably both the supreme knowledge of itself that the soul attains, in its nature restored to the image of God, and the knowledge of God as he is in himself: "the gnosis of the Holy Trinity." He says again, it is the vision of the dwelling place of God that the ancients of the people saw with Moses on the mountain, the place that God has carved out in our soul by his own presence, in such a way that we recognize ourselves as the image of God, not simply in seeing ourselves in the wholly spiritual purity of our original nature purified of its faults but in discovering ourselves as having become once more the living temples of the Trinity.

Pseudo-Dionysius, for his part, prefers to insist on the radical transcendence of the knowledge of God experienced in the divinizing union. He says that it takes place, not in the dwelling place of God within us but beyond all place; not in the image that we are called once more to become but beyond all images, all ideas; even beyond the very unity that transcends all multiplicity and also beyond all these negations themselves: in that one inaccessible light in which God dwells, which is darkness to us until we are introduced therein by his pure grace.

Evagrius also, we should note, speaks much of darkness, of going beyond all forms, of knowing in unknowing. But this is simply in relation to our ordinary ways of knowing, those which come from our senses or our reasoning mind. For Pseudo-Dionysius, the divine darkness is even more profound: we are

drawn beyond all knowing (however purified, however simplified this might be) of anything that is not God in his absolute
transcendence. Here, we truly know God only in going beyond
all knowledge (however purified, however perfect it might be)
of the world or of ourselves.

This direct attainment of the uncreated appears to St. Max-
imus the Confessor as a grace so inconceivable, so above what
we are and what any created or creatable being is, that he does
not hesitate to say that it is not only a knowing in darkness but
a real death for him who attains it. Yet, as this darkness is only
the exterior aspect of the inaccessible light in which God dwells
and to which he raises us, this death is attainment of the fullness
of life in divine charity: the very life of the risen Christ, the life
of the Spirit in us.

William of St. Thierry, for his part, describes this experience
as *unitas spiritus*, the unity (and not merely the union) which
brings it about that we are one single spirit with the Spirit of
God himself. At this supreme stage, he says, following Gregory of Nyssa, the restoration of the divine image in us is such
that the soul is no longer merely wholly present to the body,
as God is to the world—nor even does it simply reproduce,
in its complete mastery of the body, the divine rule over the
world—but, in the perfect freedom it has now attained, it is
the transcendence of God to the world that it reproduces in its
own way. This freedom, furthermore, being one with the direct
movement of the Spirit, is the final development of obedience.
Completing the interiorization of obedience, beyond obedience
to the authority of a spiritual father, beyond the obedience of
charity that puts us at the service of all our brothers in Christ,
it makes us "all things to all men" in giving us up, like Christ,
to all the opprobrium and the misunderstanding of humanity,
in the invincible radiation of love crucified but triumphant
over all hatred.

The unitive way, in other words, is like an anticipation of the resurrection. It is heaven on earth. It is the supreme goal toward which faith and asceticism tend and in which they are perfected while beginning, as much as is possible here below, to go beyond themselves. Doubtless, faith does not yet give place to the light of heavenly glory. Yet its darkness is already far more luminous than any earthly light. The cross on which the Christian must nail himself or herself is not as yet absorbed by the resurrection. But a first ray of the resurrection, and already a very real one, shines on the cross itself.

The unitive way as such is not capable of finding its proper perfection otherwise than by causing us to pass beyond death into eternal life. Here below, it is never other than the goal toward which the illuminative way tends and which it touches at best.

But when we come near to this goal, there is brought about, as it were, a supreme quieting, a higher equilibrium of the spiritual life, which still has nothing about it of a stagnation nor even of a stabilization. Rather it is the final serenity of unreserved self-abandonment to the rapture of the Spirit, carrying us with a movement that continually accelerates, as of its own accord, toward the Father.

It is at this point that the flight from the world is revealed as the best way to love the world as God himself has loved it, so much as to give his only Son for it. For the ascetic perfected in this stage beyond all asceticism, in this subjection to the Spirit, and in this union with him become unity with him, is now capable of returning to the world without further risk of being dominated by it and with the very power of God to subjugate it, to save it in saving it from itself.

This is the spiritual fatherhood which constitutes the final fruit of spiritual marriage, itself the flowering of the unitive life, according to the formulation of St. Teresa (who here takes up the theme introduced by Origen in his commentary on the Canticle and notably developed by St. Bernard in his commentary). It is by this spiritual fatherhood, as the Alexandrians already said, that perfect "gnosis" is crowned. And this is what makes possible in its purity and fullness that ideal of the "apostolic life" as St. Thomas Aquinas understood it: "to contemplate and to hand on to others what one has contemplated."

These various complementary characteristics of the unitive life, surrounding the experience of the Spirit within us which is its heart, will be given whatever greater precision may be possible when, in conclusion, we come to analyze what, according to tradition, should be understood by the mystical life. This is, as it were, the summit accessible here below toward which the Christian life tends of its very nature and in which it already attains the life of eternity to the degree to which this is possible this side of death. But, before beginning this discussion, we need, after this sketch of the development of the Christian life as a whole through the three ways or the three ages of the spiritual life, to go back and consider the rhythms that recur throughout this development.

Progress and Rhythms in the Spiritual Life

In commenting on the various vicissitudes of Israel in journeying through the desert to the promised land, Origen had already noted that the spiritual life, normally, does not progress by a continuous and regular process of development. On the contrary, its progress is marked by the alternation of phases of deprivation and enrichment, of periods of interior aridity and of growth. The periods of aridity, obviously, may be the consequence of infidelity, testifying to a regression. But they may also be sent by God to bring about, by a more intimate purification, a closer union with himself.

Much later, Aelred of Rievaulx brought out the paradoxical fact that people living in the world, strongly attached to it, perhaps even far from having renounced sin, still at certain moments have religious impressions of amazing strength and sweetness; while holy religious, perhaps heroically mortified but in any case oriented completely toward meeting God, may still live in a profound darkness, an apparently total spiritual apathy. He explains this contrast by the fact that God takes us as we are and so, at a time when we are still wholly absorbed in the sensible, he makes himself perceived sensibly by us so as to draw us to him. But when we have set ourselves in earnest on the road toward union with him, he no longer spares us the trial required by our pleasure-seeking egotism if we are truly to love him with a pure heart, a heart purified, that is, particularly of attachment to self.

Along the same line, St. Bernard shows us how Christ, God made man, draws us to him by what he calls a "carnal love"; that is, a love in which faith is certainly present but still wrapped in very miscellaneous feelings. To the extent that such a love is authentic, it spontaneously tends to go out of itself, to be transfigured into a "spiritual love" in which mere human sensibility, touched by the humanity of the Savior, is no longer what moves—or, at any rate, facilitates—our impulse toward him. At the highest stage, in Christ himself, faith and love go straight to the divinity through the humanity of Jesus. To attain this stage, our faith and love must be purified of everything which was human, too human, about them to begin with. And this is the meaning of spiritual trials.

It is St. John of the Cross, however, in his *Ascent of Mount Carmel*, and still more in his *Dark Night*, who is to be credited with giving these purifications their due position, describing their usual psychological forms and precisely defining their spiritual import. The essence of his teaching lay in two main ideas.

The first is that the soul cannot be prepared for the perfection of union with God by its own conscious efforts, even supported by grace. There must also be an intervention by God which is wholly beyond our powers and which constitutes, therefore, a "passive" purification. We should not take this to mean that we are inactive here. Quite the contrary, here, as in contemplation, in its depths the soul is more than ever active. But now its activity, far from seeming autonomous, is so completely immersed in the activity of grace as no longer to be distinguishable from it: "It is no longer I who live; it is Christ who lives in me"—this phrase of St. Paul here finds a most personal echo in each soul.

We should note that, as a general rule, during these purifications called "passive," the purely interior action of God goes along with a providential disposition of circumstances causing us to undergo exterior trials as well. These are often very painful, and the more so as they are accompanied by darkness within; but actually, as harmonized with this darkness by the all-powerful hand of God, they prove very effective in leading us to him.

The second leading idea of the Carmelite Doctor is that these purifications, in which the finger of God becomes, as it were, visible in our soul and our whole life, are to touch one after the other what he calls "the senses" and the "spirit." And so there is first the "night of the senses" which normally inaugurates the illuminative way, and then there is the "dark night of the soul," or "night of the spirit," which directly prepares for entrance into the unitive way.

Thus the "night of the senses" goes along with the progressive domination which our work of purification, founded on faith in the action of God, must achieve over our sensibility hitherto "carnal" and ruled by the *pathe*, the instinctive passions of a nature unbalanced by sin. God himself, in our relationship with him, purifies us of this attachment to sensible experiences, to feelings, and even to the best feelings which, as they drew us toward him, victoriously prevailed over feelings more human in their immediate objects but analogous in their psychological texture. This is why, at this stage, God brings it about that meditations which are imaginative, colored with a more or less easily aroused affectivity, no longer say anything to us. Instead, it is to a vision of faith far more profound and at the same time free of dross that he leads us, through the aridities that prepare us for such a vision and may even accompany it for a long time. And, in the same way, the deepening of this vision of faith, in a prayer already become contemplative, in turn opens out on the "passive night of the spirit."

God leads us, that is, beyond whatever is still too human in our thoughts about the things of God, whatever is mere reasoning, the views of human beings on the faith which God has set within them but which transcends him. It was when he had arrived at this height that St. Thomas gave up finishing even a work like his *Summa* and declared that he now saw it to be nothing but straw. It can also happen, as we see particularly with St. Thérèse of the Child Jesus, that terrible temptations against the faith may now arise. But this means in reality that God is leading us to detach ourselves from our faith inasmuch as it is *our* faith, inasmuch as it is colored by human opinions, assimilated to our own modes of thought. Thus he causes us to enter into the mysterious darkness of naked faith, which no longer amuses itself with the externals, the representations of its object, but goes straight to that object, leaving behind in its journey everything that is not him alone. . . .

St. John of the Cross, again, lets it clearly be understood in more than one place that the "nights" of which he speaks are not in the least opposed to the lights, like those of clear day, which follow them and of which they are only the converse. In this going first beyond the sensible, and then beyond the intelligible according to our habitual mode of thinking, through a faith which grace itself is making more and more pure, this faith called thus to be exercised in a wholly new way already touches, even though obscurely, that which will be revealed to it later on in an abundance of new lights.

Newman has given an independent analysis of this which is perhaps still more profound in his sermon on *Christ manifested in remembrance*. This is concerned with the disciples of Emmaus who walked and talked with the risen Christ without recognizing him, who did not recognize him until the instant when he left them but then said to one another, "Were not our hearts burning within us when he walked with us and explained the scriptures?" (Lk 24:32). In other words, the moments which seem most arid while we are living through them are seen later on as wholly permeated with light. For, here below, light is never given to us to satisfy and immobilize us, but always to make us advance further, to make greater progress in faith—that is, in pure self-abandonment to the hand of the Guide who leads us from darkness to light, from shadows and images to Truth. . . .

Behind all these considerations a basic observation of St. Gregory of Nyssa begins to stand out. We have already mentioned it, but now we need to work out its full meaning. In the spiritual life, the same experiences seem in turn first obscure and then luminous. Sin encloses us in darkness. Grace draws us out of this darkness by the first rays of faith. But what seemed so bright when it first drew us on seems like darkness once it has been reached in comparison with the higher and brighter rays that now attract us. And these rays in turn will seem dimmed, but they urge us on toward other lights only then to be discovered, and so it will be until we reach eternity.

To this we need to add one final clarification. Through all these stages, which are like so many fresh starts on a path winding higher and higher, it is the same mystery which is continually hidden and disclosed.

From which it follows that we must ceaselessly lose and rediscover the same thing. But, in between each loss and recovery, we ourselves have changed in such a way that we no longer find this mystery the same. Thus the spiritual life is wholly made of an alternation of impoverishments which we must consent to and enrichments which we must in turn leave behind, but only in order to regain them at a higher stage and then once more go beyond them. . . .

The world is the first medium in which we discover the beauty and the goodness of God. But the divine Word teaches us that we must leave the world to find God. When we have once left it in order to find him, the Word gives it back to us. But it is not the same world, the world which is the mere object of our desires, that the Word now gives back to us: it is the world as an instrument of praise. And this instrument, in turn, falls apart in our hands so that we may enter into that higher praise which is silence all filled with God. Yet, here below, we can never enclose ourselves in this silence. We must come forth from it bearing a word which is now one with our very being. And this being must in turn be broken so that the divine life will take possession of it with no further resistance. This death will be that finally preceding the resurrection, in which everything will be given back to us forever, even the body of our flesh and the world hitherto ruled by a king other than God—and given back in such a way that now God will be "all in all."

This is the final meaning of that alternation seen in the call of Abraham, the settling down in Egypt; the call of Israel to the Exodus out of Egypt, the settling in the promised land; and the new Exile of Babylon, the return from the Exile—itself only preparatory to the new Exodus in which Israel, with the Baptist, went out to the desert to await Christ. Christ himself, according to St. Luke, "accomplished his Exodus from Jerusalem" (9:31) up to his definitive entrance, and our own, into that Jerusalem from on high, which is our mother (Gal 4:26).

In the spiritual life, therefore, everything is always to be newly received as a new grace from the hands of God and to be given up, as the fruit in us of the very grace that gave it to us and that asks it back only to give it back to us transfigured. This is the unique and constant experience of the Christian life and, if this is a faithful life, an experience that must be gone through again and again. Thus it is that our present life itself becomes the purgatory preparing us to consummate our sacrifice in death, looking to the definitive restoration of ourselves and the world in God by the resurrection of the whole Christ, he in us and we in him.

Chapter 12

THE MYSTICAL LIFE

From the moment when we began to speak of contemplation, and to an increasing degree as we followed the development leading from the illuminative way toward the unitive life, our presentation has had to give an even greater place to an activity of God within us, our own perception of which constitutes the supreme experience of the Christian life. This is the experience *sui generis* of grace, of grace finally taking possession of our whole being, which in traditional Christian language has been given the epithet "mystical." An introduction to the Christian and Catholic spiritual life should necessarily, therefore, conclude with a study of the mystical life, or, if you prefer, of the mystical aspect which is inherent in every Christian life but which, it would seem, normally tends more and more to predominate in it as it progresses.

The necessary counterpart of Christian asceticism is found in Christian mysticism, just as the Cross cannot be understood apart from the Resurrection. Asceticism makes us take up and carry our cross. Mysticism inaugurates in this life the life that comes to us by the cross.

This is what makes the Christian martyrs the preeminent models of Christian mysticism as well as asceticism. As we have already said, it is a consistent feature of the oldest and most trustworthy documents of martyrdom that he or she who undergoes it appears, in its consummation, as identified with the risen Christ. More precisely, the martyr at the point of death seems to have a radiant experience of the Savior's presence within him or her. St. Polycarp, at the moment when the flames surrounded him, seemed transfigured: the bystanders thought they saw him, as it were, transubstantiated into the living Christ himself. More simply, the idea was so familiar to the early Christians that when Felicitas in prison groaned in the pains of childbirth and her jailer said to her, "What will you do in the arena?" she answered unhesitatingly, "Another will suffer in me then."

We cannot repeat too frequently that Christian asceticism would lose all its meaning without faith and is only possible on the basis of grace sustaining faith and its development throughout life. Christian mysticism is nothing other than the life of grace becoming an indubitable experience, starting from faith and in faith itself.

The Possibility and Meaning of Mystical Experience

Certainly, this word "experience" must be rightly understood. There is no question of an experience understood according to the modern notion, implying something that can be reproduced more or less at will and, even more, something that can be observed as if from without by the experimenter himself or herself. The mystical experience, conceived as the supreme "religious experience," cannot thus fall under our control, nor can it be obtained unless we are wholly engaged in it. In fact,

Catholic faith cannot admit as authentic any spiritual experience which is not entirely dependent on the sovereign liberty of God's grace and which also does not engage us unreservedly in submission to that grace.

These two correctives need constantly to be held in mind if we are to accept the notion of "religious experience" as William James introduces it, so as to see in mysticism this experience in its purest possible state. No mysticism, no Christian mysticism in any case, is worthy of the name if it pretends to be the product of any method whatever which a person might master by the appropriate techniques. Still less can it be confused, to however small a degree, with any kind of experience which we could detachedly observe in ourselves. We can in no way make trial of this experience without being wholly given up to it.

This does not mean that we cannot and should not be strictly critical with regard to our own religious experiences and, in particular, those that are apparently the most mystical. But this should be a criticism which is concerned primarily with us ourselves, with the stripping away of our lower "I," and with the sincerity of the consent given by our higher "I" to be born and to develop under the call of grace.

However, if at the time when William James wrote his work on the *Varieties of Religious Experience* it was important to be on guard against the too simplified notion of this subject which we were in danger of having imposed on us by Protestantism, today it is no less necessary to protect ourselves against an entirely negative reaction now emanating from the same Christian circles in which, not long ago, the tendency was rather toward confusionism. Contemporary Protestants have not all given up—far from it—the attraction of a "religious experience" of an equivocal nature which it would be within the power of psychological techniques to produce in us infallibly and, perhaps, to produce outside of an irrevocable commitment of our deepest personality. But there are others who, faced with this recent tendency of liberal Protestantism, have come to reject every idea of religious experience, and most particularly of the experience called mystical, as a contamination of authentic Christianity by foreign influences, and one which fidelity to the Gospel obliges us to banish unsparingly.

Thus contemporary Protestantism—following the German Friedrich Heiler and his book on *Prayer* and, above all, the Swedish writer Anders Nygren and his famous trilogy *Agape and Eros* on the doctrine of love in the New Testament writers, the Fathers, and later theologians—has come, if not as a whole, at least among the majority of its most representative theologians, to adopt a resolutely anti-mystical attitude. According to these writers, Catholicism betrays its composite origin, the mixed and impure character of its Christianity, precisely by the place that its spiritual tradition has given to mysticism.

It is curious to see how many Catholics have allowed themselves to be affected by these assertions. The activism of our contemporaries, indeed, easily persuades them that any religion which does not limit itself to active charity cannot truly be anything but an adulterated Christianity. To seek God for himself, to find our final goal in union with him, and to prize highly the experience of this union (so far as it can be achieved here below)—this is, we are told, not a Christian but a pagan ideal. It is nothing but a particularly noteworthy and also regrettable vestige in tradition of the Hellenization undergone by Christianity at the time of the Fathers of the Church.

What actually is mysticism? they say. The answer can only be: mysticism is the product, the final form of that basically Greek ideal described by Aristotle under the name of the "contemplative life." But, as they explain to us, it is by faith that the Christian lives. Not only does faith renounce "seeing" God and the things of God in any way; it has no desire to see them. It is in charity that faith is developed and fructified. But the charity of the New Testament, they go on telling us, has nothing to do with "the love of God" the mystics speak of. For Christian charity is not "the love of God" in the sense of being the love with which God is loved but rather the love with which God loves. It is, then, in ourselves as in him, a love for humanity, for the world to be saved, a love which must be translated into service, into generous devotedness.

In direct opposition to this, "the love of God" of the mystics would be nothing but a subtle and refined egotism: a flight from the world, an escape from charitable activity into experiences that do no good except to the person who has them. Authentic charity would have nothing to do with such experiences; it would even repulse them as being a dangerous diversion, an equivocal complacency in a merely aesthetic religiosity.

For, since charity is the love that God has shown us in Christ and in his Cross, it should be, in us as in him, an active, a creative love. It is a love that does not seek its own good in others, striving to possess them and enjoy them, but it rather goes out of self and goes toward the least worthy, not to seek a good which is not to be found there but to put it there, and this in the most complete disinterestedness.

Mystical love, on the contrary, is a typical product, not in the least of the *agape* of the creating and saving God, but of the *eros* natural to fallen humanity. For it is not the overflowing of a creative generosity but the mere product of a need, of a want to be satisfied. This love is made up only of desire. And what Plato described as "heavenly love," *Eros ouranios*, is in this regard in no way distinguished from "earthly love," sensual *eros*, except by the object of its desire. This is the desire of higher realities that may be described as "spiritual" in contrast to "material" ones. But it is always a desire centered on self, on its own satisfaction. This is why such a love is characteristic of humanity, and of fallen humanity, however mystical it may be or become. But, on the contrary, the *agape* that forgets itself, that does not seek its own good but only to give and to give itself, is preeminently the characteristic of God, of the Christian God revealed to us by the Gospel. While humanity remains the subject of *eros*, it is God alone who is properly the subject of *agape*, who loves in this way. For God has nothing to desire. How, then, could he love with a love wholly made of desire? No, he who is only pure generosity, and he alone loves with this love which is called *agape*, and thus he loves all beings, even those most unworthy of his love, for it is this love alone which of itself is the source of all the good in them and of their very being.

But humanity, fallen humanity, on the contrary, is made only of desire. And the acme of its insatiable desire is to desire the sovereign Good, to pretend to love God himself, but in the sense of the *eros*, of a lust that knows no bounds. Mysticism is merely the satisfaction, sought after or dreamed of, of this insane desire: this desire to possess God, to make one's own the supreme wealth that he constitutes, and, in consequence, to equal oneself to him, to identify oneself with him, by a union in some way physical with him. When one has understood this, it should be obvious that mysticism can have nothing in common with evangelical Christianity. Christians who are inclined to mysticism, they tell us, either do not really know what they desire, or else do not know God, the true God, the God of the prophets and of Jesus, or they would not thus desire him. If they did know him, they would reject as the supreme blasphemy any idea of loving God in this way, the way of *eros*.

Quite the contrary, welcoming by faith the creating and saving love with which God loves, the *agape*, and opening his or her heart to it, the true Christian receives it as, according to the words of St. Paul, "that *agape* of God poured out in our hearts by the Holy Spirit" which is to be expressed, in him or her as in Christ, through service of others. In other words, for such Christians the "love of God," the love with which God loves them and loves everything together with them in themselves, is then expressed by an unreserved dedication to the great work of saving the world and not at all by separating them from concern with the world and drawing them into a sterile intimacy with God. . . .

It is along this line of reasoning that Heiler, before Nygren's analyses of *Eros* and *Agape*, had contrasted mystical prayer—unconcerned with the world, fleeing from the world in order to be absorbed in God—with prophetic prayer—passionately concerned with the world, turning to God only to save the world, and, in consequence, never separated from a charitable activity in the service of God, which ultimately is but one with service of the world.

What are we to think of these interpretations? We should recognize that there is much that is true here (and truths that have been too frequently and too long misunderstood) inextricably intermingled with what is false, with errors or mistakes that end in a complete travesty of the whole Gospel. This mixture is the reason for the disturbing attraction that these ideas can exercise even on Catholics. And it makes all the more urgent an effort toward clarification and focusing.

It is quite true that the "love of God" which could be known to humanity without Christ, in Greek antiquity in particular, however high it may raise itself, remains a love made of desire, and so a love of humanity for God and not of God for his creatures. And above all, nothing is more true than the fact that "the love of God" spoken of in the New Testament is, on the contrary, the love with which God loves and with which he loves all beings, all his creatures, even the most unworthy sinners: love made not of desire but of generosity; creating and saving love; love that gives its life, even to dying on the Cross.

As long as Nygren limits himself to setting out in full relief this basic comparison and contrast, he is simply disengaging, as few others have been able to do, the most radical originality of the Gospel. But it is not the same when he claims to draw logical conclusions from the contrast thus described. Then, not only does he introduce a unilinear logic, wholly human and extremely narrow, into the realities which, as he himself has shown so well, transcend man, but by this very fact he parts company with scripture and finally ends in the most flagrant contradiction with it.

The Mysticism of the New Testament

In the first place, as we established in the preceding chapter sufficiently to dispense us from going back to it here, the fact cannot seriously be disputed that there is a "knowledge of God" which is fundamentally biblical, a knowledge which is the union of humanity with God, the assimilation of humanity to God. We can go even further and say unhesitatingly that the ideal of a "vision of God" in Christ, transfiguring us to his image, is purely evangelical and owes absolutely nothing of its basic elements to foreign influences, Greek or any other. The insistence of the Fourth Gospel on such themes as "to see the Son," "to know God," etc., are too well known to make it necessary to establish this fact again. It should be enough to mention the striking formula of the prologue of St. John's gospel: "No one has ever seen God, but the only Son who dwells in the bosom of the Father has made him known to us" (Jn 1:18). And if the mystical implication of this initial formula still seems doubtful, what can be said of the phrase of the First Epistle which is, as it were, the final word of St. John's spirituality: "What we shall be has not yet been made manifest, but what we do know is that when he appears (the risen Christ), we shall be like him, for we shall see him as he is" (1 Jn 3:2)?

This is so true that Nygren is too honest not to admit that St. John's writings embarrass him. And so he goes on to say that they must be the first witness to that deplorable influence of Hellenism which was to disfigure the most irreducible original characteristic of the Jewish and Christian message.

We do not even need to discuss this idea that the Hellenization of the Gospel began with St. John. Although it was generally admitted by exegetes at the end of the last century, it is no longer maintained except by some lingering defenders who themselves minimize their own positions to the limit. How could it be otherwise when the discovery of the texts of Qumran, those preeminently Jewish texts, show us that all the themes which are most specifically St. John's originated in the Palestinian Judaism of the time of Christ?

Let us simply limit ourselves to asking this question: even if it were true that St. John presents a Christianity already Hellenized and so oriented toward mysticism, what about St. Paul? It must be recognized that precisely what seems most mystical in St. John and therefore is denounced as a first foreign infiltration had already been given the most explicit and complete formulation by St. Paul. This is the text from the Second Epistle to the Corinthians which we have already cited more than once: "We all, with face unveiled, reflecting as in a mirror the glory of the Lord, are transformed into the same image, from glory to glory, as by the Lord who is Spirit" (3:18).

Is this in turn to be denounced as a Greek perversion of original Christianity? But, from the terms that St. Paul uses here as well as from the context, the fact stands out with a blinding clarity that his thought moves in an atmosphere purely biblical and Jewish. Making a comparison between Moses and Christ, on the basis of the most traditional Jewish speculations concerning what had been told us to begin with by the Bible, St. Paul was seeking simply to draw from it the explanation of the effects that the Resurrection of Christ is to produce in us. All this is derived in a direct line from rabbinical speculations on the experience of Moses on Mount Sinai as the Bible describes it for us.

Knowledge of Jewish tradition, indeed, shows clearly that Moses (like Elijah) had already become for the Jews the figure of what must be called a mystical ideal, although still purely Jewish. This is the real explanation of the account of the Transfiguration. In this account, itself belonging to the tradition common to the synoptic gospels, Jesus appears as having become the focus of that luminous cloud which, according to the Pentateuch, accompanied the Exodus of the Jews out of Egypt, later covered the Tabernacle, and still later filled the Temple in Jerusalem. The rabbis saw this cloud as "the dwelling place of the Shekinah," that is, of the presence of God among his own, half revealed, half veiled. And this is why Moses and Elijah appear in the account of the Transfiguration—not so much because in their person the Law and the prophets bring their witness to Christ (as would be said later on) but simply because, according to the Bible itself and the whole of Jewish tradition, they are the great seers of this still mysterious but already glorious presence which was to be fully revealed in the face of the glorified Christ.

When all this is taken into consideration, we are in a better position to evaluate the extent to which mysticism is or is not a true product of Christianity, to decide whether it is or is not in the line of biblical tradition. And, first, we are prepared to clarify the relationship between Christian faith and the vision of God, a vision which, as the mystics affirm, transforms us into the image of him it causes us to contemplate.

Faith and Vision, Love and Vision

It is true, of course, that faith is opposed to immediate vision. This is why, in eternity, as St. Paul himself suggests so clearly in the conclusion of chapter 13 of his First Epistle to the Corinthians, faith will "pass" when we know God as we have been known by him. But this does not mean that "believing," in the most biblical and Christian sense of the term, is opposed to all idea of "knowing" God, or even of "seeing" him. Quite the contrary, it is today's faith that will make vision possible later on.

And already in this life, to the extent that faith tends toward charity, preparing us for the expansion of the very love of God in our hearts by the Holy Spirit, it leads us toward a kind of vision as if in chiaroscuro. This is the first fruit and the pledge, as it were, of that knowing "as we have been known," spoken of by St. Paul. For in loving with the very love with which God loves us, we attain a kind of "connaturality" with him created in us by his grace which is the basis of the knowledge, the twilight vision, that can and should normally be experienced in this present life. This is, as it were, the Gospel flowering of that "knowledge of God" described by the prophets.

True enough, this is not an abstract knowledge, neither is it an "intellectual" knowledge, if by that is meant a knowledge detached from its object. But it is truly a knowledge which can, which should, become in its way as real, and more real, to us than our knowledge of sensible realities. It is to some degree truly vision—even though, according to all tradition, it is obscure vision, vision of a light which is also darkness: that inaccessible light where God dwells (cf. 1 Tm 6:16), but into which he himself can have us enter even here below, if we adhere to him by faith in the heart of the present darkness. For it is vision in that it is a knowing without any intermediary: here we know God through his own presence and his own activity in us.

Keeping this in mind, we have no difficulty in recognizing with Nygren himself that Christian *agape* (charity) is something entirely other than any egoistic, self-concerned, self-centered desire. It is rather our total self-abandonment to that divine love which is itself the total gift.

But why should we conclude from this that the *agape* poured out in our own hearts by the very Spirit of God should have no other proper object than our neighbors, loved with the very love with which God loves them in loving us? To think thus is certainly to go far afield from the New Testament, not only from the writings of St. John but also the three other Gospels. Certainly, our active and devoted love of our neighbor must be the touchstone of the reality of our love of God. No one has been more explicit on this point than St. John in his First Epistle: "He who does not love his brother whom he does see cannot love God whom he does not see" (4:20). But to make love of neighbor the touchstone of love of God is surely something quite different from reducing the one to the other. And it is quite different from what the Bible itself teaches us, particularly the Gospel, where the love of neighbor is presented as the consequence of a primary, a fundamental love *for God himself*, according to the unanimous testimony of the synoptics (cf. Mt 12:37; Mk 12:30; Lk 10:2).

In fact, if we admit that our participation in the love, the *agape*, of God is reduced to an active love of neighbor, not only do we return to a natural plane and even a pagan one (as the opponents of Christian mysticism very lightly accuse it of doing), but, as must be admitted, we descend far lower in the natural religion of fallen humanity than the level attained by Greek contemplation, at least in Neo-Platonism. In fact, whether we realize it or not, a religion—however purely evangelical it wishes to be, however suspicious it may be as to any foreign infiltration that might adulterate it—which concerns itself with God only for the good of humanity actually goes back to magic. For if our religion, our life of prayer, has no other aim than the transformation of the world, the betterment of human life by drawing divine benefits down upon it (by what is called "prophetic prayer" in unwarranted contrast to "mystical prayer"), then whether we wish it or not, whether we know it or not, our religion rejoins that of the Canaanite Baalim against which the prophets never ceased to inveigh. For then, whatever our pious verbal protestations may be, in practice we reduce God once more to a mere source of energy to be exploited in the interests of humanity.

In reality, far from appearing simply or chiefly as a super-abundant source of creative activity which one's prayer has only to draw on for all the needs of humanity, the God of the Bible, through his own Word, has revealed himself to us as a person.

And it is this very revelation of himself that reaches its height, that attains its fullness, in Christ and in Christ alone. God is not *something:* a treasure to distribute and utilize. He is *Someone:* Someone who, as he loves us and because he loves us, demands to be loved in return and to be loved for himself.

Nygren has seen this clearly, notwithstanding the one-sidedness of his developments. He has even expressed it admirably, saying that the divine *agape*, even though entirely the contrary of a "need" or a "desire" in the ordinary sense of these words, can nonetheless be defined as a "need" or a "desire" *for fellowship.* In Christ, in his Cross, God reveals to us his insatiable need to communicate his own life to us, his untiring desire to bring us to live in a society of love with him. What other response could humanity give to this overture, if not to open itself out to the same desire, to the same need? Is not this what Newman so well expressed in the dialogue of the soul with the angel in *The Dream of Gerontius:* "I would have nothing but to speak with thee for speaking's sake. I wish to hold with thee conscious communion. . . ."

To say the same thing in another way, in Christianity, to know God and to love him need no justification: this is an end in itself; it is even the supreme end. Because God is a person, is Someone, the most loving, and because the most loving, the most lovable of beings, the development of a personal relationship with him is the highest goal of human life.

It must be said that in this respect, what already was mystical—or more precisely, as we shall soon see, pre-mystical—in Neo-Platonism, not only went beyond the gross natural religions, wholly and carnally self-interested in their relationship with God, but also certainly surpassed the mutilated Christianity which an anti-mystical Christianity would be. Plotinus and his imitators (and in this, very probably, they betray, through the syncretist environment of Alexandria, a Jewish and even perhaps a Christian influence) knew at least that the search for God is an end in itself and the highest that can exist.

It goes without saying, however, that we cannot love God sincerely without loving everything that he loves. Indubitably, therefore, a love of God is worthless which does not involve us in that love of neighbor of which the Cross gives us the example. But, in return, what can be the purpose of this very love of our neighbors if not to bring them ultimately to recognize the love of God for them so that they in turn will come to know and love him? For if we do not love our neighbors in this way, we shall not love them as God loves them, we shall not love them with that creating and saving love which is only satisfied when it has communicated its supreme good.

A practical charity, consequently, which does not lead toward this does not lead anywhere. To speak truly, it is not charity at all but aimless activism. To help the poor, to care for the sick, to bring aid to those who are suffering is certainly the first gesture of love. But what is a love worth which limits itself to soothing sufferings by some anesthesia, to giving back to the sick health to be used for material purposes only, to substituting gluttons for the poor? It is incontestable, therefore, that the final purpose of everything in Christianity, and of active love of neighbor along with the rest, is that we all should know and love God together, simply in order to know him and love him, and for nothing else.

And it would also be a great error to imagine that this mystical occupation of knowing and loving God could be considered merely as our occupation in a future eternity. No form of love of neighbor can and does lead us to this future goal unless already, here and now, we begin to love God thus. We cannot accept Christ today as "the Way" without already accepting him as "the Truth" and "the Life." What will give authenticity to our active charity is that it already includes something of mystical reality. In return, it is quite certain that active charity will be the preeminent mentor for the *true* mystical life, if it is a *true* charity, supernatural in its source as in its objective; both the one and the other accepted by faith, accepted from divine grace, and not from any natural compulsion toward some kind of exterior busyness.

The Nature of the Mystical Experience

What has just been said may help us to understand more clearly how Christian mysticism is something entirely different from an extraordinary psychological experience. Neither visions, nor ecstasies, nor raptures, nor anything of the kind constitute an integral part of this mysticism. We should not even think that they are its necessary accompaniments. A great number of the prejudices against mysticism stem from the confusion that has been brought about between it and phenomena of this sort. It is true that they may appear in the course of a Christian mystical life. But, in this case, they should be recognized as being nothing other and nothing more than repercussions of an experience that transcends us: more or less inharmonious reactions of human weakness under the pressure of a grace to which it is not yet fully adapted.

Without completely rejecting the possibility that visions or interior words may play a providential role in the progress of certain souls so that God may use these phenomena to manifest his will to them and to enlighten them as to his designs, the greatest mystical writers, such as St. Teresa and St. John of the Cross, are unanimous in stating that such experiences betoken a state in the mystical life which is only embryonic. Not only should we detach ourselves to such things, not only should we keep a very critical mind with regard to what may be truly supernatural about the origin of such experiences, but, even when we have the most certain reasons for thinking that in anything like this we are not the plaything of the devil or of our own imaginations, we must still positively will to go beyond them. In fact, the masters of mysticism tell us, as a general rule, nothing of the sort any longer takes place in the "spiritual marriage," or the earthly heights of union with God.

More simply, the humor with which the Desert Fathers dealt with such things shows us the true importance to be accorded them: such as the history of the solitary to whom Satan appeared disguised as an angel of light and saying that he had been sent from heaven to assure the monk of his great progress in the interior life; to which the good man was content to reply imperturbably, "You must be making a mistake; it is certainly to some other person that you have been sent!"

It should be added, not only that the mystics canonized by the Church have all more or less gone beyond experiences like this but also that many, and among them the greatest, have never known anything of the kind. Ultimately, the substance of the highest Christian mysticism entirely consists in the knowledge and love of God attaining here below a supereminent purity and transparency to grace.

If we go more deeply into the problem, we must say that no psychological experience as such can adequately define mysticism. Here we touch again upon the error already pointed out at the beginning of this book, the error which is at the starting point of all the various mystical or pseudo-mystical forms of syncretism. So long as we concentrate all our attention on the psychological aspect of mysticism, we shall be tempted to come to the conclusion that Christian mysticism contains nothing specifically Christian, whether this be a reason for welcoming or rejecting it. It seems then as though the Hindu, Buddhist, and Islamic mysticisms are indistinguishable from Christian mysticism, which itself does not differ essentially from what Plato or other spiritual pagans of the ancient world had already experienced. Certain writers, following this line of thought, have even gone so far as to proclaim that some poetic experiences, such as those described or evoked by Wordsworth, have no different psychological substratum.

All impressions of this kind and the tendency that results from them (or is, indeed, rather their seed)—the tendency, that is, to eliminate dogmatic differences as of no importance—spring from one basic error. What authors like Aldous Huxley, in his *Perennial Philosophy*, take as the common ground of all the forms of mysticism is precisely what, for a true mystic, is of no interest in his or her own experience. As quite different mystics have said in many ways, "The man who knows that he is praying has not yet begun truly to pray"—and how much more this is true of the individuals who are concentrating all their attention on the particular psychological form their prayer is taking. What concerns the mystic in his or her experience is not this experience in itself, but the object which is the focus of it. And it could be said that the more authentic the experience, the more transcendent will that object appear to the mystic. Whence those paradoxical formulae used by the mystics to say what they then know, which is that they do not know, and whence also that disconcerting use of images of darkness together with those of light.

This is so true that—let us repeat—even a more or less agnostic liberal Protestant like Rudolf Otto, simply because he was a penetrating observer and a thinker of strict honesty, in studying a Hindu mystic like Sankara and a Christian mystic like Meister Eckhart whose expressions at first sight seem strangely similar, had to recognize their irreducible divergence. Whatever the personalist expressions that Sankara used, he tended toward nothing other, in the final analysis, than an absorption or a reabsorption of himself in a great whole that was no one. . . . And in spite of the images of fusion, of loss of self, of extinction of the "I" that Meister Eckhart may use for his part, he tends toward a reality that he never ceases to apprehend as that of Someone and in a union in which his own personality will be found not abolished at all but rather expanded. His most disconcerting expressions—which were taken up by many other writers, particularly Angelius Silesius—to the effect that to him, God no longer seems to exist except in him and for him, so much that, in the impossible case that God could cease to be in himself, God could not cease to be in him whom God loves—these expressions have no meaning other than this. They are, in truth, only an exalted affirmation of the God of love, the typically Christian God who confers, by the very absoluteness of his gift of love, a value, a transcendent existence, to the created personality.

In a word, what are called the non-Christian mysticisms can be confused with the mysticism of Christianity only so long as one continues stubbornly and against all common sense to eliminate from the mystical experience what—and, above all, the person who—is experienced.

In short, modern writers who believe they discover analogies to Christian mysticism everywhere and so go on to explain it in terms of sources foreign to evangelical and biblical tradition—these writers do not understand the fact that mysticism properly so called is a purely Christian experience. This is not to deny that outside the Church and Israel indications of it may be discerned which are remarkably convergent and yet, if they have not been touched in some way by the divine Word, all lacking in the essential point. But it is to recognize the fact, still misunderstood though so obvious, that the very notion of mysticism is one which appeared only in Christianity and that in it is distilled, as it were, what is most essential in the Christian spiritual tradition. The history of the word "mysticism" serves to establish this fact.

Mysticism, as a particular spiritual experience, has been defined in reference to the "mystery," and not simply to any mystery whatever, but to the mystery of Christ and his Cross—the mystery described by St. Paul as the great secret of the Word of God which it had finally proclaimed to the world. The use of the adjective "mystical" (in Greek *mystikos*, which simply means "hidden") to designate a special religious experience is a purely Christian affair. This use is itself the product of a slow development which took place within the Church, a development that is extremely revealing.

It makes its appearance after two other previous Christian uses of the same adjective, and it is from these that it directly proceeds. The Greek *mystikos*, outside of Christianity, had never had any other meaning than the general one: "hidden," "secret."

In the non-Christian religions and particularly in those called "mystery religions," it was always used, like the word "mystery" itself, only to describe the rites which were not to be known by non-initiates. In Christian language (prepared to a certain degree by Philo), the word came first to designate the most profound meaning of the scriptures, a meaning accessible only to faith. For Clement or Origen, the "mystical" sense is the full sense in which all the lines of revelation converge; that is, what St. Paul calls "the mystery": "Jesus Christ and him crucified" but, more particularly, the Cross of Christ seen in all its effects—what St. Paul again calls "Christ in us, the hope of glory."

After this, and concurrently with this first Christian use of the word "mystical" which was never lost, the term came to designate, in a second meaning closely bound up with the first, the profound reality of the sacraments, which is veiled at the same time as it is made present by their visible symbols. For this reality, according to Christian faith, is nothing other than the mystery of Christ, of his Cross, becoming in some way assimilable by us.

From this, finally, with the writings of the Pseudo-Dionysius presenting a third application already sketched out in St. Gregory of Nyssa, the word came to be used in our present special spiritual sense. With Pseudo-Dionysius, indeed, what is called "mysticism" is, in the context of the two preceding uses, the full and personal application by the Christian of what is proclaimed by the divine Word and given in the sacraments: the fullness of the new life, the divine life communicated in Christ dying and rising again.

The Place of Mysticism
in the Christian Life

This is the meaning that mysticism should hold for us. It is nothing other than the most profound apprehension to which we can be led by grace here below—apprehension of the truths of the Gospel, the realities of the sacramental life which the Christian accepts by faith and makes his or her own by charity. It might be said, in consequence, that the first act of charity, springing from faith in the divine Word, faith nourished by the sacraments, contains the whole of mysticism in embryo. This seed will develop more or less in each of us according to the development of our faith and our charity. It is quite certain that mysticism unfolds only in a consciousness augmented by grace at its most gratuitous, most transcendent to our own efforts. But (as Fr. Garrigou-Lagrange, first among modern writers, should be credited with emphasizing and establishing on solid theological foundations in his chief work *Christian Perfection and Contemplation)* mysticism, far from being a singular, questionable way, extraordinary in the least favorable sense of the term, must be considered the normal development of Christian perfection. Mysticism follows, that is, the vital logic of a life of faith fully consistent with itself.

Some disciples of Fr. Garrigou-Lagrange, such as Jacques and Raissa Maritain, have also pointed out quite rightly that this mystical development of every Christian life carried to holiness will be more or less conscious according to the innate tendency and capacities of the subject for reflex consciousness of what is going on within him or her. Thus saints who at first sight do not seem to be mystics actually live a mystical life without talking about it and, to a certain extent, without being aware of it. For there is no sanctity other than this "unity of Spirit" with the

Holy Spirit living in us, which is described by William of St. Thierry, as we may recall, as the height of the Christian spiritual life and which is also by far the best description of mysticism made perfect.

To say this is also to say that the mystical ascent, after all, depends wholly on the inscrutable spontaneity and liberty of the Spirit of God, who gives his graces to each according to his own good pleasure, our most accurate observations never being able to enclose him in any set of rules; his designs for each of us remain unfathomable. Yet, while no automatism is possible in mystical development any more than any infallible and necessarily effective technique, it can and must be said that no mystical life is ever anything other than the fully conscious but fully normal development of our personal apprehension of what the Word of God reveals to us of Christ in the Church, of what is given us therein through the sacraments: the gift of grace revealed to faith, working through charity.

The Summits of the Mystical Union

One last difficulty should, however, be touched on. This is one that has often troubled the mystics themselves and, it might be said, has even divided them when it occurred to them to reflect on their experience and to discuss it.

Evagrius poses the question bluntly when he states that what he himself nonetheless calls "the gnosis of the Holy Trinity" transcends and formally excludes all distinct thoughts, explaining that at this stage "pure prayer" can no longer linger even to consider the humanity of the Savior. There is no doubt that statements of this kind in his work were most shocking to Christian antiquity. The Byzantine Middle Ages, even though strongly influenced by him, reacted no less strongly if only implicitly against such formulations and what they seemed to imply by making the "prayer of Jesus," as we described it earlier, the preeminent site of the mystical experience.

Later on, at the end of the Latin Middle Ages, Eckhart seems to carry these expressions of Evagrius even further, going so far as to speak of a union with the "Godhead" in its unfathomable abyss, transcending the consideration of the three Divine Persons themselves. Without going so far as this, St. John of the Cross, for his part, certainly made his own the statement that the summit of mystical experience goes beyond any distinct consideration of the humanity of Jesus. This assertion, however, aroused the impassioned opposition of St. Teresa.

It goes without saying that expressions of this kind have been a choice prize for syncretists eager to bolster up their view that the character of the mystical experience is completely indifferent to particular dogmatic formulations. What are we to think? It would seem as though some misunderstanding usually slips into interpretations—whether shocked or too heatedly approving—of such statements.

Certainly, neither Evagrius nor Eckhart, still less St. John of the Cross, wished by such expressions to minimize the importance of dogmatic formulations in general; certainly, they did not, in particular, wish to render the Incarnation and, still less, the Trinity a matter of secondary importance to the mystic. What they wanted to say, it would seem, is that since mystical knowledge and union lead us to know and love God in Christ as he knows and loves himself, so far as this is possible to human beings, they lead us to transcend all purely human modes of knowing. The mystical life is simply the development of life in Jesus Christ, the Son of God made man, dead and risen. In consequence, the mystic ceases to consider Christ as if from without, to reach his divinity only beyond his humanity and, as it were, behind it. The mystic who can say of himself or herself,

"It is no longer I who live; it is Christ who lives in me" has not thereby ceased to know that Christ is God made man. Quite the contrary, he or she enters into this mystery better than anyone else, as the mystic begins to some extent to participate in the viewpoint that Christ himself has of it. And this viewpoint, precisely, no longer considers his humanity apart from his divinity nor even as united to his divinity but rather as subsisting in his divinity itself.

Even more profoundly, for the mystic who has arrived at this height, the dogma of the Trinity does not cease to be true; there can be no question of his somehow going beyond the Trinity in God. But what is true is that the Trinity, at this moment, is no longer so much the object of conceptual reflection as of a wholly intimate intuition of the Trinitarian life: of that current of life with a unity surpassing all multiplicity, in the communication to the Son of the life surging from that "abyss of the Godhead" opened out in the divine paternity, to which all flows back without thereby losing itself in the procession of the Spirit.

Having arrived at these heights where we hesitate and stammer in the face of mystery, we can now return with perhaps a new understanding to the beginnings of the Christian life. We can say that, at that time, the consciousness of the Christian remains dominated by his or her natural experiences, founded on the senses and laboriously disengaged from them by his or her intellect and will. The Christian believes, nonetheless, but the objects of faith remain beyond his or her experience, even though they already begin to arouse in him or her a presentiment of this "beyond." At the supreme height that this Christian life can attain, things will have changed in the sense that one's whole life and one's knowledge will have been reorganized in accordance with the new focus given by one's faith. During the whole course of this interior development, in fact, one's charity will have continually grown greater, reaching out toward this focus and little by little ordering everything in him or her in accordance with this impulse. Then this individual will no longer be centered on himself or herself but on God. So long as one dwells on this side of the veil of death, the apprehension of Christian realities will remain obscure. But, even in this relative obscurity, these realities will now seem clearer to the individual than the realities of this world ever did, even though perceived by the senses. The mystical life is simply the progressive emergence of this last state from the original state into which faith and Baptism introduce us.

AIDS IN THE SPIRITUAL LIFE

The spiritual life does not develop individually, even though it is so preeminently a personal work. We have insisted on this fact from the first pages of this book: to be authentically Christian, the spiritual life must be fully Catholic, that is, lived in the Church. This is what is realized through our sacramental practice, in the context of a participation as wide and deep as possible in the liturgical life, in the public prayer of the Church.

Thus the spiritual progress of each soul cannot be separated from the communion of saints—of those who are holy—in holy things: the unanimity of Christians in faith and love which forms, as it were, the collective, or rather interpersonal, inferiority of the Church. And it is in relation to this *communio sanctorum* in the twofold meaning of the expression (the communion of the *sancti* in the *sancta*) that all the aids of the spiritual life are best understood.

The first is making pilgrimage to holy places, to Jerusalem, or to the tombs of martyrs or other saints. To this is related the devotion of the Way of the Cross, by which we follow the traditional fourteen stations of Christ's painful road to Golgotha. Such pilgrimage, whatever forms it may take, is for the purpose of nourishing our meditation with the example of Christ and of those who have gone before us, following him in his "exodus" to the Father.

We might link up with the veneration of relics that of holy images, as expressing the enduring invisible presence of the mysteries of the Savior as well as that of all those who are already perfect in their participation in these mysteries.

Heeding their example, invoking their intercession with the Savior, and trusting in our association with their merits: that is, everything that they themselves achieved by the grace of God in the way of union with God in Christ—and which could not have brought them nearer to that union without mysteriously aiding us to come closer to it ourselves—all this constitutes what is called the "cult of the saints." We should beware of putting it on a plane with the unique adoration which we are to give to God alone, in and through Christ. But, in the sense just defined, it cannot be denied that this cult works powerfully to draw us into, and sustain us in, that life of the Spirit within us which is one with his life in the saints.

This is preeminently true of the cult of the Virgin who, as the Mother of God in Christ, is by the same token, as it were, the Mother of his grace in us. She is the eschatological image of the perfection toward which the whole Church is to tend, her Immaculate Conception being the presage of the perfect purity for which we are intended, and her Assumption that of the final victory over death that awaits us; her unparalleled union with Christ is the seed of our union with him. And also, in virtue of her unique association with the Savior, her motherly intercession is the safeguard and, as it were, the first impetus of our whole filial life in Christ, in relation to the Father.

The holy angels, after Mary, associate us with the endless praise of their unceasing contemplation, to which the Eucharistic celebration leads us back, in spite of sin. St. John the Baptist, preeminently, makes us live in expectation of the Savior's final coming, leading us out to meet him in the desert of the ascetical life. St. Joseph discloses to us the union of virginity consecrated to Christ with spiritual paternity.

The holy apostles and martyrs show us how the proclamation of faith in the mystery of Christ crucified is sealed by the crucifixion of his own after his example. The holy confessors reveal how the unbloody martyrdom of asceticism illuminated by faith can, in this regard, equal the martyrdom of blood, and so also do the holy virgins, holy married women, and penitents.

With this cult of the saints is closely connected the communion we carry on with our dead in Christ, whom our intercession accompanies to the end of their purification, just as theirs precedes us to the presence of the Father.

It is in this context that we can best understand the prayers and other pious practices to which indulgences have been attached by the Church: as acts, holy in themselves, that take on a special value for us by reason of the particular association they bring about between ourselves and the prayers and merits, above all of the saints and also of the whole Church—militant on earth, still suffering in the trials that follow death in Christ, or already triumphant in perfect union with the risen Christ.

Another manifestation of this "communion of saints," particularly important for our spiritual progress and so to be sought after, is the spiritual fatherhood to be met with here below—in proven masters in the spiritual life and, more generally, in all those who have some authority over the flock of Christ.

All forms of Christian spiritual brotherhood—whether in a parish, a family, or some group with a common religious interest—are also related to this "communion of saints." And so, we may also say, is spiritual friendship, described and extolled by Aelred of Rievaulx in one of the most beautiful works of the Middle Ages, defining it as perfect mutuality in charity, attaining on earth a first realization, a special foreshadowing, of the joy of heaven.

It is thus that the Epistle to the Hebrews invites us, "surrounded by such a great cloud of witnesses, to reject the trammels of sin, and, arming ourselves with patience, to run to the combat proposed to us, fixing our gaze on the author and the finisher of our faith: JESUS" (12:1).

NOTES

1. *The Meaning of the Monastic Life* (New York: Kennedy and Sons, 1950), ix.

2. The English translation, *Christian Initiation* (London: Burns and Oates, 1960), appeared two years later.

3. Cf. Introduction to *Le sens de la vie sacredotale* (Tournai: Desclée, 1960), 7.

4. Unfortunately, its English translation offered the somewhat misleading title *Introduction to Spirituality*; the French original is *Introduction à la vie spirituelle: précis de theologie ascetique et mystique* (1960); the term "spirituality" has come, in more recent parlance, to be both vague and amorphous, something Bouyer had clearly eschewed and sought to overcome, as will become obvious.

5. Foreword.

6. For a very recent and beautiful exposition of the relationship between the spiritual life and the liturgy, cf. David W. Fagerberg, *On Liturgical Asceticism* (Washington, DC: Catholic University of America Press, 2013).

7. *Lumen Gentium* ["The Dogmatic Constitution on the Church"], Chapter 5.

8. There is as yet no biography of Bouyer in English. For his life, see the very recent work in French by Jean Duchesne, *Louis Bouyer* (Perpignan: Editions Artège, 2011) and the study of his theology by Davide Zordan, *Connaisance et mystère: L'itinéraire théologique de Louis Bouyer* (Paris: Cerf, 2008); in English one can consult E. Leiva-Merikakis, "Louis Bouyer the Theologian," in *Communio* 16

(1989):257–282, which includes a bibliography of Bouyer's works, and the recent and very fine essay of Jake Yap, "Louis Bouyer and the Unity of Theology," in *Ressourcement: A Movement for Renewal in Twentieth-Century Catholic Theology*, edited by G. Flynn and P. Murray (Oxford: University Press, 2012), 289–302.

9. Most notably in his *The Decomposition of Catholicism* (Chicago: Franciscan Herald Press, 1969), in which he offered a critique of certain interpretations of the Council and attempts at its implementation.

10. In one of his later books, Bouyer situated the development of this Pauline idea against its pagan background, revealing how the Christian notion is not fundamentally dependent upon pagan sources (which largely postdate the New Testament), cf. *The Christian Mystery: From Pagan Myth to Christian Mysticism* (Edinburgh: T&T Clark, 1990). He also describes beautifully its particular liturgical significance in his little commentary on the liturgical reforms of the Second Vatican Council, *The Liturgy Revived* (Notre Dame: University of Notre Dame Press, 1964), 17–19.

11. *The Paschal Mystery: Meditations on the Last Three Days of Holy Week* (trans. by M. Benoit) (Chicago, Regnery, 1950), xiii. I have slightly emended the translation.

12. "Christ will never leave behind the immolation and that new life; his existence is fixed forever at the moment of the Redemption. The five wounds he showed his disciples are not merely the receipt for our ransom inscribed upon his body, but the wounds of a death from which he will never recover . . . the life of glory is a perpetuation of his death; the fire of the Spirit which consumes him keeps him as an eternal holocaust. The Lamb of God stands in glory and is surrounded by hymns of triumph, but he is still slain . . . that ever actual glorifying action coincides with Christ's death, and thus keeps the Savior forever at the moment of his death to the world, at the high point of giving himself to the Father. . . . The Church, identified with Christ finds this salvation of the Resurrection because she is incorporated into the Savior, not in this or that moment

of his life—Bethlehem, Nazareth, the roads of Palestine—not yet in a heavenly existence subsequent to the act of redemption, but in the act of Redemption itself. She is the Body of Christ in one precise, and henceforth, eternal, moment, in the moment when the redemption takes place, in the moment of his death on the cross, when Christ was glorified by the Father." F. X. Durrwell, *In the Redeeming Christ* (London: Sheed and Ward, 1963), 5.

13. 54.

14. Bouyer makes this very clear in *The Paschal Mystery*: (at xvi) "Rightly understood, the imitation of Jesus Christ is the vey essence of the Christian life. We must have in us the mind that Christ had; we must be crucified and buried and rise with him. This, of course, does not mean that we fallen human beings are to copy clumsily the God-Man. The whole matter is a mystery signifying that we are to be grafted onto him so that the same life which was in him and which He has come to give us may develop in us as in him and produce in us the same fruits of sanctity and love that it produced in him. The whole life of the Church is indeed the imitation of the life of Jesus Christ, but it is not a copy of that life. For the life of the Church is the life of Jesus Christ *propagated*."

15. Cf. Christian Smith and Melina Lundquist Denton, *Soul Searching: The Religious and Spiritual Lives of American Teenagers* (New York: Oxford, 2009).

16. There exists an interesting contrast between ancient and contemporary forms of religiosity: for many of the ancients, interior commitment was immaterial; piety consisted in the regular participation in civic (external) rites. For many contemporaries, religiosity is limited to internal dispositions and may never be externalized in practice (hence, "I'm spiritual, but not religious"). Somewhat ironically, ancient Christianity charted a course between the Scylla of Roman religion, focused on external rites, and the Charybdis of Gnosticism, which largely eschewed particular practices (and thus often espoused an antinomian morality) in favor of possessing secret "knowledge": Christians both professed particular doctrines *and* ex-

pressed and celebrated these beliefs in public worship.

17. Page 18. This theme, that faith is a response to a living *Person*, not simply assent to an idea or concept, is something Pope Emeritus Benedict XVI emphasized numerous times during his pontificate.

18. "I must insist on the fact that, in opposition to what is too often supposed by too many Christians today . . . [b]asically, essentially, there is one only one [spirituality]: that of the gospel, as it is expressed in the New Testament, and further developed through, first of all and above all, the traditional liturgy . . . However, this one spirituality, in its concrete application to varied situations, diverse in time and place and forms of existence, has to take account of a great variety of possible problems"; from "Spirituality for the Coming Years," in *Catholicism and Secularization in America*, ed. by David Schindler (Huntington, IN: Our Sunday Visitor/Communio Books, 1990), 80–92, at 80. Cf. also his caution voiced in the preface to his multi-volume *History of Christian Spirituality* (London: Burns and Oates, 1963), Volume 1, x: "It is, therefore, only with the greatest reservations that one can speak of Christian spiritualities in the plural."

19. Cf. *Introduction to the Spiritual Life*, 37–38. He adduces this precise example in his Introduction to *Le sens de la vie sacerdotale* (Tournai: Desclee, 1960), 6.

20. *Dei Verbum* ["The Dogmatic Constitution on Divine Revelation"], promulgated in November 1965.

21. Page 41.

22. Page 41; emphasis added.

23. Cf. for example, Matthew Fox, *Original Blessing* (Santa Fe: Bear Publishing, 1983).

24. Page 183.

25. Page 207.

26. Cf. *The Meaning of the Monastic Life*, in the dedication of the work to Dom Clement Lialine. It is worth noting that Bouyer anticipates by almost a decade the use of the language of "eschatological humanism" made famous by the American Jesuit, John Courtney

Murray (who used the term in contradistinction to "incarnational humanism"), cf. J. Hooper and T. Whitmore, eds., *John Courtney Murray and the Growth of Tradition* (Kansas City: Sheed and Ward, 1996), 120, n. 17. Bouyer addresses the relationship between humanism and asceticism at length in *Christian Humanism* (Westminster, MD: Newman Press, 1958).

INDEX

Aelred of Riveaulx, 353, 387
agape, 4, 10, 31–32, 119,
153, 173, 190, 192, 206,
246–47, 251, 319, 330.
342, 363–65, 370–71
See love of God
Agape and Eros, 362
"allegorical sense" of
scripture, 57–58
almsgiving, 226–30, 320
Ambrose, St., 240
anagogical sense of
scripture, 57–58
anamnesis, 48
anchorite. *See* eremitic life
angels,
cult of the holy, 386–87
sin of the, 201–3
Anointing of the Sick, 158–59
"anthological" style, 56
Antony, Life of St., 258–63
apatheia, 192, 251, 257, 310,
318–20, 325, 330, 342
apocalyptic writings,
170–73, 339–40
"apophatic theology," 105
apostles, mission of the, 26–27
"apostolic" spirituality, 24–32
"apostolic" vocations, 269–305
Ascent of Mt. Carmel, 353
ascetical life, principles of, 163–82
asceticism, 183–207
and Christian humanism,
183–207
and the Gospel, 172–73
and martyrdom, 173–75
Christian meaning of, 163–66
in ancient monasticism,
175–77
in the Old Testament, 166–71
medieval developments,
177–79

modern developments,
179–82
necessity, 183–84
Augustine, St., 103–8, 111,
116, 140–42, 192–94, 308

Baker, Dom Augustine, 116
Baptism, 58, 149–54, 156–57,
261, 280, 313, 383
baptismal commitment
to Christ, 212–15
baptismal renunciations, 213–15
baroque period, 97–99
Barth, Karl, 23
Basil, St., 262, 264–65, 296
Benedict, St., 38, 67, 88,
244, 246, 263
berakah, 48, 127, 131–32
Bernard, St., 108, 247, 352–53
Bérulle, Cardinal, 100, 113
Bible,
and tradition, 44–49
in the liturgy, 44–49
methods of reading, 68–74
study of, 68–74
traditional interpretation,
49–53
yearly reading, 68–69
See lectio divina, scripture,
Word of God
bishops,
consecration of, 155–57
functions of, 144–45, 289
mission of, 27
blessings, 127
See berakah
body and soul, relationship
between, 165 ff., 184–200
Bona, Cardinal, 115
Bossuet, 39
Bremond, Henri, 101
Buber, Martin, 22

Buddhism, 16, 14–18,
   164–65, 175

canonical life, 297
cardinal virtues, 330–33
Cassian, 79, 126, 244–45,
   253, 263, 326–27
"cataphatic theology," 105
Catholic action, 236, 277, 304–5
Catholic spirituality, 24–32
celibacy, 161,
      distinction between
      clerical and monastic,
      281–87, 243–46
   See chastity, counsels, virginity
cenobitic life, 262–65
charity, 130, 193–94, 216–22,
   226, 276, 300 ff., 330–33,
   345–48, 362–63, 370–88
   See agape, love of God,
      love of neighbor
chastity, 281–87, 243–46
Chautard, Dom, 114–15
Christ,
      and Adam, 172
      and asceticism, 172–73
      fulfillment of the Old
         Testament, 50–53
      the Incarnate Word of God,
         20–22, 26–32, 145
      modes of presence at
         Mass, 141–45
      mystery of, 53–57
   See mystery of Christ, Word
      of God, sacramental life
Christian Perfection and
   Contemplation, 379
Christian spirituality, 17–24
   use of Greek formulations,
      190–200
   See spirituality, spiritual life
Church, the, 24–32
      and the mystery of
         Christ, 141 ff.
      and prayer, 59–66
      and the Word of God, 27–29

      as the Mystical Body of
         Christ, 27–28, 148–49
   See Mystical Body of
      Christ, sacramental life
Chrysostom, St. John, 39, 319
Cicero, 14
Clement of Alexandria,
   318, 337–42, 378
Collect prayer, 60
commandments, the,
   46, 77, 240–41
communion, sacramental,
   143, 146–51
   See Mystical Body of Christ
communion of saints, 385
Compline, 88–89, 92
Condren, 113
confirmation, 149, 151–53
consciousness of self in
   modern times, 34, 94 ff.
constant prayer, 125–28
contemplation, 62–63,
   77–78, 93–101, 103–31
   See mystical life, prayer,
      unitive way
continence, 229–33, 251–54
conversion, 332–35
Cotta, 14
covenant, the, 56–58
   See Eucharist
counsels, the, 239–43, 320–22
   See monasticism,
      "religious" life (active)
cross, the, 54–57, 173–174, 181 ff.
   in Christian life,
      134, 209–234
   See following of Christ,
      mystery of Christ, sacrifice

Daniel, 170
Dark Night of the Soul, 354
Day Hours. See Little Hours
death, 184, 206–7, 224–25
desert, 258–263
   See "nomadism,"
      spiritual combat

devil. *See* evil spirit
diaconate, the, 156, 290–95
Diadocus of Photike, 261
discretion, virtue of, 109
Divine Office, 67, 81–93, 100–2
    as leaven of personal
        prayer, 84–93
    as "the prayer of the
        Church," 81–84
    "deputizing" of clergy
        and religious, 81–83
    development of, 82–84
Dream of Gerontius, 371

Eckhart, Meister, 29–30, 376, 381
Elijah, 368
episcopate, the. *See* bishops
eremitic life, 262–65
eros, 31, 173, 362–65
Eucharist, the, 139–41,
    146–49, 152–53, 154–55,
    156, 158, 174, 341
    See Mass
"Eucharistic" Prayer, 48, 63, 85
    and the Eucharist, 131–34
    See berakah, praise, petition,
        prayer of, thanksgiving
Eucharistic sacrifice, 146, 160
    See Eucharist, Mass
Evagrius of Pontus, 103–6, 128,
    192 ff., 251, 256 ff., 308–19,
    325–30, 342–50, 380 ff.
Evening Prayer, 85–87, 91
evil, 163 ff., 183 ff.
evil spirit, 119, 170 ff., 200 ff.,
    See baptismal renunciations,
        spiritual combat
examination of conscience, 321 ff.
Exodus, 46, 70, 245, 358
    See Pasch
ex opere operate, 81–82
Ezra, 48

faith, 20–24, 32, 47, 62 ff.,
    163, 311 ff., 318 ff., 321 ff.
    and vision, 369–73

Fall, the, 200–4
fallen nature, 200–4
fasting, 229–33, 318–20
Fécamp, John de, 115
Felicitas, St., 360
"the flesh," 165, 213,
    257–60, 316–20, 330
        See asceticism, *pathe*
flight from the world, 237–39
following of Christ, 172 ff., 181
Francis of Assisi, St., 38, 178

Garcia de Cisneros, 94
Garrigou-Lagrange, 379
Genesis, 8, 70, 200, 256–57, 315
gifts of the Holy Spirit, 348
Glory Be to the Father, 122
"gnosis," 310, 329, 337–44
    See knowledge of God
God,
    as "Someone," 20–22,
        140 ff., 371
    See image of God in humanity,
        knowledge of God, love
        of God, Word of God
God's pedagogy, 140 ff., 371 ff.
Gospel, the
    and asceticism, 172–73
    See mystery of Christ, New
        Testament, Word of God
Gospel of the Mass, 146
grace, 32, 101, 195–99, 308 ff.
    See Holy Spirit
Greek formulations in Christian
    spirituality, 190–200
Gregory the Great, St.,
    39, 103, 106, 194
Gregory Nazianzen, St., 197, 245
Gregory of Nyssa, St., 103,
    282, 308, 309, 319,
    337, 345–46, 356
Gregory Palamas, St., 197–99

haggadah, 309, 339 ff.
Hail Mary, 117–25
halakah, 339

Hassidim, 22
Heiler, Friedrich, 362, 365
Hermetism, 338
hesychasts, 129, 136, 139, 257
hesychia, 129, 254–57
Hinayana, 14, 18
Holy Spirit, the, 7, 25 ff., 92 ff.,
    113 ff., 120, 121 ff., 195, 216,
    260, 311, 312, 319, 332 ff., 380
    See life in the Spirit
homily, 60
hope, 170, 227, 318, 330
    See mystery of Christ
Hosea, 65, 168, 262, 334
humanism and asceticism,
    183–207
human nature, 165–68,
    183–207, 258–67
Huxley, Aldous, 36, 375

Ignatian method of
    meditation, 110–13
Ignatius of Antioch, St., 173–74
Ignatius of Loyola, St.,
    33, 38, 95, 109–15
illumination, 329–58
illuminative way, 330–33
    See illumination
image of God in humanity,
    185–88, 314, 345
indulgences, 387
intercessory prayer, 121, 134–37
interior life, 5–6, 13–24
interior peace, 254–57
Ireland, monasticism of, 178–79
Irenaeus, St., 338, 341 ff.
Isaiah, 55, 168–169, 348
    See Servant Songs

James, William, 360
Jeremiah, 169–72, 281
Jesuits, 297–99
Jesus, holy name of,
    128, 129 ff., 145
Jesus, mystery of,
    See mystery of Christ

Jewish spirituality, 24
Job, 170
John the Baptist, St., 171, 281, 386
John of the Cross, St., 33,
    309, 327, 353–56, 381
John the Evangelist, St., 58–59,
    71–74, 119, 148, 150, 165 ff.,
    176, 237, 341, 366–67
Joseph, St., 387
Josiah, 281, 387
Joyce, James, 15

keeping watch, 227–29
Kingdom of God, 118,
    170–75, 219, 320
knowledge of God, 77,
    257, 333–37

Lauds, 85–90
lauras, 265
Law of God, 56–57
    See commandments
lay vocation, 209–10,
    212–16, 269–81
    almsgiving, 226–27
    as vocation of the
        baptized, 212–15
    death, 224–25
    fasting, 229–33
    keeping watch, 227–29
    matrimony, 219–22
    parenthood, 222–24
    prayer, 79–137
    to life "in the world," 215–16
    work, 216–19
    See "liturgy" of the faithful,
        sacramental life
lectio continua, 68–69
lectio divina, 66–68,
    74–78, 109–10
life "in Christ," 154
    See baptism
life in the Spirit, 259–83
    See Holy Spirit, mystical
        life, unitive way

Litany, the (Litany of
  the Saints), 134
Little Hours, 88, 92
liturgical assembly, 45–49, 153–57
liturgy, 44–68
  pedagogy of, 53
  school of meditation, 59–66
"liturgy" of the faithful, 146–49
"liturgy" of the high
  priest, 144–56
Louis, St., 247
love of God, 30–32, 119, 133, 182,
  319–22, 323, 336–37, 363–66
  See agape, charity
love of neighbor, 370–73
  See agape, charity,
    commandments,
    love of God

Macarius, St., 103, 128, 193
Mahayana, 18
humanity, Greek and
  Christian view, 184–90
Manicheism, 164–65, 187, 237
Margaret Mary, St., 179
Maritain, Jacques, and Raissa, 379
marriage, 158–160, 219–22
  and celibacy, 175–76, 242–43
martyrdom, 173–75, 387
Mary, Mother of God,
  120–28, 386
Mass, the, 49, 141–45, 273–76
  See Eucharist
Matins, 63–66
Matthew, Gospel of, 50–51
Mazdaism, 164–65
meditating on the Bible, 53–57
  See lectio divina
meditation, 42–44
  and contemplation, 93–101
  daily, 91
  definition of ideal, 108–10
  Ignatian method, 110–13
  liturgy as school of, 59–66
  modern forms of, 95–103
  modern methods of, 114–16

object of, 101
Sulpician method,
  113–14, 149
mendicant orders, 297–300, 303
mental prayer, 79–84
  See meditation
minor orders, 156, 290–92
Mishnah, 137
monasticism
  and asceticism, 175–77
  and the search for God, 246
monastic life, 177, 243–46
monastic spirituality, 235–67
monastic vocation,
  flight from the world, 237–39
  motivation of, 247–50
  salvation of the world, 237–39
Morning Prayer, 85–90, 230
mortification, 230, 318–20
  See asceticism, purification
Moses, 46, 87, 197, 335, 367–68
"Mysteries" of the Rosary, 123–24
"mystery," history of term, 377–78
Mystery of Christ,
  53–57, 62, 141 ff.
  and meditation, 53 ff.
  and the Rosary, 123–24
  and suffering, 159
Mystical Body of Christ,
  26–31, 37–38, 45, 143–58
  See mystery of Christ
mystical experience,
  meaning and possibility,
    360–66
  nature of, 373–78
mystical life, 359–83
mystical phenomena, 373–78
"mystical theology," 105
Mystici Corporis, 149
mysticism,
  origin of term, 377 ff.
  Christian, 379–80
mysticisms, non-Christian, 377–78

Name of God, 118
Neo-Platonism, 105, 165, 188 ff.,
    190–95, 308, 313, 337, 370 ff.
New Testament, 27–30,
    50, 53–57, 366–68
    See Bible, Scripture,
        Word of God
Newman, Cardinal, 356, 371
"nomadism," 244–45, 255
None, 88
Nygren, Anders, 362,
    365–67, 370–72

obedience, 176–77, 238–43,
    251–54, 320–22
offering, 146–47
Old Testament,
    and asceticism, 166–71
    mysticism in, 368
    See Bible, Word of God
Olier, 113
orationes fidelium, 134
Orders, Holy, 154–57
Origen, 175, 247–48, 308–19,
    320, 330, 337, 342, 352, 378
Orphism, 165
Otto, Rudolf, 19–20, 35, 376
Our Father, 120–21, 132

Pachomius, St., 363–65
parenthood, 222–24
particular examen,
    See examination of conscience
Pasch, the, 48–55, 70, 142, 167
    See Eucharist, Exodus
Paschal vigil, 59
pastoral responsibilities, 273–76
pathe, 202, 251–57, 317–
    20, 340, 343, 354
Paul, St.,
    and the mystery of
        Christ, 54–57
    and the mystical life, 377–78
Pelagianism, 202
People of God, 45–49, 155–57,
    160, 167, 334, 345

Perennial Philosophy, 36, 375
Peter Damien, St., 178
Peter Lombard, 195
petition, prayer of, 130–37
phenomenological school, 34
Philo, 309, 338–39, 378
pilgrimages, 385 ff.
Pius XI, 9, 41, 236
Plato, 31, 165, 186, 335, 375
Platonic view of humanity, 186–92
Platonism, 165, 335–37
Plotinus, 31, 165,
    186–87, 262, 272
Polycarp, St. 184, 360
the "poor," 176, 280
poverty, 169–73, 176–77,
    210–12, 241–45
praise, 61–62, 84–86, 130–37
    See berakah, Eucharistic Prayer
Prayer, 362
prayer, 79–137
    activity and "passivity"
        in, 101–10
    and lectio divina, 66–68
    and "liturgy" of the
        faithful, 146–49
    constant, 125–28
    in lay life, 227–29
    liturgy as school of, 59–66
"prayer of the Church," 92
"Prayer of Jesus," 128–30, 380–81
precepts and counsels, 239–43
pride, 316
    See pathe, sin, vices
priest workers, 293–95
priesthood of the faithful, 146–49
priesthood (ministerial), 272–73
    ordination to, 155
    work of, 143–44, 161–62,
        273–76, 293–95
priestly asceticism, 277–81
priestly spirituality,
    160–62, 281–89
    See celibacy
priestly vocation, 210–12,
    271–73, 293–95

Prime, 98–99, 102
proclamation of the Word, 155–57
    See "liturgy" of the high priest
promises of God, 47–50
Proust, Marcel, 15
Pseudo-Dionysius, 103,
    308–9, 344, 348–49, 378
"psychologism," 33–40
purgative way, 308–11
    See purification
purification, 311–14, 320, 322–28

Qahal, 46–49
Qumran, 171, 340, 367

readings, liturgical, 49–53, 59–60
Reconciliation, sacrament
    of, 153–54
    See asceticism, conversion
relics, veneration of, 386
religious life, 13–17
"religious" life (active), 295–99
    contemporary
        experiments, 302–4
    forms of, 295–99
    historical development,
        295–99
    See "apostolic" vocations
religious psychology, 33
"religious" vocation, 295 ff.
    See "apostolic" vocations,
        monastic vocation
reparation, 179–81
responsorial chant, 70–73
revelation, character of, 51–53
Rosary, 117–25
Rule of St. Benedict, 67, 88, 246

sacramental life, 139–62
sacramentals, 159
sacraments, 139–62
sacrifice, 47–48, 143–44
    See cross, Eucharist
salvation, nature of, 183–84, 188
Sancta Sophia, 116
Sankara, 19, 376

Satan, 213
    See evil spirit
scete, 265
scripture, 26, 54–58
    See Bible, Word of God
secular institutes, 302–4
self-discipline, 233–34
    see asceticism
self-mastery, 318–20
seminaries, 279–81
Sermon on the Mount,
    81, 241–43, 335
Servant Songs, 70, 169, 182
"service of the Word," 47–48, 89
Sext, 88
Shekinah, the, 128, 132, 368
sin, 167 ff., 183, 209, 244, 258 ff.
    See evil spirit, spiritual
        combat, vices
Soul of the Apostolate, 114
specialized spiritualities, 36–40
"the Spirit," 165 ff.
    See Holy Spirit
"spiritual bouquet," 112, 114, 125
spiritual combat, 254–57, 315 ff.
Spiritual Exercises, 33, 95, 119–22
spiritual fatherhood, 118, 222–24,
    266–67, 351–52, 387
spiritual friendship, 387
spiritual life,
    aids of, 285–88
    and the Word of God, 42–44
    basis of, 40
    definition of, 13–17
    development of, 307–58
    in the Catholic
        Church, 24–32
    in Christianity, 17–24
    "passive" and active
        aspects, 101–10
    three ways or ages, 309–11
"spiritual marriage," 351–52, 374
spiritual reading, 66–74
spirituality and "spiritualities," 5–8
spirituality,
    for the active life, 299 ff.

for the laity, 160–62
for priests, 160–62
See spiritual life
Stoicism, 207, 240, 259, 319, 322
subdeacons, 156
suffering, 170–92
and the mystery of Christ, 159
See cross
Sulpician method of
meditation, 113–14, 149
Suso, Henry, 178
synagogue services,
50–52, 84–85
syncretism, 45–46

Taoism, 18
temptation,
See pathe, spiritual combat
Terce, 88
Teresa, St., 7, 33, 38, 93–97, 109,
115, 231, 347, 351, 374, 381
thanksgiving, 131–137, 217–18
See berakah, Eucharist
Thérèse, St., 248, 355
Thomas Aquinas, St.,
141, 197 ff., 352
Torah, 50, 60
Tosefta, 127
traditional interpretation
of scripture, 49–53
Trinity, the Most Holy,
123, 343–49
Tronson, 113–14
tropological sense, 57–58

Ulysses, 15
Umbratilis, 236
unitive way, 348–52
See mystical life

Varieties of Religious
Experience, 361
Vespers, 83–91
vices, the, 315–17
vigilance, 351–52
vigils, 59 ff., 89 ff.

virginity, 175 ff., 281–28
See celibacy, chastity
virtues, development of, 330–33
See illumination, image
of God in humanity,
purification
vocal prayer, 79–84
vocation, choice of, 215, 324–25
vocations, Christian, 210–12

Way of the Cross, 385
William of St. Thierry, 116,
320, 346, 350, 380
wisdom writings, 170
Word of God, 28 ff., 41 ff.,
127, 139–41, 204–6
Wordsworth, William, 26, 375
work,
in lay life, 216–19
of priests, 273–76
"the world," 165–66, 237–239

Rev. Louis Bouyer (1913–2004) was a member of the French Oratory and one of the most respected and versatile Catholic scholars and theologians of the twentieth century. A friend of Hans Urs von Balthasar, Joseph Ratzinger, and J.R.R. Tolkien, and a cofounder of the international review *Communio*, Bouyer was a former Lutheran minister who entered the Catholic Church in 1939. He became a leading figure in the Catholic biblical and liturgical movements of the twentieth century, was an influence on the Second Vatican Council, and became well known for his excellent books on history of Christian spirituality. In addition to his many writings, Bouyer lectured widely across Europe and America.

Michael Heintz is a priest with the Fort Wayne-South Bend Diocese and teaches both undergraduate and graduate courses in theology at the University of Notre Dame.

David Fagerberg is associate professor of theology at the University of Notre Dame. He also serves as director of the Notre Dame Center for Liturgy and as editor of the center's journal, *Assembly*. Professor Fagerberg's area of study is liturgical theology: its definition and methodology.

AVE

AVE MARIA PRESS

Founded in 1865, Ave Maria Press,
a ministry of the Congregation of
Holy Cross, is a Catholic publishing
company that serves the spiritual and
formative needs of the Church and its
schools, institutions, and ministers;
Christian individuals and families; and
others seeking spiritual nourishment.

———

For a complete listing of titles from

Ave Maria Press

Sorin Books

Forest of Peace

Christian Classics

visit www.avemariapress.com

AVE MARIA PRESS
Notre Dame, IN
A Ministry of the United States Province of Holy Cross